Major Turning Points in Jewish Intellectual History

Major Turning Points in Jewish Intellectual History

David Aberbach
Department of Jewish Studies
McGill University, Montreal, Canada;
and Department of Sociology
London School of Economics
and Political Science

First published 2003 by
PALGRAVE MACMILLAN
Houndmills, Basingstoke, Hampshire RG21 6XS and
175 Fifth Avenue, New York, N.Y. 10010
Companies and representatives throughout the world

PALGRAVE MACMILLAN is the global academic imprint of the Palgrave
Macmillan division of St. Martin's Press, LLC and of Palgrave Macmillan Ltd.
Macmillan® is a registered trademark in the United States, United Kingdom
and other countries. Palgrave is a registered trademark in the European
Union and other countries.

ISBN 1–4039–1766–3 hardback

This book is printed on paper suitable for recycling and made from fully
managed and sustained forest sources.

A catalogue record for this book is available from the British Library.

Library of Congress Cataloging-in-Publication Data
Aberbach, David, 1953–
    Major turning points in Jewish intellectual history/David Aberbach.
      p. cm.
    Includes bibliographical references and index.
    ISBN 1–4039–1766–3
    1. Jews – Civilization. I. Title.

DS113.A375 2003
909'.04924—dc21   2003053564

10 9 8 7 6 5 4 3 2 1
12 11 10 09 08 07 06 05 04 03

Printed and bound in Great Britain by
Antony Rowe Ltd, Chippenham and Eastbourne

To Mimi, Gabriella, Shulamit, and Jessica,
Shoshana, Moshe, and Mop, with love and thanks

Contents

Acknowledgments

Over a period of a decade and more of working through the complexities of a highly variegated minority civilization in a series of dominant civilizations, I have had the good fortune of being affiliated with two universities – McGill University, Montreal, and the University of London, where I have been visiting professor at London University (University College and the London School of Economics) since 1992 – without whose support and encouragement this book could not have been written.

I am deeply grateful to my colleagues in Jewish Studies at McGill University – Professors Gershon Hundert, Lawrence Kaplan, Barry Levy, and Eugene Orenstein – for allowing me exceptional conditions which let me to get on with this and other books, as well as to the Convenors of the LSE Sociology Department – Professors Paul Rock, Nik Rose, Roger Silverstone, and especially Eileen Barker – for their generous hospitality over a period of many years.

This book builds on earlier books of mine: *Surviving Trauma: Loss, Literature and Psychoanalysis; Imperialism and Biblical Prophecy 750–500 BCE; The Roman–Jewish Wars and Hebrew Cultural Nationalism* (co-written with my father, Professor Moshe Aberbach); *Revolutionary Hebrew, Empire and Crisis*; and separate studies of the three greatest Hebrew writers of the 1881–1948 period: Mendele Mocher Sefarim, Chaim Nachman Bialik, and Samuel Joseph Agnon.

I thank the editors of journals where parts of this book were first published: *British Journal of Sociology, Commentary, Ethnic and Racial Studies, Harvard Theological Review, Israel Affairs, Jewish Chronicle, Jewish Quarterly, Judaism,* and *Nations and Nationalism.*

Finally, I thank Luciana O'Flaherty, my editor at Palgrave Macmillan, and V.S. Mukesh, for their invaluable help.

Introduction

Jewish intellectual history has several watersheds, in each of which the Jews might have disappeared. Instead, they determined Jewish survival and the character of Judaism: from idolatry to monotheism in the age of the Bible; from biblical to rabbinic Judaism in the Roman period; from exclusive Jewish learning to increasing absorption of secular learning under medieval Islamic rule; and in the modern period, a cluster of overwhelming changes, from being mainly a religious, working class, rural, impoverished, diaspora-based, Yiddish-speaking people, to a secular, middle class, urban people with a reborn Jewish state in which Hebrew was revived spectacularly. This book explores these turning points largely in a comparative context. The Hebrew prophets, for example, are seen in the context of ancient near eastern culture and history; the Tannaim (Mishnah teachers) are discussed as belonging to the Greco-Roman world of Seneca, Tacitus, Epictetus, and especially Marcus Aurelius; the medieval Hebrew poets are comparable with Arabic poets such as Ibn Hazm and Ibn Zaidun; Jewish mystics such as the Baal Shem Tov may be compared with other mystics, such as John of the Cross or Krishnamurti; and the work of modern Hebrew writers owes much to European, especially Russian influence and, more recently, to English literature.

A comparative approach to Jewish intellectual history, particularly the long, ambiguous relationship between Hebraism and Hellenism, is a fascinating window into Judaism and the elements which made its survival possible. From the late-biblical period to the present, Greek culture has been the primary "Other" in Jewish life, coming to represent both that which is repugnant and alluring in Gentile culture, and one of the greatest stimulants for change in Jewish life. Hebraism and Hellenism have had an ambivalent relationship from ancient times to the foundation of modern Israel. Greek culture penetrated late-biblical, rabbinic, and medieval Judaism as well as the Jewish Enlightenment (the Haskalah) and modern Jewish nationalism. The modern revival of Hellenism in Europe influenced Jewish nationalists as they rejected rabbinic spirituality, non-belligerence, and the disdain for athleticism which had dominated Jewish life after Rome destroyed the Jewish state in 70 CE.

Messianism and mysticism were further recurrent spurs to change in Jewish life, often appearing in troughs in Jewish history, in times of defeat or exile – for example, after 586 BCE, 70 CE, and 1492 – and creating new hope that if the divine powers could be tapped by mystics, temporal human initiative and creativity could certainly create a better world. Another strand of development in crisis was the codification of Jewish law: in the Mishnah in the early third century CE, by Maimonides in the twelfth century, and by Joseph Caro in the sixteenth century. Each of these works followed breakdown in Jewish life and exile. The traditional Jewish culture of intellect as value was crucial in the phenomenal contribution to the modern world of the lapsed rabbinic elite, including figures such as Marx, Durkheim, and Freud.

The transition from idolatry to exclusive monotheism in the biblical age is the most important one in this book as it determined the course of civilization. Yet for hundreds of years, the Jews were evidently the only monotheist people, the only ones who preserved the Hebrew Bible as sacred, until the rise of Christianity and the conversion of the Roman Empire to Christianity in the fourth century CE. Why did the Jews change so much earlier than anyone else? And how did they become the first minority to maintain their identity in exile in the long term?

Similar questions arise in connection with the second major turning point in Jewish history, during the half-millennium of Roman rule. In the Roman empire, the Jews changed from being a people with their own state and a religious focal point in the Temple in Jerusalem, with its cult of sacrifices and pilgrimages, to being a stateless people scattered throughout the empire and beyond and with a predominant rabbinic leadership whose intellectually demanding teaching, preserved in the Talmud, was substantially different from that in the Bible. Why did the Jews not disappear at this point and Judaism, in fact, become the fossil that Christians said it was? And why did Rome encourage this metamorphosis, allowing the Jews to survive and flourish after inflicting the worst defeat upon them in its entire history of internal revolts?

A third turning point came with the Arab conquests in the seventh and eighth centuries, which brought most of the world Jewish population under Islamic rule until the Renaissance. How did this upheaval lead to the first "secular" literature in Hebrew, mostly in Spain in the tenth to twelfth centuries, anticipating the secularization of Jewish life in the modern period? The proliferation of Jewish philosophy in Arabic prepared the way for the transformation of Judaism amid the great changes in the modern period. Why did the Jews in Arabic-speaking countries continue to write poetry and rabbinic responses in Hebrew and not assimilate fully into Arab civilization? And why did Jewish philosophy, nourished by Arabic and Greek thinkers, come to an end by 1492, not to be revived significantly until the nineteenth century?

By the end of the Middle Ages, much of the Jewish population had shifted from Arab countries, particularly in the Middle East and North Africa, to Western Europe then to Eastern Europe. On the historical fulcrum between the Middle Ages and the modern period is Hasidism, the most influential Jewish religious movement since the age of the Tannaim. Hasidism emerged amid the turmoil of eighteenth century Polish-Jewish life, the traumatic effects of the Sabbatean heresy and Frankism, the weakening of Jewish communal organization, the widening gap between rich and poor, educated and ignorant, and the emergence of increasing individualism associated with the Romantic movement. Like many religious movements whose passionately held beliefs are threatened, Hasidism can be seen as an attempt to win social support in crisis. It reacted against the dry scholarship of Talmudic study and against Rationalism and the Enlightenment. Central to the thinking of the founder of Hasidism, Rabbi Israel ben Eliezer (also known as the Baal Shem Tov, and by his acronym, the Besht, 1700?–60), was the idea of mystical union with God, *devekut*. The popular embrace with the irrational was a turning point both in consolidating the future of Judaism on a new emotional basis and also in releasing many European Jews from religious, intellectual and social boundaries, and promoting radical change.

Finally, in the modern period, the rise of secular education has brought about the greatest upheaval in Jewish history. There has been unprecedented demographic change. Jews have defected in large numbers from traditional Judaism, but others have rediscovered it and some non-Jews have adopted Judaism. Yiddish, for all its richness and creativity, has been largely jettisoned: only Hebrew is the shared language of the scattered Jewish communities, Oriental as well as Occidental. Judaism has undergone enormous change, religious, political and cultural, in the diaspora and the State of Israel. For the first time in history, the nature of Jewish identity has become a contested issue. How did the revival of Hebrew act first as a tool of secular education, then as the culture of Jewish nationalism? In which ways did the decline of the rabbinic class lead both to the rise of a new class of secular Hebrew writers and also to founders of new "scientific" systems of thought, including Marx and Freud?

Not all the questions in this book are new. Some are frequently asked in a variety of disciplines, especially History, Sociology, Anthropology, Theology, and Political Science. What is new is the eclectic approach to the whole picture. There is no attempt to be comprehensive. Rather, particularly striking moments and personalities are emphasized, and the role of Hebrew language and literature in moments of crisis is a unifying factor. Consequently, this book is the first to be concerned exclusively with major turning points in Jewish intellectual history as reflected primarily in Hebrew literature. It explores the unique relationship between tradition and change over a period of 3000 years. This relationship was the more tangled as each major transition was accompanied by parallel changes in the non-Jewish world as well as immense efforts to prove that nothing was changing. Hebrew literature is full of living scraps of the cultures among which the Jews lived and formed a part: the ancient Near East, Greece and Rome, and medieval Islam as well as a revived Hellenism in the medieval and modern periods. How did the Jews negotiate change in such a way that they succeeded until the modern period in preserving the illusion that they were not assimilating into these cultures, that nothing fundamental had actually changed?

The Jews early on marched to a different drummer. Their religious self-consciousness and determination to preserve their distinctiveness gradually marked them out from other peoples (including many inhabitants of the nominally monotheist kingdoms of Israel and Judah) who seemed more prone to abandon their beliefs under pressure and assimilate into other cultures. In the biblical period, exile led to the exclusive perception, especially among the prophets, of an abstract God and a universal people whose identity was based on faith, not territory, and who therefore could not be exiled. Their faith was tested in the talmudic age when, deprived of their political leadership, their Temple and priestly cult, and control over their territory, the Jews became defined as an exclusively intellectual people, with a rabbinic culture that was both accommodationist and harmlessly subversive. The medieval Hebrew poets managed the self-contradiction of writing for the first time in Hebrew – unless one counts the Song of Songs – secular love poems (including homosexual poems), wine songs, poems of debauchery, while retaining strict Jewish observance. Hasidism, which encouraged the rediscovery of the mystical holiness of the Hebrew alphabet and the preservation of Hebrew and Yiddish folk tradition, was a major response to the fear of radical socio-religious change amid the upheavals threatened by the secular Enlightenment; though paradoxically it also facilitated the process of change. The most important transition in Jewish intellectual history since the eighteenth century has been from observant Judaism to secularism. For this reason, Moses Mendelssohn (1729–86) is commonly described as the first modern Jew.

Yet Mendelssohn also exemplified pitfalls of assimilation, which later generations have rebelled against: by elevating the value of German and European culture, he indirectly encouraged Jews to see their own culture as inferior; he suppressed national elements of Judaism; and his own family mostly converted and intermarried, and became so completely Germanized that by the Hitler era there were Nazis descended from him.

One argument in this book is that trauma, rather than overwhelming the Jewish people and leading to their disappearance, as was the case with most other peoples in the pre-modern world, stimulated creative cultural processes of adaptation, particularly in Hebrew. In this respect, Jewish creativity, whose greatest originality was in Hebrew, was analogous to, and comparable with that of artists and writers among whom personal trauma, far from defeating them, stimulated the quest for the new. This book then applies to Jewish intellectual history ideas explored in some of my previous books, on creative responses to loss. Yet the influence of Hebrew is not confined to the Jews: through the translation of the Bible into the vernacular throughout Europe, it determined the character of European civilization and profoundly affected the rise of modern nationalism.

A number of familiar dates in Jewish history represent turning points: 721 BCE and 586 BCE, when the kingdoms of Israel and Judah, respectively, fell; 70 CE, the destruction of Jerusalem and of the Temple by the Romans; 1096–99, the First Crusade, the decimation of the Jewish communities in the Rhineland, and 1492, the expulsion of the Jews from Spain; the mid-sixteenth century, the development in Safed in the Land of Israel of Lurianic mysticism, the basis of Hasidic mysticism; 1648–49, the Chmielnicki pogroms and the destruction of Ukrainian Jewry; 1881, the first wave of Russian pogroms, and the first *aliyah* (modern immigration to the land of Israel); 1897, the creation by Theodor Herzl of the World Zionist Organization; 1917, the Balfour Declaration; and 1948, the re-establishment of a Jewish state. Though Jewish life was significantly different after these events, the process of change was in some respects accelerated rather than caused by them, making an impact over a period of many generations. The rise of anti-Semitism and Zionism in the late nineteenth and early twentieth centuries are crucial background to modern Jewish intellectual history, but the overwhelming and as-yet not fully defined consequences of the Holocaust and the establishment of the State of Israel are beyond the scope of this book.

In which ways is a study of change in Jewish intellectual history relevant to the present? Most importantly, the Bible has so thoroughly affected the course of history that, despite the rise of secularism in the modern period, knowledge of the Bible is still invaluable in understanding much that occurs, even in nations in which religion and politics are kept apart. Elements of nationalism, imperialism, ethnic friction, fundamentalism, moral idealism which color recent history, especially in the Middle East but also elsewhere, may be traced in some form or other to biblical precedents. For example, when Iraq invaded Kuwait, precipitating the Gulf crisis of 1990–91, Saddam Hussein declared his aim of emulating the great Assyrian and Babylonian conquerors, particularly Nebuchadrezzar, who conquered Jerusalem. Similarly, the forced population transfer ("ethnic cleansing") of Bosnian Muslims by the Serbs is one of countless examples of a policy invented by the ancient Assyrians during the Iron Age in the early first millennium and used against both kingdoms of Israel and Judah in the time of the prophets. Assyria was the first state in history to use terror for calculated political ends, particularly to cow defeated peoples into submission. The Hebrew prophets represent the first cultural resistance to terror, asserting the transience of power and the supremacy of moral principles above realpolitik. A close exploration of the relationship between the poetry of the prophets and the ancient empires can, in fact, yield important clues toward interpreting socio-political and religious trends in the Middle East and elsewhere.

Similarly, the form of Jewish nationalism which evolved in the Roman period, though rare in the ancient world, anticipates more recent national movements of defeated peoples. The Roman–Jewish wars of 66–70, 115–17, and 132–35 CE destroyed the territorial, social, and political bases of militant Jewish nationalism. Successive defeats brought a Roman ban on Jewish residence in Jerusalem and on proselytization. Most of the Jewish population of Judaea, in southern Palestine, was annihilated or exiled. The creative heart of Judaism shifted to Galilee, where the study of rabbinic law and homiletics flourished, mostly in Hebrew, and the Mishnah – the basis of the Talmud – was edited by the Tannaim. This culture was an implicit rejection of Greco-Roman civilization and values in favor of a more exclusivist religious-cultural nationalism. Especially since the eighteenth century, nationalism stimulated by defeat has become increasingly common, in many cases influenced directly, via the Bible, by the Jewish example. In the medieval and modern periods, too, Hebrew acted as an antenna of change, anticipating and attempting to define a secular way of life in which tradition is, nevertheless, preserved.

As we shall see, modern Hebrew literature has given stability and direction to a people which in less than a century experienced almost total demographic change, moved from the *shtetls* (small towns) in Eastern Europe to urban centers; largely gave up its religious character and abandoned its primary language of daily communication, Yiddish; mostly exchanged its high valuation of Torah study and poverty for secular learning, professional training, and social mobility; experienced unparalleled anti-Semitism and lost a third of its numbers in the Holocaust; and recreated in the Land of Israel a Jewish state. The strains caused by such massive religious, social, political, and cultural change are the subject and motive of much modern Jewish literature.

The Jewish experience has more than purely historical interest and relevance in multicultural societies which aim to preserve minority languages and cultures. An analysis of the vicissitudes of Hebrew can help weigh advantages and disadvantages both of assimilation and the preservation of minority cultures. The Jewish experience warns that assimilation, however rational, just, and beneficial, can exact a high cost to the minority culture. Consequently, minorities are right to be protective of their cultures and cautious and critical of the education provided by the dominant culture.

The struggles of a tiny minority to preserve and revivify its identity in the major upheavals in world history are of general interest in a pluralistic global polity consisting of countless minorities faced with conflict between the desire to preserve tradition and the pressing need to adapt to change. In this perspective, the Jewish example is full of warnings but also gives much hope.

Part I
From Idolatry to Monotheism

1

The Iron Age, Imperialism, and the Prophets

Hebrew prophecy and much else in the Bible was a product of the two and a half centuries from 750 to 500 BCE,* the historical juncture when the center of civilization was about to be wrenched from the Near East to Europe. Hebrew prophecy is generally regarded as the greatest and most lasting and influential artistic creation of a powerful but dying near eastern civilization built upon imperialism and the newly harnessed technology of the Iron Age. We know of three major waves of Hebrew prophecy. Each accompanied a wave of imperial conquest, first by Assyria in the late eighth century, then by Babylonia in the late seventh and early sixth centuries, and finally by Persia in the mid-sixth century. Each empire had its own character and motives and stimulated a distinct wave of prophecy, led by Isaiah ben Amoz during the Assyrian heyday, by Jeremiah and Ezekiel at the time of Babylonian supremacy and by Second Isaiah (the anonymous poetry appended to the book of Isaiah) during the rise of Persian hegemony. While prophecy was not confined to Israel, the phenomenon of prophetic poetry as it developed in Israel was unique and without a real parallel elsewhere (Bright 1965, p. xix). It is one of the outstanding creative achievements in literary history and its impact on civilization is incalculable. It represents the triumph of the spiritual empire over the mortal empire; of the invisible God, king of the universe, over the human king of the civilized world; of losers over victors; of moral ideas over military force; and also, in a sense, of the creative imagination over historical facts. It is the only surviving body of poetry from the ancient Near East which, for the most part, belongs to a clearly defined historical period – 750–500 being the

---

* All dates referred to in Chapters 1 and 2 are BCE.

period marking the rise of the Assyrian empire until the restoration of the exiled Judeans to their land from Babylonia.

Although this poetry was written (or spoken) largely in response to the rise and fall of the Assyrian and Babylonian empires, it gives an extremely sketchy and misleading picture of the period. Judging from the prophets, Israel and Judah were central powers of the Fertile Crescent, equal in might and influence not just to the surrounding nations – Edom, Moab, Ammon, Philistia, Aram, and Phoenicia – but also to the Mesopotamian nations which posed a constant threat. The fall of the kingdom of Israel around 720 and of Judah just over a century later did not occur because they were tiny, mostly insignificant pawns in the politics and economics of the region. Their defeats were not inevitable consequences of military weakness, of geographic vulnerability, of unavoidably inferior manpower and resources. They fell because of moral backsliding: had they retained their faith in God and observed the Law, the prophets imply, they might have been victorious.

Historically (though not theologically), this biblical picture distorts the facts, as archaeologists and biblical scholars have discovered in the past 150 years.[1] Assyria, by the late eighth century, had built the most powerful empire in history to date, over a hundred times larger than Judah, with most of the population of the Near East under its rule. It had the strongest army ever to be assembled and pioneered revolutionary techniques of warfare, for example, in the use of cavalry and the implements of siege – these would be used for the next two and a half millennia. Its success was owed not just to its military power but also to a highly effective bureaucracy based in Assyria, with a network of administration and trade stretching from the Persian Gulf to the Egyptian border (by 663 the Assyrians had conquered Egypt, thus gaining control of the entire Fertile Crescent). In addition, Mesopotamia had a sophisticated civilization, was a leader in many of the arts and sciences and had an elaborate polytheistic religion with a remarkable mythology, traces of which survive in the Bible, especially in the opening chapters of the book of Genesis.

The true character and might of Mesopotamia do not emerge in the prophets. Assyria and Babylonia (like Persia after them) are depicted at best as agents of God's will, commanded to punish Israel and Judah for their sins, and at worst as tyrants and idol-worshippers doomed to extinction. And this image of the ancient empires came down in history because the Bible survived while Assyria and Babylonia vanished. Their superb temples and palaces, their art, language and literature were buried and obliterated. Whereas Jerusalem has been inhabited by Jews during most of its 3000-year history from biblical times until the present, the great cities of Mesopotamia – Asshur, Calah, Khorsabad, Nineveh, Babylon – were so completely forgotten that their very sites were for the most part unknown prior to the nineteenth century. While Hebrew was venerated and studied as the word of God, Akkadian, the cuneiform language of Mesopotamia, was lost for well over 1500 years and deciphered only in the mid-nineteenth century.

If the Bible grossly misrepresents Mesopotamia, the hundreds of thousands of cuneiform tablets recovered in archaeological digs over the past 150 years yield little insight into the kingdoms of Israel and Judah (Pritchard 1969). These kingdoms are mentioned rarely, almost invariably as minor participants in extensive military campaigns or swallowed up in long lists of nations forced to pay tribute. While some biblical kings appear – Jehu, Ahaz, and Hezekiah among them – no other biblical character, not even Isaiah ben Amoz or Jeremiah, has yet been identified in Mesopotamian writings. The destruction of the two kingdoms is given brief mention. The fact that they were, according to the Bible a unique monotheistic enclave (albeit a flawed monotheism) in a polytheistic world is passed over in silence. The extraordinary characters and literature of the Bible left no known mark on Mesopotamian culture.

However, in their most brilliant creative achievements, Mesopotamian and Israelite cultures were not dissimilar and have echoes to the present day: the toughness, violence, and emotiveness of prophetic poetry have their visual counterpart in the magnificent wall reliefs of war scenes and lion hunts which hung in the palaces of the Assyrian kings. The prophets rarely condemn the Mesopotamian empires for their barbarity – for flaying their enemies alive, chaining them in cages, immuring them, cutting out their tongues and eyes, cutting off their genitals and feeding them to dogs, burning, impaling, piling up their heads or corpses, as depicted in their inscriptions. Violence and cruelty were part of the biblical world. No peace was ever permanent. Passages from poems attributed to Moses and Deborah – both described as prophets – underline the violent thrust of biblical poetry. In the "Song of Moses", a bloodthirsty Yahweh thunders at his people for turning after strange gods of wood and stone, this being a frequent motif in prophetic invective:

> ... fire burns in me, devouring
> the earth and its fruits, blasting the base
> of mountains, grasping out to hell –
> I'll heap misfortune on them, wasted with hunger,
> burnt-out by the plague of Meriri –
> fanged beasts I'll set on them, and maddened snakes.

The sword will kill in the street ...
As I live forever –
I will make sharp my lightning sword!
I will make my arrows drunk
with the blood of captive and slain!
My flesh-devouring sword
on the heads of the wild-haired foe!
(Deuteronomy 32:22–5, 40–2)

If these lines were spoken not by God but by an Assyrian conqueror – Shalmaneser III or Sargon II, for example – they would be equally, if not more, convincing as the outburst of a king believed to have the authority of a god.

The "Song of Deborah", likewise, illustrates several features of the prophetic style, particularly in the rhetoric, the repetition, the imagery and the intense rhythmic excitement of Deborah's victory over the Canaanites:

The kings came and fought.
The kings of Canaan fought in Ta'anach
by the waters of Megiddo –
no silver spoil for them!
The heavens fought,
the stars fought Sisera in their orbits,
the river Kishon swept them away,
ancient river, river Kishon ...
(Judges 5:19–21)

Here again, the triumphant mood is not unlike that in Assyrian art, the Lachish reliefs, for example, and also, occasionally, in the annals of the kings. The touching vignette of Sisera's mother at the close of the poem also recalls the Assyrian engravings of their enemies in defeat and exile.

Each of the surviving three major waves of Hebrew prophecy came about in wartime, and war is the subject of, or background to, most of the prophetic poetry, even that depicting the golden age at the end of days when swords are beaten into ploughshares and the wolf lies down with the lamb: at that time Israel and Judah will gain resounding victories over their enemies (Isaiah 11). Only then will God be "king of the whole earth" (Zechariah 14:9), an image of imperial rule deeply influenced, no doubt, by the Mesopotamian kings who used an identical phrase to describe the extent of their power (e.g. Pritchard 1969, p. 297).[2]

Thus, by identifying itself with a spiritual empire, an immortal kingdom of God mirroring and rivalling Mesopotamian kingdoms with their feet of clay, Judah stretched the range of creative imagination and in doing so held on to its unique identity even, and perhaps especially, in exile.

While the prophets extol the virtues of submission, justice, kindness, and mercy, their strongest moods are of angry defiance, accusation, and bitter guilt; and this might be explained in the context of imperial expansion in the 200 years starting from the mid-eighth century. It cannot be accidental that the first written prophecies – of Isaiah ben Amoz, Hosea, Amos, and Micah – coincide with an astounding series of Assyrian conquests in the second half of the eighth century. During that time, hardly a year passed without a military campaign. The cataclysmic effect of these wars of expansion may be gauged in Isaiah's impassioned prophecies to surrounding nations – Egypt, Ethiopia, Arabia, Aram, Edom, Phoenicia, Philistia, as well as Assyria and Babylonia. These prophecies barely acknowledge Assyria as the main cause of upheaval, perhaps because this was self-evident or as a slap at Assyria by attributing its victories not to its superior power but to God. The prophecies to the nations in Isaiah and later prophets, Jeremiah and Ezekiel particularly – there are about three dozen such prophecies in all – chart the course and impact of imperial expansion and give a unique outsider's view of the great events of the age. The threat of being overrun and the experience of vassaldom contributed in bringing about an explosion of creativity in Judah starting from the mid-eighth century. Prophecy served to control and make sense of otherwise uncontrollable, incomprehensible, earth-shaking events, to create something of permanent theological and aesthetic value in the face of impending disaster.

To explore the meaning of this simultaneous growth of empire and prophecy, it is useful first to outline the extent of the Assyrian conquests and to offer some interpretation of Assyrian imperialism in the light of modern theories.

Tiglath Pileser III, a general who usurped the throne around 745, was chiefly responsible for Assyria's rise as the first extended empire in history: he conquered most of the Fertile Crescent, made the northern and eastern borders safe from marauding tribes, and divided the territory into administrative units designed to protect the trade routes and to collect taxes with maximum ease. To these ends, he built a network of roads – the finest prior to the Romans – together with a chain of resting posts and forts. To ensure the disorientation of his defeated enemies, to make use of them and, finally, to assimilate them into Assyrian cities, he instituted a policy of deportation to the Mesopotamian heartland where the exiles were put to work on public building projects. This policy inadvertently had momentous consequences for civilization. It broke down ethnic barriers and opened the way for the future expansion of prophetic influence and of Judaism (and through Judaism, Hellenism and, later, Christianity and Islam) as a universal religion. But at the time, deportation was a catastrophe: Israel was exiled by the Assyrians and Judah by the Babylonians, and this policy was reversed only by the Persians in the late sixth century. The over-extension of the Assyrian empire, civil war in the time of Ashurbanipal and the natural hatred engendered by a tyrannical regime, weakened the empire. In the late seventh century it collapsed and disappeared.

The phenomenon of Assyrian imperialism is crucial in the poetry of the prophets. Why did the Assyrians build their empire? Why did it fall, while Judah, for all its insignificance, survived? Interpretations of imperialism have originated mostly since the late nineteenth century, based upon studies of modern empires. The word "imperialism" was originally used specifically to describe modern, not ancient, empires, and there is a view among some scholars that it should be confined to modern empires. However, scholars specializing in ancient Mesoptamian kingdoms agree almost unanimously that the word is applicable also to Assyria, Babylonia, and Persia in the prophetic age, inasmuch as the human forces underlying imperialism have not changed greatly and its means and ends remain fundamentally the same.

Historical and theoretical evidence suggests that imperialism results from diverse factors: nationalism and economic pressure; the drive for power and prestige; greed, cruelty, and raw energy; the struggle for security; and surprisingly, even humanitarianism and a desire to enlighten. Among these and other forces, the ones most obviously applicable to Mesopotamia are geography and economics, though religious motives are stressed in the ancient inscriptions ("The God Asshur, My Lord, commanded me to march ..."). Geographically, Assyria had no clearly defined borders: it was surrounded by often-hostile nations and tribes. While it had much fertile land by the Tigris and its tributaries, which attracted invaders, Assyria had few raw materials and had to import wood, stone, bronze, copper, wool, flax, and, above all, iron. (This economic reality may have influenced the Mesopotamian worship of idols of wood and stone, which the prophets mock and condemn ceaselessly – such commodities, plentiful to the Judeans, were precious to the Assyrians.) A further destabilizing factor was the irregular rise and fall of the Tigris and Euphrates, which could lead to inadequate irrigation one year and flooding the next, and which required an elaborate and not always effective network of dykes and canals. These conditions forced Assyria to maintain a strong army and to look beyond its borders, especially to the Mediterranean coast, for raw materials. The eighth century was a time of expanding Mediterranean trade, and one of Tiglath Pileser's chief military feats was the conquest of the east Mediterranean coast, with its trade routes and ports. His successors, Shalmaneser V, Sargon II, Sennacherib, Esarhaddon, and Ashurbanipal, were largely successful in consolidating the empire and maintaining control over trade from Egypt to Persia and northwards to the Taurus mountains. The growth of international trade increased the strategic importance of Israel and Judah, straddling the land bridge between Asia and Africa. The prophets did not entirely exaggerate when they spoke of their land as central.

The picture of Assyria as the wolf come down on the sheep in the fold has blocked the impartial assessment of its campaigns for territorial expansion in the eighth century. Assyrian imperialism is easily condemned as a sport, motivated by the basest instincts which are never entirely absent in modern imperialism (or, for that matter, in human nature) – bloodlust, greed, power-hunger, sadism, and perverted sexuality:

> Foreign peoples were the favorite game and toward them the hunter's zeal assumed the forms of bitter national hatred and religious fanaticism. War and conquest were not means but ends. They were brutal, stark naked imperialism (Schumpeter 1951, p. 44).

Only in recent years, through evidence discovered in cuneiform, have scholars begun to regard Assyrian imperialism with any sympathy. If not for Assyria, Judah and Judaism might not have survived:

> Imperialism is not necessarily wrong: there are circumstances in which it might be both morally right and necessary. Such was the case in the Near East in the early first millennium. But for the Assyrian Empire the whole of the achievements of the previous 2000 years might have been lost in anarchy, as a host of tiny kingdoms (like Israel, Judah and Moab) played at war amongst themselves, or it might have been swamped under hordes of the savage peoples who were constantly attempting to push southwards from beyond the Caucasus (Saggs 1965, p. 118).

It is hard to see Tiglath Pileser III, Sargon II or Sennacherib as an unwitting savior of Judah, but there is reason to believe that this was so.

For in a sense, Assyrian imperialism forced upon Judah the discipline of monotheism and its teachers, the prophets. If left alone, Judah might have abandoned its faith and submitted to the paganism which dominated the Near East, making it far more vulnerable to assimilation and disappearance.

The discovery of the uses of iron – the greatest technological advance of the biblical era – made possible the type of imperialism created by Assyria as well as the defences against imperialism, the military ones and also, indirectly, the spiritual ones of the prophets. The Assyrians were the first to create a large iron weapons industry and, through the mass production of iron weapons, to put these instruments of destruction into the hands of sizeable armies. Iron changed forever the nature of warfare, travel and trade, all crucial to imperialism. The phenomenal Assyrian military successes of the late eighth century, news of which came to Europe via the Greek trading posts in the east Mediterranean, accelerated the growth of an iron-based urban economy in Europe, paving the way for the rise of the Greek and Roman empires. Assyrian improvements in the design of the bow, the quiver, the shield, body armor, and the chariot (making it heavier, strengthening the wheels), as well as increasingly effective battering rams to penetrate siege walls and city gates, were largely made possible by iron tools and materials (Yadin 1963). Iron played its part in military training and combat techniques, in the building of roads and new means of rapid, flexible deployment of troops, logistics, and administration. The poetry of the prophets echoes with iron: soldiers on the march, horses galloping, the glint of javelins, the thrust of swords, the clang of chariots.

While Assyria built the finest offensive army in history to date, Israel and Judah and other nations in the Near East developed some of the most sophisticated means of defense: walls, siege fortifications, gates, towers, and protective structures on the walls, and engineering, notably Hezekiah's 500-meter conduit hacked through the rock from the stream of Gihon into the city of Jerusalem. Jerusalem was never conquered by the Assyrians. Samaria, which in some places had walls 33 feet thick, resisted Assyrian siege for three years.

The prophets were part of these defenses, strengthening resolve against the moral "breach in the wall" (Isaiah 30:13), depicting God as the only king and warrior-protector – "shield", "wall", "bow-man", "chariot-driver" as well as a type of smith-creator, removing impurities, battering the heart of his people into new shape, using the prophets as tools and fortifications. The prophet Jeremiah, for example, is chosen by God to be a "bronze wall", an "iron pillar," and a "walled city" protecting the faithful (Jeremiah 1:18, 15:20). Significant, too, is other prophetic imagery of iron: the iron axe wielded by God in leading the Assyrians to victory over his faithless people (Isaiah 10:34), the iron yoke made by God to symbolize the supremacy of Nebuchadrezzar (Jeremiah 28:14), the iron pen to inscribe the sins of Judah (*ibid.* 17:1). At the same time, the prophets denigrate the uses of iron in war as in idol-worship, and the iron-smith is the target of the most vituperative mockery in Second Isaiah.

While Assyria's imperial growth stiffened Judah's will to survive, it also led to the destruction of Assyria within a century. The cruel force needed to build and sustain the empire aroused violent hatred throughout the Fertile Crescent; it died, as Napoleon put it, of indigestion. Demographically weak, Assyria could not hold down its huge empire. At practically every opportunity, the subject nations, who provided much of the Assyrian military and administrative manpower, rebelled. Power was so centralized that the death of the king, who was believed to have divine authority, weakened the empire still further and often provided the best conditions for revolt. The seismic effects of the deaths of Assyrian kings are among the main events of the century preceding the annihilation of Assyria, and they decisively influenced the growth and character of prophetic poetry. After the death of Tiglath Pileser III in 727, Israel rebelled and was crushed and exiled. Against the background of revolt in the western provinces of the empire, Babylonia followed suit and waged a long and initially successful war against Assyria after the death of Shalmaneser V in 722. The death of Sargon in 705 led to widespread revolt in both the eastern and western sides of the empire. The death of Sennacherib in 689 again set off unrest which Assyria this time managed to contain rapidly. The death of Esarhaddon in 669 brought civil war and wars with Babylonia and Egypt. And finally, the death of Ashurbanipal in 627 triggered a massive revolt and the collapse and disappearance of Assyria. The prophets' response to Assyria was inherently ambivalent. On the one hand, Assyria was hated and feared as the piratical empire that had crushed Israel and came within a hairbreadth of doing the same to Judah. This empire had an enviably attractive polytheistic culture, needing little or no military coercion to impose it on subject nations: the people of Israel, for example, seem to have assimilated willingly, though they had fought hard to keep their independence, and their kingdom and faith were lost in exile. On the other hand, if monotheistic faith was to survive, the Judeans had to learn to accept Assyrian victory as the will of God. This may be why no extended prophecies against Assyria are found in the period of its greatest military successes. Isaiah has no "burden of Asshur," neither does Micah or Hosea; and the prophecies against the nations which start the book of Amos do not include Assyria. The vivid memory of Israel's exile challenged the prophets: how to maintain a monotheistic faith strong enough to keep alive a national–religious identity in exile as well as the hope of return. The lack of unity which had led to Israel's split into two kingdoms in the tenth century was another force which, paradoxically, helped Judah to survive. For after Israel's fall, Judah had over a century to ready itself psychologically for the possibility of exile, to avoid being swallowed up like Israel. The threat of exile concentrates a nation's mind wonderfully, and the prophets' writings are the full creative flowering of this concentration.

The prophets, then, were leaders in a war against cultural imperialism, and perhaps this was initially the main reason for the writing and preservation of their teachings. Though they accepted submission to the superior military power as a condition of survival, they subverted imperial rule in a number of ways: in their attacks on the materialism and injustice which were inevitable consequences of imperialism; in their apparent lack of concern with economic realities, which may be seen as a backhanded attack on the very foundation of Assyrian expansionism; in their insistence that the divine word was not the monopoly of priest and king in the sanctuary, but could inspire the common man, even a shepherd such as Amos; in their undying hope for the ingathering of exiles, which ran directly counter to Assyrian and Babylonian policy; in their readiness to admit defeat, to depict it graphically and to accept it as the will of God; in maintaining belief in one omnipotent God in opposition to what they saw as the paltry polytheism of Mesopotamia. "The prophetic ideal was the kingdom of God, the kingdom of righteousness and justice. This was the basis of the first Isaiah's negation of war and of dominion acquired by warfare. This ideal implied the negation of world rule generally, of empire" (Kaufmann 1970, p. 117). The unique ferocity of the prophets' attacks on idols and idol-worship, while largely ignoring the rich mythology of pagan beliefs, might have been less a sign of hatred for idol-worship *per se* than of the empires which were odiously identified with the false gods and the magic and superstition associated with them.

The late eighth-century prophets were torn between detestation, hatred, and fear of Assyria and identification with Assyria as the rod of God's wrath. Consequently, their hatred of Assyria was shunted to a large extent onto various targets: idols, idol-worshipping nations, and Judeans who failed in moral self-discipline. But only with the fall of

Assyria could this hatred burst out freely and without terror of reprisal. Loathing and fear of Assyrian tyranny are spelt out in the relish and glee with which the prophet Nahum depicts the fall of Nineveh and of the Assyrian empire:

> Blasted, blank and bare:
> No end of the slain.
> Everywhere corpses strewn.
> Mountainous dead.
> Soldiers stumble on the bodies...
>
> How your shepherds slumber,
> king of Asshur!
> Your warriors lie in peace.
> Your people are scattered over the mountains –
> no one gathers them.
>
> There's no balm to ease your pain,
> the wound too deep:
> All who hear of it
> clap hands in glee...
> for over whom did your evil
> scourge not pass?
>
> (Nahum 2:11; 3:3, 18–19)

During the more stable period of the empire, from the middle of Sennacherib's rule until the death of Ashurbanipal, from about 700 to 627, there is no datable Hebrew prophecy. It is likely that Hebrew prophecy was suppressed, perhaps even by royal command, during this period. Manasseh, the Judean king for much of this time, reportedly spilt much blood, and the prophets might have been among his victims.

With the collapse of Assyria, Hebrew prophecy re-emerged and entered its second great period, against the background of Babylonian and Egyptian rivalry and the defeat and exile of Judah by the Babylonians. For a short time at the end of the seventh century, Judah seemed within reach of independence, but with the defeat of Josiah by Egypt in 609, it reverted to vassaldom. The motif of God's injustice – why do the righteous suffer and the wicked prosper? – emerges in prophetic poetry at this time, as if in response to the death of the righteous Judean king and the failure to gain independence at a time of the breaking of nations. The Babylonian defeat of Egypt at Carchemish in 605 was a watershed which left a strong mark upon prophetic poetry.

With this victory, Babylonia took over the mantle of imperial conqueror left by Assyria. As in the previous century, Judah was caught up in the jockeying for power of Egypt and Mesopotamia, the prophets warning against alliances, especially with Egypt, which could lead to disaster. Jeremiah was jailed in besieged Jerusalem for his pro-Babylonian views and let go only after Nebuchadrezzar defeated Judah, burned down the Temple in Jerusalem and exiled most of its inhabitants.

Had the Babylonian empire survived for a century or two rather than a half-century, the Judean exiles might have assimilated into Babylonian society as the Israelites had in Assyria. The rise of the Persian empire saved Judah and, in effect, made possible the survival and growth of Judaism. Following his defeat of Babylon in 539, the Persian king Cyrus issued an edict allowing the Jews exiled by the Babylonians to go back to their homes in Judah. This act stimulated the third and final wave of biblical prophecy, dominated by Second Isaiah, which for the first time conveys the ecstasy of vindication, of having come through, the sheer relief of regaining the territorial homeland, and the gratitude to God and commitment to his Law.

The Jews, having survived, alone, as it turned out, among the minority peoples of the ancient Near East, felt an enormous sense of privilege, specialness, responsibility, and chosenness. In the course of a single lifetime, the two most powerful empires in history, Assyria and Babylonia, had disappeared, while Judah miraculously held on. From the ecstatic viewpoint of Second Isaiah and his contemporaries, the earlier prophets such as Isaiah and Jeremiah had been proved right: faith in the end was indeed stronger than military force. In their desperate search for defenses against imperialism, the prophets discovered an alternative to empire which became the basis of Judaism in exile and, later, of Christianity and Islam. Faith is independent of time and place – this was their discovery – and they prepared the way for what Isaiah Berlin called "a culture on wheels", a mobile culture built upon faith and viable in exile.

It is striking in the biblical account how the weakening of imperial rule both in the late eighth century and the late seventh century was accompanied by a turning back to Yahweh-worship and the destruction of idols, and how the discovery of the Book of the Law (believed to be Deuteronomy) occurred just when Assyria lost its military grip at the end of the seventh century. Most of the main elements of Judaism in exile appear to have crystallized into a religious way of life under Persian rule, at the tail end of the prophetic period (the prophets vanished, one feels, because their task was done): belief in one invisible universal God and the total rejection of idols and magic; attachment to the memory of the Land of Israel; the introduction of synagogue worship as a substitute for Temple worship, and of prayer and study in place of the sacrifices; the repudiation of intermarriage; the invention of proselytization, this being almost a religious warfare equivalent to imperialism, and of the idea of martyrdom to defend the faith (as suggested in the book of Daniel which, although written much later, describes the Persian period), as well as the concept of the Messiah who would appear at the end of days and restore the Davidic kingdom of Judah. As indicated earlier, the exposure of the exiled Judeans to a kaleidoscopic group of other exiled peoples inclined them to develop their religion along far more universalistic lines than would have been possible in Judah. At the same time, it may be that the alienation and aggressiveness of some of the exiles aroused hatred, which was to develop into full-blown anti-Semitism during the Hellenistic period and after.

In condemning the greed and cruelty of imperial power, and in their creation of a spiritual alternative, the prophets became, in effect, the archetypal dissident artists, the most influential in history. The prophets are the voice of a minority society struggling to survive amid a dominant, often hostile, majority, and it is unlikely therefore that they will ever be passé. Every political and religious movement which stresses the value of social justice and compassion, opposes materialism and the unjust distribution of wealth, objects to ritual at the expense of spirituality and to the emphasis on the letter of the law rather than its spirit, and fights the abuse of power, owes something to the prophets. According to Weber (1961, p. 265), the prophets freed the world from magic, and in doing so created the rational basis for modern science and technology and for capitalism. However, from a creative standpoint the prophets' impact is most striking: all poets who write religious or political poetry, or in a rhetorical, confessional or lyrical mode are part of a tradition in which the prophets are among the prime movers, their taut, rhythmic, gritty Hebrew rich in imagery, contrasts and emotional range, of anger and tenderness, devastation and hope, vision and sarcasm.

The prophets, above all, helped transform Judaism from a national and parochial religion to a universal one, progenitor of Christianity and Islam. For all its bitterness, their poetry is remarkably hopeful and life-affirming, coming as it does from a people under constant threat of annihilation, whereas the outstanding Mesopotamian art is possessed by death. Death is the main subject of the finest poem of this civilization, the epic of Gilgamesh, which ends with Gilgamesh awaiting death by the magnificent city walls which he has built. Gilgamesh weeps to

Urshanabi, the ferryman across the waters of death: "O Urshanabi, was it for this that I toiled with my hands, is it for this that I have wrung out my heart's blood?" (1960, p. 114).

The most memorable representations in Assyrian art – the lions caged and trapped, pierced by arrows and spears, convulsed in dying agonies – may be taken in the end as a symbol of empire, violent and unloved, lacking spiritual direction, turning upon itself in a *Götterdämmerung* of despair.

The prophets, then, largely determined the character of the Jewish people and their faith and set the mold of Hebrew literature as a minority culture in an often-ambivalent relationship with dominant imperial cultures – the Greco-Roman, medieval Arab and Christian, and Tsarist Russian in particular – up to 1948. Since the time of the prophets, the Jews, even when they assimilated into other cultures, preserved the teachings of the prophets (without which Christianity and Islam would be hard to imagine) with its explosive revolutionary potential.

2
Trauma and Abstract Monotheism
Jewish Exile and Recovery in the Sixth Century BCE

The exile of the Judeans in the sixth century BCE is often linked to the emergence of Judaism as a universal, exclusively monotheist religion.[1] However, exile alone cannot account for the revolutionary nature of the Jewish acceptance of monotheism. It does not answer central questions relating to the biblical world: Why did non-monotheist religion in Jewish life, "the idols of wood and stone," suffer a mortal blow just then, ultimately vanishing from mainstream Judaism as completely as the dinosaurs? Why were the Jews solitary heretics of the ancient world, accepting principles of faith which apparently no other entire people did for a thousand years? Why did they no longer tolerate idol-worship – which they had done until the sixth century, at times to the exclusion of the worship of God? Why did most other defeated and exiled peoples, rather than become monotheists as the Jews did, evidently lose their faith in their local gods and fuse into the general pagan culture of their victors?[2] And why did the sixth century mark a crucial stage in human development when for the first time a people, rather than go to war against its enemies, insults and threatens their religious culture instead – though, as seen in Chapter 1, there is no evidence that pagan societies were at all aware of Judean monotheism, let alone its danger to them – and looks forward to an apocalyptic age when there will be universal harmony and the end of war? The Judean acceptance of monotheism calls for a broad framework of explanation that takes into account not only historical, theological and aesthetic factors but also psychological ones.

Circumstances in the late sixth century near east were favorable for Jewish monotheism. The need for unity of the surviving remnants of the two monotheist kingdoms, whose mutual hostility was now past, might have impelled them to escape further divine wrath by adopting the uncompromising faith of the prophets. General religious trends in the late sixth century, particularly Zoroastrianism, might have contributed to the Jewish acceptance of exclusive monotheism (Cohn 1993). It may be that Judean monotheism was supported by the Persians – the cost of rebuilding the Temple was paid by the royal treasury (Ezra 6:4; 7:20) – in part because of its likeness to Zoroastrianism. Furthermore, Judean monotheism was in many ways similar to the image of Ahura Mazda as taught by Zoroaster and accepted by Darius I (522–486), in whose reign the Second Temple was completed. Ahura Mazda was believed to be creator of heaven and earth, source of light and darkness, sovereign lawgiver, center of nature, originator of the moral order, judge of the whole world. Boyce (1984) has pointed out that "Jews and Zoroastrians would have found a minor bond in their rejection of images of worship" (p. 263). Still, the fact that Ahura Mazda was creator of Ahriman, his rival, was a major point of difference. Also, no people who came under Persian rule is known to have followed the Jews in their exclusive turn to abstract ethical monotheism. These social and political factors were undoubtedly important in their time, but they hardly explain the power of monotheism among the Jews in the long term.

The acceptance of one abstract God, to the exclusion of all others, by the exiled Judeans of the sixth century cannot be attributed to exile alone. There might have been a number of interrelated causes, unique in their configuration. Four are of paramount importance:

1. The fall of the kingdom of Israel in the eighth century inoculated Judah against the loss of identity when it, too, was exiled, in the sixth century. This disaster gave Judah a terrifying picture of what its fate might be if it did not strengthen its national and religious identity and prepare for the possibility of exile. Grief for both kingdoms, particularly in the form of guilt over the betrayal of God and anger at false gods and idolators (which had not saved Israel from exile) as well as the hope of restoration, helped preserve Judah's identity. By the sixth century the Judeans were, to some extent, ready to fight assimilation in exile and to grieve their exile. A key to survival, they found, was to split themselves off from what they regarded as the impure world of idolatry, to define themselves in hostile opposition to polytheism, and to offer a faith with a then unique missionary character, superior in ideas and in human and aesthetic content.

2. A critical mass of Judeans were consequently inclined toward universal abstract ideals and principles which could not be defeated or exiled.

In contrast, material gods and territorial identity were seen by the Judeans as weak and transient.

3. The destruction of the empires of Assyria and Babylonia within one lifetime (612, 539) confirmed Judah in its anxiety to worship correctly an abstract and indestructible God, rather than gods of wood and stone, and fortify itself against destruction. The fall of these empires and the Persian Edict of Return appeared to vindicate Judean faith in one invisible God and the devaluation of worldly power and material gods. Judah, comprising little more than 1 percent of the Assyrian and Babylonian empires, survived while these empires vanished. Its survival was evidence of the superiority of abstract moral ideas over military might, the trappings of state, and the exiled gods of the fallen empires. Principles of faith are indestructible, unlike territorial sovereignty, material objects, and the physical representations of gods and their edifices, which can be plundered, exiled or destroyed. The need for the unity of the surviving fragments of both kingdoms of Israel and Judah as well as the general direction of ancient religion, especially Zoroastrianism, would have further inclined the Jews to monotheism.

4. The aesthetic revolution led by the prophets was a key factor in the turn to the abstract God. The poetry of monotheism was revered and recited in public worship as the word of God: non-Hebrew literature of the ancient near east was abandoned and lost. Poetry helped turn the Judeans from a monotheist people who had vacillated to and from paganism into an international people who rejected idol worship and welcomed believers into a community of faith. At least some Jews in the sixth century found the spiritual inspiration and beauty of the prophets' poetry so manifestly above most other near eastern culture that it drew them away from that natural, endemic cure for their chronic wound of defeat, exile, and humiliation: assimilation. They were, as Spinoza might have put it, too intoxicated by the divine poetry of the prophets to seek the sobriety of what seemed to them a more materialist faith. The particular form of national trauma experienced by the Jews, coupled with their historic traditions, evidently enhanced their need for and receptiveness to creative repair through poetic art in the sixth century and later. The biblical prophets, then, may be seen as literary progenitors of later poets and philosophers seeking insight into and cure of trauma, whether personal or collective, in the quest for an abstract God.

Two and a half millennia on, the effect of the prophets on their first listeners and readers can only be imagined. A generation before the

exile, King Josiah on hearing the words of the Scroll of the Law (presumably Deuteronomy) was awestruck and inspired into a total reform
of religious practice in Judah (II Kings ch. 19). The prophets' words
thundered in the ears of the exiled Judeans, left with little but memories
and words, possessed with guilt and fear at having been untrue to their
God and consequently exiled, then miraculously given the chance to
rebuild their lives in their homeland. The release given by this second
chance bonded them in hatred of idols coupled with faith in their God,
whose fearful threats were now the realization of a promise:

> If it crosses your mind – it shall never, never be! – that "We'll be
> like the nations, like the families of the earth, serving wood and
> stone" – I swear says Adonai Yahweh, that with a strong hand and
> outstretched arm and with outpoured fury I will rule over you!
> (Ezekiel 20:32–3).

Modern studies of catastrophe and grief, personal as well as collective,
throw light on the movement to abstract monotheism among the
sixth-century Jews. These Jews suffered unusually complex upheaval
in their physical existence, their loss of sovereignty, land, property, pride,
and continuity as the monarchy and Temple were lost. In this crisis, the
idea of the Bible – of intellectual territory as their inheritance – became
possible and necessary for Jewish survival. The concept of a "new identity"
as the outcome of the grieving process after a severe loss (Parkes 1986)
helps us understand what happened to the sixth-century Jews.

Consider the Hebrew Bible, especially the prophets, like other writings
deriving from trauma as a tool of creative repair (cf. Brink 1977;
Aberbach 1989), setting abstract, spiritual values above material ones.
The turn to abstraction might have served an adaptive, therapeutic
function, for "The capacity for abstraction gives man a sense of mastery
over that from which he is detaching himself" (Storr 1972, p. 182).

The prophets' depiction of God as an abstract being is a radically
original aesthetic as well as theological phenomenon. It is striking how
frequently the prophets use concrete imagery to depict abstract concepts: "I will betroth you to me in faith" (Hosea 2:21), "let justice roll
down like waters" (Amos 5:24); "fountains of salvation" (Isaiah 12:3);
"to go humbly with your god" (Micah 6:8); "the righteous shall live by
his faith" (Habakkuk 2:4); "seek humility, perhaps you will find shelter"
(Zephaniah 2:3); "righteousness the plumbline" (Isaiah 28:17); "circumcision of the heart" (Jeremiah 3:4); "like a fire shut in my bones" (20:9);
"a God in hiding" (Isaiah 45:18); "prisoners of hope" (Zechariah 9:12).

These and many other phrases point to a quality of mind substantially different from that which evidently prevailed in the ancient world, though there are occasional parallels, notably in Homer. To the mind capable of such creative leaps, material reality is not enough. Consequently, the Bible mocks pagan worship and totally ignores the vibrant, affirmative, moral qualities of the "strange" gods (Curtis 1992):

> They – their kings and princes,
>   priests and prophets –
> say "Hi, Dad!" to a tree
> and "Hello, Mom!" to a stone.
>   (Jeremiah 2:26–7)

The abstract imagination, which rejects "gods of wood and stone," must work harder, enriching itself in the struggle; traumatic sources are transcended by such creativity. The idea took root that the world is governed by invisible, immutable forces. The importance of this development was not, of course, confined to theology but marked a crucial advance in human intellectual growth: the imagining of an abstract God is one step away from the imagining of invisible particles, gravity, sound and light waves, and microorganisms.

What brought about these changes among sixth-century Jews? What set them on a theological path followed by no other people in the biblical world? One notable factor was multiple grief. There were two monotheist kingdoms. Both were destroyed in a period of 135 years. The destruction of the kingdom of Israel in 721 drew the surviving kingdom of Judah toward exclusive abstract monotheism. At the time of Israel's fall, Judah embarked on a massive reform aiming to uproot idolatry (II Kings ch. 18). Judah's exile in 586 reinforced the shift away from idolatry. Some Judeans and surviving Israelites who preserved their identity evidently denied at first the permanence of the exile of the ten lost tribes of Israel. They thought that the kingdom of Israel would be restored. This hope is found among all the written prophets of the eighth century: Amos (9:14–15), Hosea (11:11), Isaiah (11:16), and Micah (2:12), and it never entirely died (e.g. Ezekiel 37:15–25). Still, as time passed, denial gave way to a more sober recognition: Israel was probably gone for good. Judah remained vulnerable. To avoid Israel's fate, it had to prepare for the possibility of exile.

This situation was rare in the ancient world. The common biblical explanation of Israel's fall was its idol-worship: hence the purges of idols and idolators in Judah. The fall of Judah was felt more strongly than that of Israel.

Never before had God's covenanted partner – at least that half that had survived the devastation of Israel and her capital city, Samaria – experienced, or even witnessed, such violence against the people, the land, and the fortified as well as unwalled cities. Even more shattering was the incredible fact that God's own sanctuary, His very own Zion, was taken by Gentiles and lay defiled by them (Orlinsky 1977, p. 49).

The exiled Judeans, therefore, had greater need and capacity than the Israelites to mourn their loss and in so doing retain their distinctive identity. Elements of grief such as guilt and anger were expressed more openly, in the form of self-blame for moral corruption and exile and attacks on idols and idolators.

No survival can occur without severe guilt (Lifton 1967). Similarly, "in normal mourning anger expressed towards one target or another is the rule" (Bowlby 1980, p. 29). Anger might have inclined the exiled Judeans to differentiate themselves totally from pagan beliefs. They did so by accepting the abstract God taught by the prophets, and rejected the idolatry odiously identified with empires. To the Judeans, the collapse and disappearance of Assyria and Babylonia confirmed the impotence of their gods and enhanced the credibility of the abstract God, who cannot be exiled.

> Bel is bowed, Nebo bent double –
> a heavy load of gods
> carried by weary beasts
> buckling under the weight –
> They did not save a soul,
> exiles all ...
> (Isaiah 46:1)

The centrality of the Land of Israel in one of the major trade routes in the ancient world – between Egypt and Mesopotamia – as well as exile itself, which brought the Jews into close contact with numerous beliefs and practices of other peoples, seems to have inclined some to a critical rather than empathetic view of this foreign culture.

The prophetic teaching of faith in one abstract God helped overcome the great fear underlying Judah's theological vicissitudes – exile and loss of national identity. In grieving their lost kingdom and that of Israel, the Judeans were drawn more than before to an exclusive, invisible, omnipotent God of the universe and to God's kingdom of Truth and

Justice as the only source of power. This was a slow process, affected by a variety of factors and not completed until the late sixth century, perhaps not even then.[3] The Jews took strength and courage from a faith which denied the need for territorial existence and material objects. As a universal people, they, like God, could no longer be exiled. Their spiritual existence alone made them viable as a people, though it did not obliterate hope for the restoration of their land.

Clinical studies of multiple losses of siblings in childhood offer insight into the role of multiple grief in ancient Judah. A frequently observed phenomenon among bereaved children is failure to absorb the meaning of death and the inability to grieve (Bowlby 1980). A second loss might trigger off an unusually powerful grief reaction in which long-suppressed mourning for the first loss is also felt (Furman 1974). A powerful example of this phenomenon appears in De Quincey's autobiographical *Suspiria de Profundis* (1845), the never-finished sequel to *Confessions of an Opium Eater* (1821). In the *Suspiria*, De Quincey writes that his first knowledge of death came at age four-and-a-half, when his sister Jane died. He writes movingly of his ignorance of the meaning of death and of his disbelief that the loss was permanent:

> I knew little more of mortality than that Jane had disappeared. She had gone away; but, perhaps, she would come back. Happy interval of heaven-born ignorance! Gracious immunity of infancy from sorrow disproportionate to its strength! I was sad for Jane's absence. But in my heart I trusted that she would come again. Summer and winter came again, crocuses and roses, why not little Jane? (1966, p. 125).

In contrast with Jane's death, the illness and death of his sister Elizabeth when he was seven was a blow whose effects he felt for the rest of his life. De Quincey's mother was rather cold and aloof (he wrote of her, "She delighted not in infancy, nor infancy in her"), and Elizabeth had mothered him and was his favorite companion. News of Elizabeth's impending death set off an unusually strong grief reaction in which, no doubt, the long bottled-up mourning for Jane was also expressed:

> Rightly is it said of utter, utter misery that it "cannot be remembered." Itself as a remarkable thing, is swallowed up in its own chaos. Blind anarchy and confusion of mind fell upon me. Deaf and blind I was, as I reeled under the revelation (p. 128).

He describes how he would search the inanimate world for some sign of his sister:

> Into the woods or the desert air, I gazed, as if some comfort lay hid in them. I wearied the heavens with my inquest of beseeching looks. Obstinately I tormented the blue depths with my scrutiny, sweeping them for ever with my eyes and searching them for one angelic face that might, perhaps, have permission to reveal itself for a moment (p. 137).

How close this yearning and searching for the lost person is to the religious quest for an invisible God.

The importance of abstraction and detachment in creativity has been noted by psychoanalysts, literary scholars and historians.[4] According to Worringer (1953), the "urge to abstraction" originates in anxiety, in the drive for self-preservation and the need to create order in a chaotic world. The tendency to abstract philosophical thought is further linked to difficulties in relationships, especially in childhood, in which loss is often a factor.[5] Storr (1972) links contentment with the physical world with familial love and stability and discontent with trauma. Those like Poe, Descartes, Buber, Newton, and Bialik, who experienced the destruction of family bonds in childhood, perhaps for that reason found readier access to the world of imagination and abstract thought. Bereavement in some cases might lead to creative striving for mystical union with abstract ideas[6] (though most bereaved persons show no especial proclivity for abstract thought after bereavement). Among certain individuals, however, irrational though normal grief responses might trigger a creative engagement with abstractions.

Consider the following passage from René Descartes' *Second Meditation* (1641):

> Let us take, for example, this piece of wax: it has been taken quite freshly from the hive, and it has not yet lost the sweetness of the honey which it contains: it still retains somewhat of the odor of the flowers from which it has been culled; its color, its figure, its size are apparent; it is hard, cold, easily handled, and if you strike it with the finger, it will emit a sound. Finally all the things which are requisite to cause us distinctly to recognize a body, are met with in it. But notice that while I speak and approach the fire what remained of the taste is exhaled, the smell evaporates, the color alters, the figure is destroyed, the size increases, it becomes liquid, it heats, scarcely can one handle it, and when one strikes it, no sound is emitted. Does

the same wax remain after this change? We must confess that it remains; none would judge otherwise. What then did I know so distinctly in this piece of wax? It could certainly be nothing of all that the senses brought to my notice, since all these things which fall under taste, smell, sight, touch, and hearing, are found to be changed, and yet the same wax remains.

Perhaps it was what I now think, that this wax was not that sweetness of honey, nor that agreeable scent of flowers, nor that particular whiteness, nor that figure, nor that sound, but simply a body which a little while before appeared to me as perceptible under these forms, which is now perceptible under others. But what, precisely, is it that I imagine when I form such conceptions? Let us attentively consider thus, and, abstracting from all that does not belong to the wax, let us see what remains. Certainly nothing remains excepting a certain extended thing which is flexible and movable. But what is the meaning of flexible and movable? (Descartes 1970, I 154).

This reveals both the evolution of Descartes' method of reasoning and his distrust of the evidence of his senses in favor of belief in an abstract God. The imagination cannot grasp the physical nature of the wax: "It is my mind alone which perceives it" (p. 155). To Descartes, Truth cannot be found in sensory perceptions, only in abstract thought.

What caused Descartes' distrust of his senses? Why did he search relentlessly for abstract Truth? A number of psychological studies[7] have found insight in the fact that Descartes' mother died when he was an infant. Until he was nine, he was raised by his father and stepmother. Then he was sent to a Jesuit boarding school. The results, Descartes' dreams suggest (see Feuer 1963; Aberbach 1983), were confusion, weakness, isolation, a sense of being whirled about by irrational, uncontrollable forces, and fear of physical and mental collapse.

In general, loss in early childhood may lead to deep mistrust, both of human beings and, by extension, of physical objects and the senses. The growth of what Erikson (1963) calls "basic trust" comes through consistent loving care in infancy. Slowly the baby perceives that it is "in good hands." Disruption of the maternal bond in infancy may lead to chronic distrust, or what Laing (1969) describes as "ontological insecurity." Descartes' system of thought has an objective philosophical value of its own. But it might also be seen as a struggle to overcome insecurity, to hang on to something after the mother's death, to find what is real and true, to be convinced that the world is stable and reliable after all. Thought, to Descartes, is proof of God's existence.

Were there analogous motives in the Jews' rejection of the sensory, of material gods, and their acceptance of an abstract God – to create a believable world governed not by blind forces but by immutable, sacred ethical principles?

Another illustration of the possible connection between childhood bereavement and abstract thought is found in Martin Buber's *I and Thou* (1923):

> Every developing human child rests, like all developing beings, in the womb of the great mother – the undifferentiated, not yet formed primal world. From this it detaches itself to enter a personal life, and it is only in dark hours when we slip out of this again (as happens even to the healthy, night after night) that we are close to her again. But this detachment is not sudden and catastrophic like that from a bodily mother. The human child is granted some time to exchange the natural association with the world that is slipping away for a spiritual association – a relationship … The innateness of the longing for relation is apparent even in the earliest and dimmest stage. Before any particulars can be perceived, dull glances push into the unclear space toward the indefinite; and at times when there is obviously no desire for nourishment, soft projections of the hands reach, aimlessly to all appearances, into the empty air toward the indefinite (1970, pp. 76–7).

Buber is describing a movement from physical to spiritual attachment, from detachment from the "eternal mother" to a spiritual quest for a relationship with an abstract God. Underlying this thinking is childhood trauma: when Buber was three, his mother vanished, and for the rest of his life he saw her only once, when he was 33 (Friedman 1981, I 4, 11). This loss was "the decisive experience of Martin Buber's life, the one without which neither his early seeking for unity nor his later focus on dialogue and on meeting with the 'eternal Thou' is understandable" (p. 15).

Could we deduce from the example of Buber, too, that the movement to abstraction in sixth-century Judaism was possibly facilitated by a parallel collective trauma, of abandonment and exile, and a quest for an "eternal Thou" who would never fail his believers?

Consider a third passage, from Edgar Allan Poe's prose-poem, *Eureka* (1848):

> Each atom, forming one of a generally uniform globe of atoms, finds more atoms in the direction of the centre, of course, than in any

other, and in that direction, therefore, is impelled – but is thus impelled because the centre is the point of its origin. It is not to any point that the atoms are allied. It is not to any locality, either in the concrete or in the abstract, to which I suppose them bound. Nothing like location was conceived as their origin. Their source lies in the principle, Unity. This is their lost parent. This they seek always – immediately – in all directions – wherever it is even partially to be found ... I am not so sure that I speak and see I am not so sure that my heart beats and that my soul lives: of the rising of to-morrow's sun – a probability that as yet lies in the Future – I do not pretend to be one-thousandth part as sure – as I am of the irretrievably by-gone Fact that All Things and All Thoughts of Things, with the ineffable Multiplicity of Relation, sprang at once into being from the primordial and irrelative One (1984, pp. 1287–9).

In *Eureka*, Poe expounds his theory of cosmic unity, in which the uncertainties of physical existence are relieved by faith in an abstract God. Unity is a "lost parent" which, by extension – in contrast with real parents – can be found and retrieved. Poe lost both parents by age three (Symons 1978). His semi-mystical vision might be linked to these losses (Aberbach 1989). The abstraction Unity is more secure than a parent. It gives solace and hope in a world of disunity and fear.

Did the Jews in sixth-century Babylonia, having lost their motherland, find the idea of the unity of the abstract God – the credo of Judaism (Deuteronomy 6:4) – similarly consolatory and hope inspiring?

Consider, finally, this passage from Chaim Nachman Bialik's *Random Harvest* (1923):

Every stone and pebble, every splinter of wood, was an inexplicable text, and in every ditch and hollow external secrets lurked. How can a spark be contained in a mute stone, and who puts the dumb shadows on the house walls? Who heaps up the fiery mountains in the skirts of heaven, and who holds the moon in the thickets of the forest? Whither stream the caravans of clouds, and whom does the wind in the field pursue? Why does my flesh sing in the morning, and what is the yearning in my heart at evening time? What is wrong with the waters of the spring that they weep quietly, and why does my heart leap at the sound? These wonders were all about me, caught me up, passed over my poor little head – and refuge or escape there was none. They widened my eyes and deepened my heart, until I could sense mysteries even in commonplace things and secrets everywhere (Bialik 1999, p. 22).

Random Harvest is a semi-biographical prose-poem in which the poet writes of his "abandonment" by his parents and his 'adoption' by the God of Nature. Bialik, though best-known as the great poet of Jewish nationalism, is also a poet of private grief, having suffered the complete break-up of his family by age seven: his father died and he was separated from his mother (Aberbach 1982, 1988). These losses are connected in his poetry (e.g. *The Scroll of Fire*) with the decisive tragedies of Jewish history, such as the destruction of the Temple in Jerusalem and the exile. At times, one cannot separate Bialik's depiction of personal from national disaster. In clinical literature, similarly, the language of collective catastrophe (including the Holocaust) is to a greater or lesser extent the language of personal loss.[8] For good or bad, the search for an abstract ideal – whether theological or secular – links modern writers and thinkers with the Biblical prophets: for them, too, "The power of abstraction is the beginning of wisdom" (Storr 1972, p. 181).

Part II
From State to Scripture

3
The Roman–Jewish Wars and Hebrew Cultural Nationalism

The three Jewish revolts against the Roman empire in 66–70, 115–17, and 132–35 CE, in which the Jews were crushed each time, led to the total ban on Jewish residence in Jerusalem as the focal point of militant messianic Jewish nationalism. The Jewish population of Judaea (southern Palestine) was destroyed, enslaved, or exiled. A large part of the territory of Judaea was confiscated by the Romans as its Jewish owners had fought against Rome. Dozens of Jewish villages in Judaea were wiped off the map (Avi-Yonah 1976, pp. 15–16). The wholesale replacement of a Jewish by a gentile population is described by Millar (1993) as "the decisive transformation in the religious demography of the Holy Land in the Imperial Age" (p. 348). As a result, the living centre of Jewish culture moved north, to Galilee, where many Judaeans fled. In Galilee, synagogues and schools were built, and the legal and homiletic traditions flourished. Here the Mishnah, the basis of the Talmud, was edited by Judah Hanasi around 200 CE. This culture, mostly in Hebrew but also in Aramaic, fortified the Jews for what became, in Isaiah Berlin's words, "an unbroken struggle against greater odds than any other human community has ever had to contend with" (1979, p. 253).

Prior to the wars, Jewish political and religious identity were tied together; now, the Temple was destroyed, the priesthood and ruling class deprived of their political power, and Jewish identity was defined almost exclusively in terms of religious culture. Jewish leaders were no longer kings, priests, politicians, and warriors, but masters of Halakhah (law) and Aggadah (legend). Yet, this cultural renaissance was nationalistic insofar as Jews mourned the memory of the land from which they were exiled and kept alive the hope of return. They maintained and developed their traditions, they preserved their holy scriptures and the Hebrew language as well as their sense of chosenness. The Tannaim (rabbis of the Mishnah) were crucial in the survival and growth of living Hebrew: "In the tannaitic age, Hebrew was evidently not widespread among the Jews, and only the Tannaim used it in daily life" (Even-Shoshan 1983, III, p. 1566). At the same time, they entered to a greater extent than previously a world of their own making, of inner reality. The imaginary celestial Jerusalem became all the more potent as the earthly Jerusalem was out of reach.[1] This form of cultural nationalism spurred by defeat was practically unique in the ancient world.

Nationalism bred of victory is a common and rationally explicable precipitant of cultural achievement and ethnic identity. Military victory – of ancient Greece over Persia, for example, or of Rome and later Islam over most of the civilized world, of the Italian city-states over their enemies, the English over the Spanish Armada and Napoleon, the Allied powers over Germany in the two world wars – heralded cultural victory of various forms and degrees. The form of cultural nationalism set off by defeat evolved in the Middle Ages and has become familiar in modern history: the Armenians, the Finns, the French Canadians, the Irish, the Poles, the Ukrainians, the Bosnian Muslims, the Basques, Kurds, Tamils, and Palestinians are among many peoples whose identity has been galvanized and shaped by the frustration and humiliation of defeat.

Many defeated peoples in modern times have taken strength from their religious–cultural heritage, making it a powerful force of nationalism. Cultural nationalism, even when rooted in defeat and grievance, can sometimes transcend these as a moral value of its own (Hutchinson 1987). In Ireland, for example, defeats by Cromwell in 1649 and William of Orange in 1690 heightened the sense of Irish national identity, reflected in Irish literature both in Gaelic and English, and culminating in the poetry of Yeats. Defeat and partition of Poland in the late eighteenth century and the failure of its revolts against Tsarist Russia in 1830 and 1863 led, again, to enhanced Polish national feeling and creative activity, notably in the writings of Mickiewicz. The Finns, Ukraininans, and other subject peoples produced equally significant works during the same period. Russia's military disaster in the Crimean War of 1854–56 and the reforms which followed triggered off what is, arguably, most creative period of literary fiction in history. Indian literature developed remarkably after the failed mutiny of 1857, notably in the writings of Tagore, as the sense of Indian identity was enhanced by oppressive British colonial rule. The French defeat by Prussia in 1870–71 and the German defeat in World War I led, in each case, to heightened nationalism and a flowering of the arts.

In ancient history, however, defeat as a lasting spur to national identity was rare. Defeated peoples – even great empires such as Assyria and Babylonia – were mostly decimated or destroyed or they assimilated and died and their culture was lost or incorporated into other cultures. In ancient near eastern literature, victory is trumpeted; defeat is usually passed over in silence. It seems that no ancient people reacted to defeat as the Jews did. This does not mean that the Jews would not have preferred victory. The first six books of the Hebrew Bible have as their main theme the emergence of the Israelites from slavery in Egypt and their conquest of Canaan. The study and recital in synagogue of Scripture was a constant reminder of the possibility of a victorious struggle against the odds. Yet Judaism in practice evolved as an anti-triumphalist religion in which defeat was given unique emphasis as the communication of God's judgment and will and as a challenge to moral renewal. As a defeated people, the Jews underwent a variety of metamorphoses but kept their identity until modern times.

Defeated and exiled by the ancient near-eastern empires, the Jews turned to their religious culture as an exclusive means of preserving in sacred texts and memory their religious–national identity. The nature of this defeat in the biblical age was little different from that inflicted on many other small nations who got in the way of the great powers of the time. What was unusual, perhaps, was the perspective in exile of a defeated kingdom, Judah, whose people had witnessed the fatal defeats of the two greatest empires the world had yet seen – Assyria and Babylonia. The Judeans in sixth-century Babylonia are the first known example in history of an exiled diaspora community that in the long run did not totally assimilate but kept its identity and the hope of return to its homeland. Some Jews did return when given the chance by the Persians around 538 BCE, and the post-exilic state survived for six centuries.

However, the Jewish defeats by Rome in the three wars of 66–70, 115–17, and 132–35 CE were massive and virtually unprecedented, certainly in the internal history of the Roman empire. There was no return from exile and no rebuilding of Jerusalem and the Temple, as in the sixth century BCE. The Romans destroyed the Jews' political independence and state-based national identity, as well as their militant, messianic fervor, and banned Jewish proselytizing. They crushed and humiliated the Jews with a ferocity that largely determined the socio-psychological and religious character of the Jews and Judaism until modern times. These defeats contributed to the emergence of anti-Semitism as an important social and political force. Defeat effectively fixed, up to the modern period, the character of the Jews – especially those living in Christian countries – as an oppressed, exploited semi-pariah people who, nevertheless, had a rich civilization. Defeat labelled the Jews as deviant and amplified their cultural–national awareness, driving them more than previously into their own culture and educational system, sharpening their sense of distinctiveness and separation from the imperial system and their perception of the external world as the hostile impure Other. Defeat inclined some Jews to a lachrymose psychology of grief for the lost homeland, even in periods when the Jews were not persecuted. Defeat was decisive in the evolution of the Mishnah and the tradition of Jewish Law and of Midrash, the Jewish homiletical tradition.[2]

The national identity of the Jews – their common religion and language (Hebrew), sacred texts (the Bible), territory (the land of Israel), and history – has led some scholars (e.g. Kohn 1946; Smith 1991) to suggest that Jewish nationalism was the closest in the ancient world to modern nationalism. Though there is debate among scholars of nationalism as to the existence of genuine pre-modern nationalism,[3] many classical scholars – including Schürer (1909), Jones (1938), Smallwood, (1976), Avi-Yonah (1976), Brunt (1977), Mendels (1992), and Millar (1993) – accept the idea of Jewish nationalism in the Roman empire as a given. This nationalism might be seen as an antecedent of the modern nationalism of defeated peoples.

Before 66 CE, the Jews and Judaism were more variegated than after 70 CE. At no time, however, could the Jews be described as one single, simple organism reacting to external stimuli in a uniform, self-preservative manner. The picture of Jews in the Roman empire is mostly seen through rabbinic eyes. Yet not all Jews accepted the authority and ethical message of the rabbis. Jewish reactions to defeat included some that were not influenced greatly – if at all – by the rabbis. There are occasional glimpses of Jews who did not subscribe to, and even challenged, rabbinic teachings, for instance in 4 Ezra, in Martial's epigrams, and in the Talmud (e.g. *Pesahim* 49b). Still, the Jewish defeats affected all Jews, uniting them in the end as sovereignty never did. To suggest a parallel with the Holocaust is exaggerated, but there is a common unifying effect of heterogeneous groups in the aftermath of both collective disasters. Jewish survival under Roman was best ensured by rabbinic Judaism, which for this reason became mainstream Judaism by the end of the tannaitic age, when the Mishnah was edited at the start of the third century CE.

Largely deprived of the territorial, social, and political bases of their nationalism, the Jews were forced to base their identity and hopes of survival not on political but cultural and moral power, by things that could not be taken from them: the sacred word, the belief in being chosen, widespread education in Torah, legal justice, and the grief-stricken yearning for restoration to their ancestral homeland. Their religious life strengthened the Jews to tolerate the low social and political status and the psychological inferiority which came from taking up arms and losing. It gave them not just hope of ultimate freedom from Rome but also an inner freedom, out of the empire's cultural radius. Hebrew literature, both in the Bible and newly emerging from the Bet Midrash and Bet Knesset (Houses of Study and Prayer), salved their wounded ethnic identity after the destruction of Jerusalem and the Temple and the exile from Judaea. It helped to overcome the ensuing crisis of confidence and social division, and sublimated militant aggression into religious creativity. Defeat forced the Jews to test the strength of their culture, whose essence was indifference to worldly power and submission to God, to the law of the only true, eternal imperial ruler. Survival confirmed belief in being chosen. The forced split between political and cultural nationalism was a major factor in Jewish survival.

These combined elements of cultural nationalism were a unique mutation in the ancient world: a defeated people refusing to die but, instead, building and taking strength from a religious–national heritage; the split between political and cultural nationalism; the sense of uniqueness and chosenness nourished by defeat; the defence of this historical community, its ideals and dignity, expressed in a readiness to fight against the odds and die, if necessary, for ideals. Since the French Revolution, all these have become common features of national identities throughout the world. Even when major differences are taken into account – for example, that the Jews created a religious legal system independent of the dominant power, and they blamed themselves for their defeats – these similarities are striking.

Hebrew creativity in the Roman empire of the second century CE is, therefore, of especial interest to students of modern nationalism as a source of insight into the varieties of cultural nationalism stimulated by defeat. This culture, different in many ways from that of the Bible, was the "home territory" of the Jewish people and the basis of their religious–cultural nationalism. As Goodman (1983, p. 180) writes, the rabbinic world view

> made a virtue of, and gave sense to, the need for protection of national identity and group solidarity against external hostility that Palestinian Jews were bound to feel after the bloody failure of two

revolts [in 66–70 and 132–35 CE] and the accompanying surge of anti-Jewish feeling among the gentiles of nearby cities.

While Greek culture itself derived much impetus from the defeat of Greece by Rome in the second century BCE, the Hellenists hitched their cultural wagon not to Greek nationalism and the hope of Greek independence from Rome, but to the Roman empire. Still, the Hellenists were the first to show that a culture could conquer an empire. This revolution in civilization pointed out the dangers of Judaism and undermined Jewish hopes of independence from Rome. It set into motion prejudice toward and hatred of the Jews which, taken up by Christianity, survived long after the Roman empire vanished, culminating in the Holocaust and the re-establishment of a Jewish state (cf. Poliakov 1965; Alexander 1992).

Hebrew cultural nationalism in the Roman empire may be linked to a group of interconnected forces: Hellenism in the Roman empire; Jewish demographic expansion throughout the empire; anti-Semitic ideology and provocation; procuratorial misrule and the social and economic decline of Judaea; Jewish revolts and defeats; the retreat to cultural nationalism and to Hebrew creativity. Two new, more or less simultaneous, seemingly contradictory movements appeared at the start of Roman imperial rule: first, large numbers of pagans began to see Judaism as a strong, attractive religion and adopted Jewish customs or converted to Judaism; and second, ideological anti-Semitism became a virulent lasting force.[4] Judaism was portrayed as a barbaric superstition, the Jews as lepers, the plague and enemy of mankind. Jewish expansion evidently contributed to this hostility. In the broadest sense, the Roman–Jewish wars had one cause: the incompatibility of Judaism as a political force with the unity of the Roman empire (Mommsen 1996, p. 195). It was no accident that Judaea, the province that posed the greatest ideological threat to Rome, had practically the worst Roman administration. As Jewish political and religious hopes were inseparable from each other, Roman attempts to curtail Jewish political power inevitably threatened Jewish religious freedom and brought unforgiveable insult to the Jews. The main arena for conflict was what amounted to a *Religionskrieg* between Jews and Greeks, Judaism and Hellenism. According to Goodman (1987, p. 12ff.), the depth of hostility and ferocity of violence among Jews and Greeks in the first and second centuries CE was unusual in the history of inter-ethnic relations in the empire. The reasons are not hard to find. Hellenism and Judaism were powerful rival civilizations, the first to adopt the simplified alphabet at the start of the first millennium BCE and to develop sacred literary cultures (Homer and the Bible) with longlasting universal appeal. Both were conquered by Rome, the Greek city states by 146 BCE and Judaea in 63 BCE. Their cultures were to some extent mutually intolerant. Greek and Jewish communities co-existed uneasily in many of the major cities of the Roman empire, including Rome, Alexandria, and Antioch, with sporadic outbreaks of violence.[5] Rivalry between Greeks and Jews was exacerbated by the fact the both had cultures superior to that of Rome which, Feldman (1996) observes, "had an inferiority complex about arriving so late on the scene of history" (p. 22) and needed an imperial culture. Rome adopted Hellenism and, as Rostovtzeff (1957) points out, the empire became increasingly Hellenized in the years just before the 66–70 CE war:

> Greek civilization, art, and literature were again regarded even by the Romans as *the* civilization, *the* art, *the* literature. Nero was the first to proclaim *urbi et orbi* the new gospel and to act on it (pp. 117–18).

Even before Nero's rule, in the reigns of Caligula (37–41 CE) and Claudius (41–54 CE), the central government bureaucracy in Rome had come largely under Hellenistic control. Hellenistic ex-slaves (freedmen), whose sympathies in the Greek–Jewish rivalry were naturally with fellow-Greeks, had at crucial moments powers equal to, if not greater than, the emperors themselves (Duff 1958). Egregious misrule of Judaea and maltreatment of diaspora Jews (primarily in Rome and Alexandria) became most bitter and violent when freedmen had most power in Rome (Aberbach and Aberbach 2000). This was the environment in which the war of 66–70 CE broke out.

Judaism was a somewhat unwilling rival to imperial culture. Most diaspora Jews in the Roman empire – the majority of the world Jewish population – accepted Roman rule and assimilated to some extent at least into the culture of the empire. But whether they liked it or not, they had a powerful, attractive religious civilization of their own to which anyone could convert. Their influence and numbers were growing, apparently reaching a peak in Nero's reign, in the years prior to the 66 CE revolt (Stern 1974, I, p. 429).[6] Jewish expansionism could be seen as a vote of no confidence in the Roman empire and its Hellenistic culture. These demographic and cultural changes evidently caused alarm and hatred in the empire, especially among anti-Jewish Hellenists in Rome, where Jewish influence in the imperial court also reached its height in the years leading up the 66 CE revolt (Feldman 1993, p. 428).

True, the empire had many concerns other than the Jews. Also, although tension was always there, Roman–Jewish relations were sometimes good, and diaspora Jews were in most cases protected by Roman authorities. Still, Rome had more trouble with the Jews than with any other people in its empire. In the long run, negative elements – mutual suspicion and hostility leading to war and Jewish defeat – won out.

The roots of anti-Semitism in the Roman empire – and, indeed, as a significant historical phenomenon – may be found in the early years of Roman rule, after the conquest of Judaea in 63 BCE. As in fifteenth century Spain or in the Soviet Union after the Bolshevik revolution, Judaism was perceived, whether in fact or exaggeratedly, as a potential danger to the unity of the ruling power. Of all the peoples in the Roman empire, only the Jews, because of their religion, felt strongly about the retention of their distinctiveness (Roberts 1997, p. 241). Consequently, until 135 CE, the Jews were in an almost constant mood of revolt (Stern 1977, p. 244). Titus reportedly declared as much to the besieged Jews of Jerusalem (*BJ* VI 6, 2 [329]).[7] To some pagans, Judaism offered a welcome humanist antidote to the brutality of Roman culture. Weber (1952) explains the attraction of Judaism in the Roman empire to proselytes:

> What was most appealing were the conception of God which appeared as grandiose and majestic, the radical elimination of the cult of deities and idols felt to be insincere, and, above all, Jewish ethics appearing as pure and vigorous, and besides the plain and clear promises for the future, hence rational elements (pp. 419–20).

According to Smallwood (1976, p. 541), the high moral code of Judaism was politically a subversive force in the Roman empire because it was inseparably tied to messianic nationalism.[8] The fact that a number of Roman client-kingdoms situated near the border of Rome's enemy, Parthia, were temporarily at least ruled by Judaizing royal families was a further source of friction in Roman–Jewish relations: "in conjunction with Parthia and its allies, a concerted rising of such Judaizing kingdoms might have proved a formidable threat to Rome's Eastern frontiers" (Aberbach 1966, p. 39).[9]

Rome and Parthia clashed over zones of influence in the East. In particular, Parthia was dangerous to Rome as it aimed to emulate the ancient Persians and conquer the Roman-held east Mediterranean territory. It had better cavalry than Rome and inflicted two of the worst military disasters in Roman history, against Crassus (53 BCE) and Mark Antony (36 BCE). This might not have affected the position of the Jews in the Roman empire, except that Parthia also had large Jewish communities with close ties to Palestinian Jewry: "Palestine and Babylonian Jewries [almost all of whom lived under Parthian rule] formed in fact one national body separated by an artificial boundary" (Avi-Yonah 1976, p. 38). The Palestinian Jews thus became vulnerable to Roman suspicion of divided loyalty and guilt by association. Rome in any case did not like peoples that were half in and half out of the empire. (The conquest of Britain was undertaken partly to bring the Celts of Gaul and of Britain under Roman rule.) The international character of Judaism was out of Roman control, and this inadvertently made Judaism a natural focal point for dissidence in the empire, expressed partly in the large number of proselytes, sympathizers, and adherents to Jewish customs in the empire.

Rome naturally reacted with hostility. To some Greco-Romans, the reduction of the power and attraction of Jewish political identity and the proselytizing messianic fervor which drove it was a long-term *sine qua non* for the survival of the empire. In the case of the Jews and Judaism, official religious tolerance in the empire could sometimes be inimical to Roman interests. Rome dealt with the problem prior to 66 CE not by officially changing its policy of tolerance but through what might be called an elective affinity for misrule and provocation, persecution and anarchy in Judaea and, occasionally, the diaspora. In the context of the history of Roman provincial administration, the rule of Judaea was exceptionally poor (Grant 1971, p. 221), especially as Roman administration generally improved under imperial rule by comparison with the corruption of the last century of the republic (Roberts 1997, p. 240). Schürer observes that the Judaean procurators behaved as though they set out to drive Judaea to revolt (1973, I, p. 455); and more recently Schäfer has written that the incompetence of the procurators, their exploitation and insults to Judaean national and religious feelings, made war almost inevitable (1995, p. 114). Procuratorial policy must have had the approval or at least the tacit consent of the government in Rome. The treatment of the Jews, though generally localized and temporary, had no parallel in Roman treatment of its minorities. It was calculated to weaken the prestige and influence which the Jews and Judaism were perceived as having. The extraordinary military force deployed by Rome against the Jews, which included large numbers of Greeks from Hellenistic cities in Palestine, is an indication of the importance which Rome attached to the Jewish threat (Millar 1993, p. 73). The ban on Jewish proselytization by Hadrian was an implicit admission of the dynamic attraction of Judaism as a rival culture

(Feldman 1993). The closure of Jerusalem to Jews and the de-judaization of Judaea after the Bar-Kokhba revolt of 132–35 CE acknowledged the symbolic power of this territory as a unifying force of Jewish nationalism inimical to Rome (Mendels 1992). Aberbach (1966), Smallwood (1976), and Gager (1983), among others, describe anti-Semitism as part of the background to the Great Revolt of 66–70 CE. Goodman (1996, p. 781) writes that "wilful hostility" of Romans toward Judaism led not just to the 66–70 CE revolt but also to the other two.[10]

The failed Jewish revolts prepared the ground for the culturally revolutionary Hebrew literature in the age of the Tannaim.[11] Greek involvement in the Jewish defeats contributed in turning many Jews – certainly the rabbinic leadership – against Hellenistic culture. The consequent explosion of Hebrew literature – partly under the influence of Hellenism – led to an enhanced sense of Jewish national–religious identity which has survived to the present.

The trauma of defeat, though lasting, was offset somewhat by changing sociological conditions in the Roman empire of the second century CE which aided recovery. The wars against Rome ended the Jewish internecine conflict that had erupted in civil war during the Great Revolt of 66–70 CE. Rome achieved a form of social electrolysis: it virtually destroyed the Sadducees, the Essenes, and the Zealots, and by defeating the Jews helped split Christianity off from Judaism. Rome also made imperial Greco-Roman culture unpalatable to many Jews – leaving only Pharisaic Judaism and its leaders, the rabbis. The paradox of defeat was that it "led to the triumph of rabbinic Judaism" (Schürer 1973, I, p. 555).

The razing of Jerusalem and the ban on Jewish residence there after the Bar-Kokhba revolt gave life to the imaginative idea of the celestial Jerusalem and the Temple, as it was in its glory and as it might someday become. In much the same way, exile has been the nursery of modern nationalisms such as that of the Irish:

> The massive exile which followed the famines of the 1840s left hundreds of thousands of Irish man and women in the major cities of Britain, North America and Australia dreaming of a homeland, and committed to carrying a burden which few enough on native grounds still bothered to shoulder: *an idea of Ireland* (Kiberd 1995, p. 2).

Perhaps partly for this reason, most of the greatest Irish literature was written outside Ireland. Similarly, Hebrew literature after the

Roman–Jewish wars (and, indeed, until modern times) evolved and was edited in exile from Judaea. It may be a universal truth, Salman Rushdie suggests, that various forms of exile can stimulate remarkable creativity:

> The writer who is out-of-country and even out-of-language may experience this loss in an intensified form. It is made more concrete to him by the physical fact of discontinuity, of his present being in a different place from his past, of his being "elsewhere". This may enable him to speak properly and concretely on a subject of universal significance and appeal (1991, p. 12).

Mutual hostility between Jews and Greco-Romans sharpened group boundaries and promoted Jewish cultural separatism: "historical consciousness that is so essential a part of the definition of what we mean by the term 'ethnic *community'* is very often a product of warfare or the recurrent threat thereof" (Smith 1981, p. 379).

The failed Jewish revolts brought the secondary gain of an international community united in trauma and prepared the way for the culturally revolutionary age of the Tannaim. War, like exile, is often associated with periods of cultural creativity. For example, Hebrew prophecy flourished between the eighth and sixth centuries BCE against the background of conquest of the kingdoms of Israel and Judah, the exile of many of their inhabitants, and the rise and fall of the empires of Assyria and Babylonia (Aberbach 1993). The birth of tragedy in the drama of Aeschylus, Sophocles, and Euripides (fifth century BCE) came in an age dominated by major wars, first between Greece and Persia, then between Athens and Sparta, in the Peloponnesian wars. In the fifth–third centuries BCE, the literature of Confucianism emerged amid constant civil war in China. In the High Renaissance (c. 1495–1527), similarly, the explosion of original art by Leonardo, Michelangelo, and Raphael was accompanied by frequent wars as France and Spain struggled for hegemony over Italy. Many of the artistic achievements of the Romantic movement – the poetry of Goethe and Wordsworth, the music of Beethoven and Schubert – were created under the impact of the French revolution and the Napoleonic wars. In the early twentieth century, too, the creative flowering of writers such as Yeats, Joyce, Eliot, and Pound, among others, was inseparably bound up with the massive blow to the ideals of Western civilization – the "old bitch gone in the teeth" as Pound called it – in World War I. Of the tannaitic age, as of these other periods of outstanding creativity, an observation of Goldmann's is apt: "On the social as well as the individual plane, it is the sick organ which creates awareness, and it is in moments of crisis that men are most aware of the enigma of their presence in the world" (1964, p. 49). The growth of Jewish legal and homiletic traditions was facilitated by conditions in the Roman empire in the late second century CE, by the *Pax Romana*, the waning of Roman imperialism, and improvements in the economy of Galilee and in Roman–Jewish relations. Much Roman animosity toward Jews was evidently transferred to Christianity, which unlike Judaism was not a *religio licita*. The originality of the Tannaim might be linked to their muted, ambivalent relationship with the dominant imperial culture. Hellenism permeated Jewish urban life. The cultural ambience of Hebrew literature was largely Greek, literary and archaeological evidence has shown (Lieberman 1950; Hengel 1981). No Greek writings have survived from any of the Tannaim. Few of them lived in major Hellenistic cities such as Caesarea and Scythopolis (Beth-Shean). Their lingua franca was Aramaic. There is little evidence that they knew Homer, but some of them possibly spoke Greek better than Hebrew as Greek was more widely used. The limited immersion in Greek culture – their use of Greek vocabulary, Greek rhetorical devices, and Greek styles and motifs in their architecture as well as their unprecedented emphasis on the importance of education and law – might be interpreted as a sign of admiration toward a rival culture. Yet, in its assimilation of elements of Hellenism, Hebrew literature could signify Jewish resignation to imperial rule: it drew strength from the strength of the empire and addressed some of the empire's weaknesses.

At the same time, the Jews inevitably associated Greco-Roman culture with their military defeats. Once Jewish political–messianic nationalism was broken by the Roman army in the 132–35 CE war and the Hadrianic persecution, the Jews were let alone, to remake their religious culture and develop the Hebrew language and literature as they wanted, independently of imperial culture.[12] In some ways, the Jews reacted to defeat as they had during the persecution of Antiochus IV in 168–65 BCE: with hatred of pagan culture and a sharp psychological turn inward (though the Hasmoneans kept the trappings of Hellenistic civilization, including their administration and military organization). In general, a tendency to retreat from Greco-Roman civilization had existed among Jews prior to the Roman–Jewish wars, notably in the monastic sect of Qumran. However, Hebrew literature of the Tannaitic period and after expresses what Millar (1993, p. 352) describes as a wholesale retreat from Hellenism, representing what was becoming the Jewish mainstream, to the consolation of what was perceived as uniquely Jewish. While Greek and Aramaic were used by Jews and pagans alike, Hebrew was used only by Jews. It was unstained by enemy use. There is much artistry in tannaitic literature but little of the overt aestheticism associated with Greek culture. Defeat evidently led to a revulsion among many Jews toward Greek culture (cf. Mishnah *Sotah* IX 14, *Hagigah* 15b, *Menahot* 99b). The wars initially undermined Jewish communal cohesion and self-image and endangered Jewish survival. They spurred some Jews to develop their educational system and homiletic tradition and to edit oral teachings to ensure these would not be lost. In this way, Jewish cultural nationalism, with Hebrew literature at its core, became vital to Jewish survival. It kept alive the possibility, however faint, of a political awakening.

The achievement of the Tannaim is ironically among the legacies of Rome. Hebrew flourished in the volcanic ash of defeat, spreading roots of Talmud and Midrash, of Halakhah (law) and Aggadah (legend). Defeat converted an untolerated Jewish militant messianism, challenging the empire, into a tolerated cultural nationalism. It drove the Jews into their own Hebrew cultural identity, forcing unity, distinctiveness, and a form of divorce from the imperial system.

Jewish cultural nationalism after 70 CE had its chief impetus in the reconstitution of Judaism around the synagogue. This meant sermons by rabbis and imaginative development of aggadic as well as halakhic thought. While the Mishnah was the most lasting achievement of the Tannaim, tannaitic midrash set a similarly high standard of excellence in its originality, insight, and stylistic felicity which later midrash rarely equalled. There is a view that the tannaitic midrashim on the Pentateuch – *Mekhilta* (on Exodus), *Sifra* (on Leviticus), and *Sifre* (on Numbers and Deuteronomy) – "reached a high point never since surpassed" (Epstein 1959, p. 116). Though midrash evolved for at least a millennium after the tannaitic period, at times with much beauty and charm, its basic form and content did not change substantially (de Lange 1987, p. 157); much of it is at best an echo of tannaitic midrash.

A re-examination of the Roman–Jewish wars and the ways in which defeat entered the national consciousness and cultural fabric of the Jews, is more than an academic exercise. It gives insight into modern nationalism born of defeat and humiliation, which in the absence of a creative outlet could lead to frustration, spite, bitterness, depression, rage, and the lust for revenge. Tannaitic writings are eminently dignified and, at times, beautiful and moving. They are a reminder that defeat can sometimes be a more powerful, longlasting spur to national identity than victory. They also show how a defeated minority can learn from the dominant culture and enrich its own. History suggests that victors do not always know what they want and who they are; the defeated often do. Victory may lead to ultimate failure to adapt effectively to social change. Defeat and subjugation, in contrast, can promote sensitivity and caution and be a covertly subversive adaptive force. Power is not confined to the ruling body but may be found in various forms also among the subjugated. The many nations which sprang up with the fall of the Soviet empire are proof of the power of nationalism among defeated peoples. To the ardent nationalist crushed by an imperial power, the inversion of Vince Lombardi's famous quote is more than a *bon mot*: Losing isn't everything, it's the only thing.

The suicidal readiness of many modern nationalists to fight in fanatic defence of national and religious ideals and dignity has its closest ancient analogue in the Roman–Jewish war of 66–70 CE. Josephus conveys an almost modern spirit when in the *Jewish War* he has Eleazar ben Yair, commander of Masada, declare that he and his followers will die heroically, in defense of their liberty: "let us do each other an ungrudging kindness, preserving our freedom as a glorious winding-sheet" (VII 8, 6 [370]). The act of revolt against Rome, writes Schürer (1973, I, p. 357), was suicidal. Its chief aim – as among the Poles in 1830 and 1863, the Irish in 1916, or the Hungarians in 1956 – was to assert defiance and national pride. In their cultural nationalism, the Tannaim preserved a different form of national freedom, with survival at its heart.

4

Entry to Powerlessness

The Tannaim, Marcus Aurelius, and the Politics of Stoicized Judaism

In the second century CE, after three failed revolts against Rome, in 66–70, 115–17, and 132–35 CE, the Jews turned from political to religious aims, from suicidally militant messianism to pacifist resignation. If, as Josephus writes of the Great Revolt of 66–70, the Jews had "preferred to perish at one fell swoop than piecemeal" (AJ XX 11,1 [256]), after 135 CE survival within the "four cubits of the Law" (*Berakhot* 8a) was their aim. Resistance to Roman rule was now sublimated into the cut and thrust of talmudic argument (cf. *Megillah* 15b, *Kiddushin* 30b). The tannaitic Midrash, *Sifre* on Deuteronomy 32:35 identifies the "craftsmen and smiths" exiled to Babylonia by Nebuchadnezzar (597 BCE) with gifted scholars engaged in "the warfare of Torah" (321).

The point at which the survival of Judaism became predicated upon a pacifist philosophy, after the Bar-Kokhba revolt of 132–35 CE, coincided with the Antonine dynasty. At this time, a parallel philosophy, of Stoicism, associated with thinkers such as Zeno, Cleanthes, Chrysippus, Seneca, Musonius Rufus, Epictetus, and especially Marcus Aurelius, became prominent to an unprecedented degree – in theory at least – in the highest circles of power in Rome while at the same time enjoying widespread popularity in the Roman empire as a "middlebrow philosophy" (Goodman 1997, p. 155). Though the Roman empire contained many forms of religion, Stoicism was notable for its emphasis on ethics.[1] In its ethical concerns, tannaitic literature – particularly tractate *Avot* in the Mishnah (edited by Judah Hanasi, c. 200 CE) – seems closer to contemporary Stoics, notably Epictetus and Marcus Aurelius, than to the earlier Stoics.

There is reason to believe that similarities between tannaitic and late Stoic literature may have different social, political, and psychological significance from that of parallels between Greek and Jewish literature observed by Hellenistic Jews such as Philo before the Roman–Jewish wars. Before 66 CE, the idea of "Hellenistic Judaism" was more viable than after 135 CE. "The world of Greek culture," writes Gruen (1998), "was not an alien one to Hellenistic Jews. They thrived within it and they made its conventions their own. They engaged in Hellenic discourse but addressed their message to fellow Jews. Their free adaptation of the Scriptures, imaginative fiction, and light-hearted recreations of Hellenistic history gave readers pride in Jewish heritage and amusement in its novel reformulation" (p. 297). There were various motives for pressing the similarities between Jewish and Greek culture. Most importantly: as a defense of and apology for Jewish culture in an empire that had adopted Greek culture and was using it to unify its fissiparous parts, so that Judaism should not be seen hostilely as foolish and strange, or worse, a heresy and a threat to Rome; pride that Jewish culture was ancient, rich and sophisticated, and should be taken seriously by the non-Jewish majority; or as an expression of competition with Greek culture, propaganda aimed to persuade Gentiles of the superiority of Judaism. Defeat made these motives largely anachronistic as Hellenistic Judaism faded in the second century CE: "inconsistent Hellenistic Judaism was unable to hold its own in the face of the greater consistency of the Pharisees" (Schürer 1973, p. 2).

Yet Greek culture remained a powerful influence on Judaism both because of physical proximity of Jews and Greeks and, perhaps primarily, because the Greeks, especially the Stoics, had developed a philosophy which could make defeat and humiliation more bearable. Post-135 CE amalgamation of Stoic ideas into Judaism helped Jewish survival: not just as a form of identification with the aggressor, or a means of softening Roman hostility toward the Jews through necessary political accommodation while appearing to "blend in" with a Greek cultural veneer, but as a spiritual need. For Stoicism was closest in the Roman world not just to Judaism but also to psychotherapy. No people had been so completely crushed as the Jews were by Rome and survived in the long term. The Stoicization of Judaism after 135 CE may be taken to reflect both the psychological and political terms for Jewish survival under Roman rule and consolidation of common ground between Greek and Jewish civilizations after the failed Jewish revolts. Stoic ideals in any case became more pronounced in Roman public life after the destruction of the Temple in Jerusalem in 70 CE. The Flavians brought a new spirit of severity and a consciousness of public service to the principate (Rutherford 1989).

Defeat forced the Jews to test and enhance the strength of their religious culture, whose essence was indifference to worldly power and submission to God, to the law of the only true, eternal imperial ruler. According to Schürer, the Jews derived paradoxical advantage from defeat: "...after the political collapse, the whole of the nation's energy was concentrated on its true and supreme task...It was, in effect, precisely the annihilation of Israel's political existence which led to the triumph of rabbinic Judaism" (1973, I 524, 555). However, withdrawal from politics can itself be seen as a political act necessary for Jewish survival. Judaism was in any case depleted of its political variety. Rome had virtually destroyed the Sadducees, the Essenes and the Zealots, and by defeating the Jews helped split Christianity off from Judaism and made Hellenistic Judaism unviable in the long term. This left only Pharisaic Judaism and its leaders, the rabbis, whose teachings, Josephus writes (*Life* 2), in an exaggeration intended to appeal to the pagan intelligentsia, were similar to those of Stoics. In particular, the destruction of Jerusalem and, after 135 CE, the banning of Jews from residence in Jerusalem, could be seen as ultimately strengthening Judaism by forcing the Jews to rebuild their religion on the exclusive basis of prayer and study rather than political power and Temple ritual: "In destroying Jerusalem the Romans forcibly dissociated the Jewish religion from the Jewish state...In this the Romans in the long run did Judaism a service" (Simon 1996, p. 35). At the same time, as we shall see, the Tannaim evidently expropriated elements of the enemy culture – from Stoic philosophy in particular – which, in altered form, could promote healing, facilitate submission to Roman rule, and increase the chances of the survival of Judaism.

The *locus classicus* in the Talmud of the separation of rabbinic Judaism from war with the aim of political accommodation with Rome is the account of the escape of Rabbi Yochanan ben Zakkai from Jerusalem during the siege of 70 CE. Though rabbinic literature has a number of versions of the story,[2] its main line is clear. Carried from the doomed city in a coffin, the rabbi emerges before Vespasian [*sic*] and hails him as the new emperor. When a few moments later an envoy arrives and declares that Vespasian has indeed been chosen, the new emperor offers the rabbi a gift of his choosing. Rabbi Yochanan does not hestitate: "Give me Yavneh [Jamnia] and its wise men" (*Gittin* 56).

The implications of this aggadah, however implausible historically, were momentous: if Judaism was to emerge from the coffin of its self-destructive militancy, it would have to defer to Rome and create a way of life in which Jewish education was central and revolt discouraged. Some knowledge of the Greco-Roman world was evidently also taught at certain times: when Gamaliel the Second, grandfather of Judah Hanasi, was head of the academy at Yavneh, half the students reportedly studied

Greek wisdom, presumably including Stoic thought (*Bava Kamma* 83a). The futility of the Great Revolt against Rome was a hard lesson, as later Jewish revolts, in 115–17 and 132–35 CE, showed. The Tannaim had an upward struggle to restore confidence in Judaism and to assert their authority: "Probably everywhere the failure of the revolts led to disaffection with and attrition from Judaism" (Schwartz 2001, p. 108). The school of Yavneh became a model for Jewish adaptation and survival, whose chief intellectual tool evolved as the Mishnah. The Tannaim taught that it was not necessary or desirable to perish suicidally but possible, as Joshua ben Hananiah put it in an Aesop-like parable, to be useful to Rome and survive:

> A wild lion ate its prey and a bone got stuck in its throat. He declared: "I will reward the one who pulls the bone out!" An Egyptian heron stuck its beak in, pulled the bone out and demanded its reward. "Go," said the lion, "boast that you've been in the lion's jaws and survived." So we too should be content that we survived the jaws of Rome (*Genesis Rabbah* LXIV 10).

The overwhelming conclusiveness of the Roman victories prepared the way both for improved Roman–Jewish relations, as the Jews could no longer be seen as a threat, and also for a new form of Judaism, based upon the synagogue cult that took the place of the Temple. The number of synagogues increased after 70 CE (Levine 1998). Many elements of Hebrew prayer (as well as the canon of the Hebrew Bible) were fixed in the post-Destruction era (Reif 1993). There was a growing need for buildings in which to pray and spiritual preparation for the survival of Judaism in a Temple-less world. Rabbis were now essential: no other form of Jewish leadership was tolerated by Rome. The synagogue, which was also a school, came to represent more than previously intellectual endeavor and a pacifist outlook. Rabbi Haninah, a disciple of Judah Hanasi, is reported to have said that "Torah scholars increase peace in the world" (*Berakhot* 64a).

Such views had less force prior to 135 CE. Many scholars were evidently caught up in the national revolts. In particular, the School of Shammai was associated with anti-Roman Zealotry in the years prior to and during the 66–70 CE revolt (Ben Shalom 1993). Insurrectionary agitation was "a virtually permanent phenomenon in the life of [Judaea until 135 CE] and not a passing phase as elsewhere" (Stern 1977, p. 244). Josephus has Titus declare to the besieged Jews on the verge of his conquest of Jerusalem in 70 CE, "You have been in a state of revolt from the time Pompey's army crushed you [in 63 BCE]" (BJ VI 6,2 [329]). Despair over the futility of the Jewish wars against Rome evidently underlines the rabbinic saying "neither suffering nor the reward of suffering" (*Berakhot* 5b). The Jewish survivors of the revolts could do worse than to adopt a philosophy of resignation such as that taught by Epictetus and Marcus Aurelius. Stoic ideals are compatible with pacifism and, at times, might be described as pacifist (e.g. Seneca, *Naturales Quaestiones* 5.18). Not having to run an empire, the Jews were better placed than the Romans to put Stoic ideals into practice. Among the Jews, for example, the treatment of slaves was considerably more humane than among Romans (Aberbach and Aberbach 2000, p. 55, 61); but although Stoicism never produced an abolitionist movement (Manning 1986), neither did traditional Judaism.

From a Jewish viewpoint, Stoic ideals did not have to be seen as specifically Greek. They represented what the Jews needed if they were to survive as a people: to live with sorrow, disappointment and misfortune, to renounce worldly things, to attain calm imperturbability, to continue to believe in Providence, and in one universal God unconfined by temples. The hedonism taught by the Epicureans, the enemies of the Stoics, was incompatible with Judaism (cf. *Avot* II 14). Stoic puritanism was far closer to the spirit of the Tannaim. The Stoic has faith in the essential goodness of the world and the purpose of existence, in the virtues of the simple life, the ethos of work, good citizenship achieved through reason and good deeds, and in the intrinsic value of the study of the art of living.[3] The Stoic conception of ethical social life was not dissimilar from Jewish communal responsibility according to Halakhah. Seneca, for example, "frequently subjects to ethical scrutiny areas of conduct that are more social than individual, more public than private" (Griffin 2000, p. 533); and Josephus could claim (*Against Apion* 2.168) that the Stoic view of the nature of God was similar to that of Moses. Stoic philosophy corresponded in practically every detail with some facet of rabbinic teaching. Both Stoic and rabbinic literature have as their ideal not power but well-being: wealth is found in *apatheia* or *euthymia*, most completely achieved through the emulation of the deity. Halakhah may be translated "The Way" – that is the way to find and imitate God (cf. *Shabbat* 133b). Intimacy between man and God as taught by some Stoics, notably Epictetus, a major influence on Marcus Aurelius, was a more desirable and controllable ideal than political agitation and revolt. Attractive though Stoic ideas were to Jews before the wars against Rome, they had particular value afterwards. Stoic theology could lessen the pain of defeat: life belongs to God and must be returned to God, the soul of the world; suffering is proof of God's love for his creations; human beings, imperfect as they are, should strive toward divine perfection. It is sin that should be eliminated, not the sinner. The Stoic belief that "man is a sacred thing for man" (Seneca, *Letters to Lucilius* 95, 33) may be compared with the rabbinic view of the holiness of life, summed up by Akiva: "Beloved is man, created in God's image" (*Avot* III 15).

The Mishnah is itself clear evidence of the success of the Tannaim in achieving a Jewish form of *apatheia*; though in the context of modern grief studies, it may also be seen as a numbing of emotion which characterizes denial of trauma (Aberbach 1989):

> From the perspective of Torah, from the point of view of holiness at its most ideal, there was no catastrophe and there were no sufferings – to speak of. All of that was unimportant. What was important – and ever continues to be – was the utopian, ideal, biblical, and messianic world of the eternal Torah (Kraemer 1995, p. 60).

In contrast, pre-135 CE Jews, with their immersion in politics and war, were evidently far less willing to surrender to pacifist spiritual aims. The anti-military thrust of Stoic literature, including the *Meditations*, was shared by the Tannaim and is summed up in the Mishnah: "Who is a man of valor? He who conquers his [Evil] Inclination" (*Avot* IV 1). The concept of *yetzer* (Inclination, or Impulse) here may be compared with the Greek *pathos* (irrational passion), though *yetzer* has a dynamic meaning: the Good and Evil Inclination at war with each other. Similarly, the calm, magisterial style of the Mishnah contrasts with the apocalyptic fervor of Jewish (and Christian) writings of previous generations – such as 2 Baruch, 4 Ezra, the Apocalypse of Abraham and 3 Baruch – as if in realization that if the messiah had not yet come it was not the end of the world. The sober authority of the Mishnah belies its revolutionary character, for it violates the tradition against writing down oral law.

Rabbinic literature suggests that defeat inclined some Jews more than previously to elevate the virtues of humility and self-blame. In this respect, they seem to have out-Stoic-ed the Stoics. However great the value of modesty and resignation to that which cannot be changed – another teaching associated with Epictetus and repeated in the *Meditations* (e.g. V 8, XII 1) – humility is generally counted by the Stoics a regrettable *pathos*. The idea that "suffering is precious" is attributed to Akiva and Judah Hanasi (*Bava Metziah* 85a, *Sanhedrin* 101a). The value of extreme humility is emphasized by rabbis of the post-70 CE period: "Rabbi Levitas of Yavneh said: 'Be very very humble, for the hope of humanity is worms' " (*Avot* IV 4). Rabbi Meir concurred: "Be humble before everyone" (*ibid.* 10). According to Joshua ben Levi, a contemporary of Judah Hanasi, true humility was worth all the sacrifices a man could offer in the Temple (*Sotah* 5b); and "He who accepts sufferings gladly brings salvation to the world" (*Ta'anit* 8a). The rabbis praise "those who are insulted and do not insult, who act out of love and find joy in suffering" (*Shabbat* 88b). The virtues of humility and submission characterize pre-rabbinic Judaism as well,[4] but there is no sense of the "joy of suffering"; and military power and prowess are often extolled (e.g. Psalms 18, 29, 144). The Stoic aim to change not the world but the self was in line with Roman policy as in theory it discouraged political dissent. An equivalent among the Tannaim may be found in the tendency to self-blame, originating in the Bible. In a theological perspective, the Romans, however much hated, could not be blamed. On the contrary, they – like the Assyrians and Babylonians before them – were the rod of God's wrath, inflicting punishment on his backsliding people. In particular, the Jewish defeats were attributed to fraternal strife, idolatry, and love of Mammon.[5] The development of Halakhah was motivated to a large extent by the consequent yearning for self-purification and return to the true worship of God.

Whereas revolt implied letting go, adherence to Halakhah meant restraint comparable to the Stoic ideal. Stoic control of emotion even when one's child dies (Epictetus, *Discourses* 3.3.15; 3.8.2; see *Meditations* I 8, XI 34) is paralleled in rabbinic literature, in accounts of the deaths of the sons of Yochanan ben Zakkai and Rabbi Meir (*Avot de-Rabbi Nathan* 14, *Midrash Mishle* 31). The idea that truth to one's nature involves using adversity to advantage (*Meditations* IV 1) is illustrated in the midrashic story of Akiva's martyrdom (c. 134 CE). The martyr transforms a gruesome death into the fulfilment of a divine commandment denied him in life:

> When [the Romans] took Akiva out for execution, it was time to say the *Shema*. They raked his flesh with steel combs, and he concentrated on the loving acceptance of the yoke of heaven. His pupils said: "Our rabbi! Even unto this?" He replied: "All my life I was troubled by the passage 'And you shall love the Lord your God with all your soul' – even if He takes your life. I asked: when will I ever have the chance to fulfil this? Now that I have the chance, shall I not fulfil it?" (*Berakhot* 61b).

The need for "loving acceptance" in the attainment of holiness is echoed by Marcus Aurelius. Despite differences in context and nuance between the Hebrew and Greek, the general sense is not dissimilar:

> Commit the future to providence, and simply seek to direct the present hour aright into the paths of holiness and justice: holiness by a loving acceptance of your appointed lot (XII 1).*

There is irony – possibly even hypocrisy – in the ideal of resignation in both the Greek and Hebrew sources. As emperor (161–180 CE), Marcus Aurelius could hardly attack the military policies of Rome. He persecuted the Christians and spent much of his reign fighting on the northern border of the empire, where he died. Akiva, according to one Jewish tradition, far from accepting a pacifist philosophy, was spiritual leader of the Bar-Kokhba revolt. Resignation, though helped by defeat and Rome's supreme power, did not come easily but had to be fought for inwardly. To some Jews, part of the attraction of Stoic philosophy might have been that the Stoics could be seen as "symbolic opponents of the state" (Goodman 1997, p. 162).

Mutual influences of Greek and Jewish civilizations

In the half millennium between the conquests of Alexander the Great and Marcus Aurelius, Greek–Jewish relations underwent many vicissitudes, ranging from extreme mutual emulation to murderous hostility. It is a cliché to say that Jews in the Roman empire lived in a Greek environment: "they found themselves cheek by jowl with Hellenistic communities in Palestine, and they were part and parcel of Hellenistic societies in the Diaspora" (Gruen 1998, p. 292). Greek and Jewish culture challenged and enriched each other (e.g. Lieberman 1950, Hengel, 1981, Feldman 1993). The Greeks and Jews provided the two most powerful definitions of humanity dividing the Roman empire: this is implicit in St Paul's declaration that through Christianity there would be neither Jew nor Greek (*Colossians* 3:9). Hellenistic-Jewish writers such as Philo wrote Greek and used Greek ideas in defense of Judaism. The Tannaim did not have a uniformly exclusive Jewish background. Some of them, including Rabbi Meir and Rabbi Akiva, were evidently descended from converts. Others, notably Elisha ben Avuya, who was excommunicated, had Greek education. Large numbers of pagans joined Jewish communities, took part in Jewish divine service and observed Jewish precepts and customs (Millar 1986, pp. 160–1). Even after the Jewish wars, "Much the most attractive belief was full-fledged

---

* Translation from the Greek is by Staniforth (Marcus Aurelius 1964).

Judaism" (Fox 1986, p. 271). Some of those drawn to Judaism, especially from the Roman upper class, were probably familiar with Stoic literature. Hellenized Jews such as Philo and Josephus envisaged the ideal of Hellenized Judaism as a synthesis of Greek, particularly Stoic, thought and Jewish tradition in which revolutionary Jewish politics was shunned (cf. Rajak 1983; Barraclough 1984). The aims of Stoic ethics and Jewish ethics, Philo taught, were essentially the same: peace, harmony, and justice (Winston 1984).

Consequently, many parallels have been noted in Greek and Jewish literature, in Stoicism and Judaism.[6] Among the most remarkable are those in the *Meditations* and *Avot*, the only tractate in the Mishnah devoted exclusively to ethics. Kaminka, in translating the *Meditations* into Hebrew (1923), discovered frequent echoes of rabbinic texts. Still, the parallels being in different languages are rarely exact and individually perhaps unconvincing; as a Gestalt they are impressive. For example: Marcus Aurelius' self-exhortation to be Antoninus' disciple (VI 30) and live in harmony with oneself and others is matched by the rabbinic "Be a disciple of Aaron, a lover of peace and pursuer of peace" (*Avot* I 12); the *Meditations* and tannaitic literature emphasize the need for individuals to stand up for themselves (*Meditations* III 5, *Avot* I 14); the ascetic spirit of both requires sin to be fenced in (*Meditations* VII 55, *Avot* I 1); both sing the virtues of poverty (*Meditations* V 15, *Hagigah* 9b). Marcus Aurelius draws on imagery similar to that in rabbinic literature, though often used in different ways: the severed head (*Meditations* VIII 34, *Avot* II 6), the clusters of "three things" (e.g. *Meditations* VII 55, XII 24; *Avot* I 2, III 1), the corruptible body (*Meditations* II 17, *Avot* III 1), the seeming insignificance of life (*Meditations* IV 48, *Avot* III 1); the need to accept one's lot in life (*Meditations* IV 29, *Avot* IV 1). The *Meditations* and *Avot* depict predestination in somewhat similar language, the first as a woven tapestry of causation (X 5), and the second, while also asserting free will, as a net over all living things (III 16). Both works stress the need to refrain from passing judgment on others and to be aware of personal shortcomings (*Meditations* X 30, *Avot* II 4). Both oppose anger (*Meditations* VII 24, *Avot* II 10). The reminder of life's brevity (e.g. *Avot* II 15) is echoed frequently in the *Meditations*, though the latter accepts with equanimity the possibility of suicide, which is against Jewish law. Marcus Aurelius and the rabbis agree that one should live each day as if it were the last (*Meditations* II 5, *Avot* II 10; see also *Avot de-Rabbi Nathan* 14, 4).

What does one make of this evidence? The complexities in Greco-Roman and Jewish relations over a period of several centuries have been a source of scholarly bafflement. Do the copious parallels in Greek and Jewish literature reflect common wisdom, or was there direct influence one on the other? Lieberman (1963), for example, points out that many fundamental teachings of Stoicism appear in some form in the Bible. Greek translations of the Bible contain stylistic similarities both to rabbinic and Stoic literature. Herr (1968) expresses the view that actual influence runs deep:

> Greek and Hellenistic influence is particularly marked in mainstream rabbinic Judaism, in the content and especially the form of aggadah, in public sermons and in methods of Torah exposition. In many instances, aggadah bears a relationship to Scripture like that of Hellenistic grammarians to Homer...a parallel of which the rabbis occasionally showed awareness (p. 625).

These issues are clouded by the fact that mutual hatred and suspicion among Jews and Greeks made difficult the open acknowledgment of the influence of one civilization on the other.

In the three centuries between the ban on Judaism by the Seleucid Greeks (c. 168 BCE) and Hadrian's ban on Judaism (c. 135–38 CE) – two brutal reminders of the problematic nature of Judaism as a powerful and deeply attractive rival to Hellenistic culture – attitudes of Jews and Greeks toward each other varied markedly, from friendly cooperation and mutual influence to genocidal hatred and mass slaughter. Hellenistic Judaism, with its relative tolerance of cultural pluralism, was promoted with greatest optimism in such works as the third book of the Sibylline Oracles and in the book of Aristeas, which evidently date mostly before the Roman conquest of Judaea in 63 BCE. A Jewish form of Stoicism would have been viable to the extent that "for most Jews, Judaism may have been little more than a vestigial identity, bits and pieces of which they were happy to incorporate into a religious and cultural system that was essentially Greco-Roman and pagan" (Schwartz 2001, p. 15). However, Hellenistic Judaism – if, indeed, it can be called Judaism – was stifled by Roman rule as Hellenism became identified first with oppressive imperial Roman culture and the emperor cult and the growth of anti-Semitism; then with defeat, exile and humiliation. These factors coupled with Greek–Jewish ethnic rivalry, Greek involvement against the Jews in the Roman–Jewish wars, the adoption by Christianity of Greek as its lingua franca and the Septuagint to the exclusion of the Hebrew Bible, as well as the attraction of rabbinic Judaism, broke the back of Hellenistic Judaism and, to a large extent, stigmatized Greek culture among the Jews. Judaism suffered a similar fate among pagans. The nadir of Greek–Jewish relations may have been reached during the diaspora revolts in 115–17 CE, when the teaching of Greek wisdom was apparently proscribed by the rabbis (Mishnah *Sotah* IX 14). Even the singing of Greek songs (or reading of Greek poetry, particularly Homer) was considered offensive (*Hagigah* 15b). Loyal Jews ideally spent all available time in Torah study, leaving no time for Greek wisdom (*Menahot* 99b).

Though hostility to Rome became fixed in rabbinic thought, the overt zero tolerance for Greco-Roman culture which emerged in the 66–135 CE period evidently ceased by the time of the editing of the Mishnah (c. 200 CE). Roman cultural imperialism had waned, and Greek freedmen, whose power, at times equal to that of emperors, was a significant factor in the decades leading up to the 66–70 CE war, no longer held high executive positions in the central Roman government (Duff 1958, pp. 170, 181; Aberbach and Aberbach 2000, pp. 69–78). Under Marcus Aurelius a senate decree was passed (Paulus, *Dig.* XXXIV.5.20) which enabled Jewish communities as *collegia licita* to receive legacies (Lindner 1987, pp. 107–10). The very creation of the Mishnah was symptomatic of improved relations with Rome, and it subtly alludes to the changes: in referring to the ban on teaching Greek wisdom during the 115–17 CE war, it uses the Greek *polemos*, not the Hebrew *milḥama* (*Sotah* IX 14); indeed, rabbinic literature has a large Greek vocabulary. The study of Greek philosophy could be justified to the extent that it was compatible with Jewish teaching. Also, Greek culture retained aesthetic appeal. The third century CE rabbi, Hiyyah bar Abba, supported the opinion of Simeon ben Gamaliel that books of the Hebrew Bible may be translated only into Greek "because it is written, 'Let God enlarge [*yaft*] Japheth [Genesis 9:27]': let the chief beauty of Japheth [i.e. the Greek language] be in the tents of Shem" (*Megillah* 9b). But by this time Hellenized Judaism was a relic of the past: the writings of Philo and Josephus, in which the assimilation of Stoicism into Judaism is overt, were not preserved by the rabbis who, instead, assimilated Stoic thought covertly, not as Greek culture but as original Jewish culture. Some striking parallels between the two cultures are found in Marcus Aurelius' *Meditations* and the Mishnah, above all tractate *Avot* which performs the remarkable balancing act of being both wholly Jewish, in a line of tradition pointedly going back to Moses, yet in its basic ethical outlook and mode of expression hardly different from that of the emperor.

The *Meditations* and the Mishnah

As works of literature, the *Meditations* and the Mishnah are exceptional. The *Meditations*, written in Greek in the late second century CE, are often described as the most profound literary survival of Stoicism, though Marcus Aurelius never identifies himself as a Stoic: "Stoicism serves as a starting-point for Marcus' reflections and provides the core of his beliefs; but Marcus ranges widely and, by taking diverse approaches, adds flexibility and complexity to Stoic beliefs" (Asmis 1986, p. 2229). The same could be said of the relationship of the Mishnah to pre-rabbinic Judaism. As the basis of the legal discussions of the Talmud, the Mishnah is highly idiosyncratic, a Hebrew legal and ethical code in which the illusions are maintained that the Temple was still standing or would soon be rebuilt and that the Roman empire did not exist. In common with Greek law, which as Diogenes Laertius, a contemporary of Judah Hanasi, observes (*Lives of Eminent Philosophers* 1.89–90), combines the written and oral traditions, the Mishnah draws on an oral tradition going back many generations, with its ultimate authority in the Hebrew Bible (*Avot* I 1). The *Meditations*, too, come from ancient traditions which the Stoics committed to writing. They were not intended for publication and remained in private hands for many generations after Marcus Aurelius' death.[7] These works are rarely spoken of in the same breath. They come from different worlds: the solitary philosopher-emperor, and the opinions of a hundred or so Tannaim edited by Judah Hanasi, the Patriarch of the Jewish community (cf. Cohen 1992). The Patriarchate was effectively the last survival of Jewish self-government after the destruction of the Temple as the priesthood and the Judaean ruling class were not reinstated. The Mishnah does not refer to Marcus Aurelius or Stoicism. The *Meditations* do not mention Jews or Judaism (or, for that matter, Christianity). Indeed, Judaism and the philosophy in the *Meditations* have many points of difference. Belief in revelation at Sinai, the chosenness of the Jews, their sacred texts, distinctive calendar, and rituals – not to speak of their historical experience and the continuity of their religious–national identity – are uniquely Jewish. Jewish laws of purity and tithes were crucial characteristics of second century CE Judaism, setting the Jews apart as a chosen people with memories of sovereignty, the Temple, and the vanished priesthood (Goodman 1983). The Stoic religion of pantheism was intolerable to Judaism. Though the *Meditations* are the closest pagan literature to Jewish–Christian monotheism (and for this reason they were preserved by the Church), their henotheism, or kathenotheism – in some passages they refer to "God" and in others to "the gods" – would have made them totally unacceptable to the rabbis, who represented a tradition violently hostile to idolatry. Stoics and the rabbis had divergent views of sin and charity. The bases of their ethical teachings were different. Judaism could not accept Stoicism with its lack of divine authority and of religious fervor (Bergmann 1912). The Stoics, unlike the Jews, did not believe in a final judgment or in life after death. Some leading Stoics, including Seneca, were hostile to Jews and Judaism. The fascinating tension between Marcus Aurelius' longing for philosophical calm and his pressing sense of duty to serve society and preoccupation with imminent death is largely absent in rabbinic literature. Apart from this, the Greeks in the Jewish mind were implicated in the loss of the Jewish state, the destruction of the Temple, the mass slaughter and exile, the ban on residence in Jerusalem. For these reasons and others, the Mishnah evidently aims to create a Greek-free space and to achieve an impression of "wholesale retreat from a Hellenised environment" (Millar 1993, p. 352). Yet the intensity of hostility itself betrays a close relationship, hinted at in the similarities between the *Meditations* and rabbinic literature. These may be divided in two groups: socio-cultural and literary-ideological.

Socio-cultural similarities

1. The *Meditations* and the Mishnah are creations of the same empire at roughly the same time. Marcus Aurelius (born 121 CE) was an older contemporary of Judah Hanasi (born c. 135 CE). Improved relations and greater openness to mutual influences between Jews and Greco-Romans in the latter half of the second century CE might be reflected in rabbinic legends telling of the friendship between Judah Hanasi and the Roman emperor "Antoninus". This emperor (perhaps a composite of several) belonged to the Antonine dynasty and is probably best identified with Caracalla (206–17 CE) (Avi-Yonah 1976, pp. 40–2), though he might have been (or included) Marcus Aurelius (cf. Wallach 1940–41; Stemberger 1996). The only recorded view attributed to Marcus Aurelius on the Jews outside rabbinic literature is a negative one cited by Ammianus Marcellinus in the fourth century, expressing somewhat un-Stoical disgust at the "stinking, rebellious Jews" (*Iudaeorum fetentium et tumultuantium*) (Whittaker 1984, p. 122): on the bright side, Feldman (1993, p. 101) points out, this was an expression of sorrow and did not lead to persecution. The rabbinic picture of the Antonines glows in comparison. During the Antonine period, it was conceivable to Jews, and presumably to non-Jews, that a rabbi and an emperor could have personal relations based on tolerance and respect, even reverence, and discuss as equals philosophical matters common to Judaism and Stoicism: the emperor's wisdom is sometimes superior to that of the rabbi. Such a relationship is hard to imagine prior to 138 CE. Mention of

some emperors – particularly Titus, Trajan, and Hadrian – is commonly accompanied by the curse, "May his bones rot!" Yet the attraction of the wisdom of "Antoninus" to Judah Hanasi is not its Greekness but its Jewishness: indeed, Antoninus ultimately converts to Judaism (Jerusalem Talmud, *Sanhedrin* 29a, *Megillah* 72b). It may be assumed, therefore, that the Tannaim could be influenced by Stoic thinkers such as Epictetus or Marcus Aurelius (as by Socrates and earlier Greek philosophy) as revealers of "Jewish" wisdom. This form of Jewish cultural assimilation is consistent both with the past (as indicated, for example, in the similarities between the biblical stories of the creation and the flood and parts of the *Epic of Gilgamesh*) and with the future (e.g. the medieval Hebrew verse influenced by Arabic secular poetry but brought into line with Jewish tradition). The discourse of Roman power entered the content of rabbinic teaching. Rabbis who could find a positive side to Roman rule were evidently more likely to find acceptance of their teachings than those who remained hostile to Rome. The most frequently quoted Tanna is Judah bar Ilai, a teacher of Judah Hanasi (Margalioth 1976, I 397). Over 600 rulings attributed to him appear in the Mishnah alone. He is also the most frequently cited rabbi in *Sifra* and the Tosefta. In an aggadah in which a group of rabbis discusses the Roman government of Judaea, he is the only one to praise Rome (*Shabbat* 33b).

2. The Stoics and the Tannaim elevated education to unprecedented importance as an activity not for a privileged elite but as a social necessity for everyone. A slave such as Epictetus, and an emperor, Marcus Aurelius, were equals in the quest for wisdom. Ordinary men must work at moral perfection through reason. The relative lack of concern with class and wealth among the Tannaim is strikingly illustrated in an aggadah telling of the wealthy Rabban Gamaliel and his deputy, the impoverished blacksmith Rabbi Joshua. Gamaliel visits Joshua at home and realizes for the first time that he is a poor man (*Berakhot* 28a). Among Stoics and rabbis, wisdom transcends not just class and wealth but also time. Thought lives, and discussion continues, among individuals who lived generations apart as though they were in the same room. Intellectual activity is the essence of life. Consequently, according to Epictetus, an error in reasoning is as serious as parricide (*Discourses* 1.7.31–3); similarly, the Jewish father who fails to teach his children is guilty of spiritual infanticide (*Sifre* on Deuteronomy 11:19).

3. By the time of the editing of the Mishnah, Stoicism was well-known in the Roman empire, particularly among the educated classes. Judah Hanasi belonged to this social stratum. He was born into

the family of Gamaliel, which traditionally had dealings with Roman authorities (*Bava Kamma* 83a). His upbringing was aristocratic and included Greek language and Greek thought (e.g. *Sotah* 49b). As representative of the Palestinian Jews to the Roman authorities, he had to be well-acquainted with Greco-Roman culture. But as Patriarch he also spoke for diaspora Jewry in the Roman empire, the majority of the world Jewish population at the time, numbering perhaps as many as eight million (Baron 1952, I 170; 1971, col. 871), an estimated 10 percent of the empire and 20 percent of its eastern half. Most of these Jews were Greek-speaking. They lived in a Greek cultural milieu in which Stoicism was current. The adaptation and Judaization of Greek ideas, though unacknowledged, in the Mishnah was both politically correct and attractive culturally to diaspora Jews tempted to Hellenization or Christianity but mostly loyal to Judaism and to Rome.

4. The Jewish need to master grief and achieve resignation to political and military powerlessness was vital if the Jews were to survive. According to the Jerusalem Talmud (*Ta'anit* 4:5), Judah Hanasi preached extensively on the destruction of the Temple. His audiences, overcome with weeping, would fall silent and file out. Judah himself would break down in tears (*Lamentations Rabbah* II 4). These *aggadot* were written down two centuries or more after the death of Judah Hanasi. Yet historic truth is preserved in the memory of spiritual distress caused by defeat. Solace could be found not in the militancy which had led to disaster but in philosophical ideas mutual to Greek and Jewish civilization of the late second century CE. The need for such consolation as that offered by the Tannaim after the Jewish revolts did not exist among the Jews prior to 66 CE.

5. Stoicism and Judaism stressed ethics and personal virtue, unlike the declining Roman religion. "For the spiritually hungry," writes Jenkyns (1992), "Roman religion had nothing to give: it lacked moral or theological content, and it was incapable of growth or adaptation; in the midst of a sophisticated, Hellenized civilization, it remained stubbornly primitive" (p. 8). Stoicism, as pointed out earlier, was closer to Judaism than any other philosophy in the ancient world. The *Meditations* have little with which the Tannaim would have disagreed and much that accords with their thinking. The rabbis, despite Josephus' claim (*Life* 2) were not Stoics. Yet the moral vision of Marcus Aurelius is essentially that of the rabbis: the commitment to truth, justice and duty, with a quiet piety leading to good deeds in the community, a constant awareness of human insignificance in the face of death, for life is short and one must make the best of it (e.g. *Meditations* VI 30, *Avot* II 15). The basis

of virtue in Stoic theory is reason, which unites man and God. Wisdom is better than ignorance, and the highest wisdom leads to good deeds. Ethics do not come out of blissfully ignorant goodness but out of the struggle of thought, reason, and argument (cf. Long 1978). The emperor and the rabbis often praise the same traits – asceticism, self-questioning, self-mastery, self-reliance – and oppose anger and despair, gladiatorial displays, and sexual immorality. The moral optimism of Judaism, which entered Christianity, was an important point of contact with Stoicism (Wasserstein 1994). Though Marcus Aurelius occasionally lapses into polytheism, he also frequently alludes to belief in one God. He believes in the human soul, predestination, and the unity and equality of all before God. The rabbinic idea that life is a preparation for judgment (*Avot* IV 16) is in line with Marcus Aurelius' view that God – or the so-called Reason the Helmsman – requires individuals to judge themselves and act in such a way as to give their life an aim and meaning (II 7).

6. The *Meditations* and rabbinic literature hint that the wisdom of equanimity and moral optimism come out of despair and struggle. Marcus Aurelius refers to his physical pain, bereavement, and sickness and takes comfort – in a manner the rabbis would have found abhorrent – in the thought of suicide (I 8, II 11). He admits finding himself hard to live with (V 10): life was more like wrestling than dancing (VII 61). His belief in Providence does not cure him of scepticism, for the world – again, in contrast with rabbinic Judaism – might be "a mere hotch-potch of random cohesions and dispersions … why wish to survive in such a purposeless and chaotic confusion; why care about anything save the manner of the ultimate return to dust" (VI 10). There is the extraordinary, unstoical outburst:

> A black heart! A womanish, wilful heart; the heart of a brute, a beast of the field; childish, stupid, and false; a huckster's heart; a tyrant's heart (IV 28).

On the Jewish side, a dark struggle to keep the faith may be read in the following anecdote:

> The schools of Shammai and Hillel debated two and a half years: one school that it is better not to be born, the other that life is preferable. Their verdict: better not to be born, but once in the world, one should be sin-fearing [lit. he should examine his deeds] (*Eruvin* 13b).

Bitter experiences and memories of the wars against Rome could weaken faith. In the 66–70 CE war alone, perhaps as many as one-third of the Jewish population of Palestine were casualties (Schäfer 1995, p. 131).

The Roman humiliation of the Jews was intended to weaken Judaism (Aberbach and Aberbach 2000, chs 7 and 8) and, to some extent, succeeded. Defeat could be interpreted as a sign that God had abandoned his people. The rabbinic scholar Elisha ben Avuya is said to have given up his faith after seeing the ripped-out tongue of the scholar, Hutzpit the Interpreter, eaten by a pig (*Kiddushin* 39b). Unlike the Stoics, the rabbis regarded God as ultimately good (Urbach 1975, p. 273). Consequently they occasionally felt anger at the supposedly omnipotent God for the destruction of the Temple in Jerusalem by Titus:

> Abba Hanan says: " 'Who is mighty as thou art, O Lord?' [Psalms 89:8]. Who is powerful and hard as you, for you hear the abuse and blasphemy of that wicked man [Titus] and you remain silent." In the name of Rabbi Ishmael it was taught: " 'Who is like you, O Lord, among the gods [*elim*]' [Exodus 15:11]. Who is like you among the silent [*ilmim*]" (*Gittin* 56b).

Jewish adaptation of Stoic ideas could be seen as a form of therapy by which depression, despair, and anger could be mastered. Rabbinic sources (e.g. *Eruvin* 54a) refer to the healing qualities of the Torah as Marcus Aurelius writes of Philosophy as medicine (V 9).

7. Archaeological evidence suggests a fruitful meeting of Hebrew and Greek cultures in second century CE Galilee, where the Mishnah was edited. It, too, points to improved Greco-Roman and Jewish relations in the Antonine period. Sepphoris, where Judah Hanasi lived and the final editing of the Mishnah was probably done, was a *polis* with a mixed population, including Greeks and Jews. Excavations have uncovered a Roman villa with superb mosaics (which apparently date from the post-Mishnaic period) depicting scenes from Greek mythology and a theater seating close to 5000. A thriving Greek world co-existed with creative rabbinic activity within a radius of a few hundred meters. Though the interaction between Hebrew creativity and Hellenistic art is vague, Meyers (1992) concludes that "These creative bursts in great art and literature most probably were unleashed as a result of complementary synergistic forces" (p. 331).

8. The Mishnah and the *Meditations* appear to represent cultural peaks in Jewish and Greek civilization, after which both declined. This coincidence corroborates the likelihood of close links between them. The Mishnah was the outstanding creative achievement of the Tannaim. While Daube (1949) perhaps exaggerates in writing that after the Mishnah, "there was a distinct lack of vitality and originality, the most

prominent tendency now being greater specialization" (p. 334), the post-tannaitic rabbis (the Amoraim), creative though they often were, remained in the shadow of the Tannaim and acknowledged their own secondary authority and status. The same was apparently true of tannaitic Midrash which, according to one view "reached a high point never since surpassed" (Epstein 1959, p. 116). MacMullen (1989) identifies major decline in Greco-Roman civilization at roughly the same time as the Mishnah:

> The line of major later poets ends before the prose-writers are done; that of philosophers in the favoured, Stoic line does not extend past Marcus Aurelius; the line of physicians rises to Galen (d. 199 CE), no further; that of jurisconsults does not run past the second decade of the third century, after which the lights of jurisprudence, that quintessentially Roman power of illumination, are abruptly dimmed and mere compilers take over (pp. 4–5).

Though in the second century, "Stoic teachers ranked high in the popularity stakes," they were displaced by Platonists by the third century (Chadwick 1999, p. 61).

9. Just as the Mishnah, as the basis of the Talmud, largely determined Jewish religious-cultural identity for the next two millennia, so also Greek culture of the same period became the chief cultural model in the West until the threshold of the modern age. According to Brown (1973), in the entire history of the Roman empire the Antonine period was most crucial in the future development of world civilization:

> It is just at the end of the second and the beginning of the third centuries that the Greek culture was garnered which formed the ballast of the classical tradition throughout the Middle Ages. The encyclopedias, the handbooks of medicine, natural science and astronomy, to which all cultivated men – Latins, Byzantines, Arabs – turned for the next fifteen hundred years, were compiled then. Literary tastes and political attitudes that continued, in the Greek world, until the end of the Middle Ages, were first formed in the age of the Antonines: Byzantine gentlemen of the fifteenth century were still using a recondite Attic Greek deployed by the Sophists of the age of Hadrian (p. 17).

The *Meditations* and the Mishnah might, therefore, be claimed to sum up much of the ancient world while having one foot, as it were, in the Middle Ages.

10. The need for a philosophy of resignation united Jews and Romans by the late second century CE despite residual hate and suspicion. The Jews were forced to confront the futility of military power and of

the nationalist-messianic hopes which fueled the Bar-Kokhba revolt of 132–35 CE. The Jewish revolts were the last and most ferocious outbreaks of internal dissent in the Roman empire. By the time of Marcus Aurelius, it was apparent that Christians and barbarians might be chronic threats that could not be crushed – as the Jews were – by force. The Romans became increasingly aware that already in the time of Hadrian the empire, though still overwhelmingly powerful, had passed the peak of its power. Even the rabbis, generally hostile to the empire, came to recognize that their survival was linked to the empire's fate. Rome could not only crush the Jews but also defend them from anarchy, self-destruction, and external threats: the rabbis shared Roman concern at invasions of Germanic tribes and other barbarians who spread terror in the empire (cf. *Avot* III 2, *Megillah* 6b). Rome is even complimented at times for preserving the rule of law. Resh Lakish, a younger contemporary of Judah Hanasi, went so far as to interpret the passage "and it was very good" (Genesis 1:31) as referring to Rome (reading "Edom" for "Adam") as Rome "exacts justice for men" (*Genesis Rabbah* IX 13). There was a rabbinic view that Roman rule was divinely ordained (*Avodah Zarah* 18a). Widespread plague during the reign of Marcus Aurelius might have contributed to the tendency toward a Roman–Jewish rapprochement, with common resignation to human frailty. The Patriarchate confirmed the recognition of mutual Roman–Jewish interests: the Romans by allowing this unique institution of non-territorial authority, and the Jews by accepting this unpromising cultural niche and making it a powerful instrument of Jewish unity under Roman rule; beyond that it became the foundation of Jewish survival. Accommodation with Rome was *faute de mieux*. Ultimately, the rabbis believed, observance of the Law would free Israel from Roman rule. The fixed elements in rabbinic theology of the kingdom of God and the messianic age are based on the envisaged triumph of the empire of the spirit over the "evil empire" (Schechter 1975, p. 102). After 135 CE, the Romans did not need to worry about this theology among the Jews but, rather, among the Christians. Yet, the *Meditations* themselves may be accounted a triumph of the "empire of the spirit," an anticipation of the end of the greatest – but morally flawed – pagan empire.

Literary–ideological parallels

Inner freedom

Stoic and rabbinic literature emphasize limitations of political power and freedom. Especially in the writings of Stoics with power, such as

Seneca and Marcus Aurelius (cf. Colish 1985, p. 40; *Meditations* II 1), philosophy allows the contemplative sage to escape the vicious machinations of public life. A Jewish tendency to withdraw from Greco-Roman life had existed long before 70 CE, notably in Qumran. However, the recoil from Greek education (particularly rhetoric) during and after the revolts ensured that Jews would play virtually no significant part in public life in the Roman empire (Goodman 1983). The subversive power of this philosophy of withdrawal is distilled in a tannaitic saying which sets temporal power beneath spiritual power: "Lust not after the tables of kings: your table is greater than theirs, your crown too" (*Avot* VI 5). Jewish and Christian literature share with Stoic sources the notion that victory is not achieved by subjugating others but one's own passions (Aune 1994). The true man of valor is he who masters himself (*Meditations* III 4, *Avot* IV 1). The downgrading of worldly power gives piquant irony to the *Meditations* as an intimate portrait of a man with supreme authority, to whom the only true power is that over the self. At times, Marcus Aurelius seems less an emperor than a monk. The goal of submission to the divine to avoid subjugation to man is shared by Judaism and Greek philosophy. The rabbis taught that freedom could be had not through political power but through Torah study: "There is no free man but he who studies Torah" (*Avot* VI 2). This view is uniquely Jewish, has been crucial in the development and survival of Judaism, and had especial relevance during and after the Roman–Jewish wars, when many Jews were sold as slaves. Yet, the idea that a religious philosophy can be liberating appears also in Stoic philosophy, notably Epictetus ("Only the educated are free", *Discourses* 2.1.21) and in the *Meditations* (IV 31). The freedom alluded to here appears to be more than the usual Stoic freedom from passion. It might reflect Marcus Aurelius' awareness that Epictetus was a freed slave:

> Let the rest of your days be spent as one who has wholeheartedly committed his all to the gods, and is therefore no man's master or slave. Invulnerability to external forces ensures the godliness of the human soul (V 34).

Universalist elements in tannaitic Judaism and the *Meditations*

Though Judaism continued to be a *religio licita* after 138 CE, many Jews in the Roman empire, overwhelmed by the effects of defeat and humiliation, by the *fiscus Judaicus* and the ban on proselytization and Jewish residence in and even pilgrimage to Jerusalem, must have felt like pariahs. The Stoic ideal of the Brotherhood of Man and the assuaging of personal suffering through the awareness of being part of a Whole was not unattractive to some Jews. The Stoics taught that all human beings are citizens in a single cosmic city governed by divine natural laws and distinguished from one another not by power, wealth, class, social status or gender, but by moral virtue (Balbry 1965, Schofield 1999). This philosophy recalls biblical universalism. The Roman victory in the Bar-Kokhba war suppressed the missionary-messianic thrust of Judaism while increasing its universalism by de-emphasizing its cultic and political-nationalist elements. Judah ben Shamua, a survivor of the Hadrianic persecution, is reported to have organized a night-demonstration in Rome to protest anti-Jewish decrees (presumably those passed by Hadrian). The language of his protest recalls Marcus Aurelius on the Brotherhood of Man (it also echoes the language of the book of Malachi [2:20]):

"Are we not children of one father and one mother? Are we different from any other nation and language that you impose such harsh decrees on us alone?" The Romans then declared these decrees null and void (*Rosh Hashana* 19a).

Perhaps the classic expression of this universalism is in the *Meditations*: "as Antonius my city and country is Rome, and as a human being the universe" (VI 44). Some Tannaim (e.g. *Sifre* on Deut. 11:12) evidently objected to biblical passages that seemed too narrowly Jewish or Israel-based. This tendency was more likely a feature of the Antonine age than of the pre-138 CE period (cf. Aberbach and Aberbach 2000, pp. 50–62, 114–17).

The importance of law

The codification of law uniting diverse communities was the main cultural achievement both of Romans and Jews in the second century CE. At no time in recorded history up to the second century CE was the codification of law regarded as having such high importance, by Jews and Gentiles alike. Although Stoicism had only a superficial relationship to Roman jurisprudence (Colish 1985), its emphasis upon a divinely given natural law makes it the origin of the modern notion of human rights (Hadot 1998). To many Jews, already familiar with human rights from the Hebrew Bible, particularly in the treatment of society's unfortunates – the widow, the orphan, the slave, the poor, the stranger (e.g. Leviticus 19:9–10, 33f., Deuteronomy 23:16–17, 24:10f.) – it might have seemed that the Gentiles were finally catching up. The *Meditations* insist on divine universal law (*nomos*) based on reason (*nous*), uniting all mankind, making them citizens of one city (IV 4, V 21). This conception of law gave those who accepted it a sense of belonging to a greater whole than the empire. True, much rabbinic law strengthened the boundary between the Jews and the allegedly impure Gentile world, while the Stoic concept of law was designed to obliterate social boundaries and build human unity in the belief that human beings are good or can be made good. Yet, the moral aims of both systems, the emphasis on holiness, justice and inner freedom, are essentially alike.

Intellect, the key to divine virtue

Marcus Aurelius' high valuation of the scholar and philosopher and his conviction that truth can be reached through study and contemplation were shared by the rabbis. The unprecedentedly high value attached to the intellect by the Tannaim – in contrast with the stark expressions of simple biblical faith (e.g. Micah 6:8, Habakkuk 2:4), adopted by Christianity – is paralleled among Stoic thinkers. In the *Meditations*, Asmis (1986) observes, the intellect is elevated into a deity to be worshipped: "Nothing matters except the intellect; and its activities are wholly within our power" (p. 2236). Rabbinic methods of argument derived partly from Stoic influence (Feldman 1996, p. 25). As in Stoic theory, dialectic in rabbinic discussion is a means for discovering the truth.

Exile and resignation

Many Jews in the second half of the second century CE, including most of the Tannaim, were exiles. Jerusalem was rebuilt as an exclusively pagan city and much of Judaea was de-judaized. Yet exile was not a Jewish monopoly. Epictetus and other Stoics were exiles. Although Marcus Aurelius was not an exile, the imagery of exile which pervades the *Meditations* suggests that he often felt like one. Most of Marcus Aurelius' reign, as pointed out, was spent at war abroad. He was preoccupied with the existential dilemma of being a stranger in his homeland (XII 1), of banishment from his city (XII 36). One can accept one's lot through knowing the universe. Failure to do so leads to self-exile (IV 29). However, Marcus Aurelius expresses a view of man in God's image familiar in the Hebrew Bible (e.g. Genesis 1:26). The realization of the divine in man can overcome exile (e.g. VIII 45, *Megillah* 11a). Marcus Aurelius advises those who feel injured by life to put aside the sense of wrong, and the injury will itself vanish (IV 7). Everything that happens should be accepted as part of nature (IV 44). The recovery of the Jews after 138 CE depended on putting this philosophy into practice. Everything that God does, the rabbis taught, is for the good (*Berakhot* 60b); and one is obliged to accept the bad even as one accepts the good (*ibid*. 54a). There is even a view expressed by Rabbi Oshayah, a younger contemporary of Judah Hanasi, that God had benefited the Jews by exiling them, making them less vulnerable to extermination (*Pesahim* 87b). In fact, the survival of Judaism depended both on resignation to exile and the faith that the exile would end. The majority opinion in the Talmud and later is that exile was an unmitigated disaster but could not be overcome through military means. Rather, the Jews should submit to God's will and wait for the messianic age. Rome could not object to this theology, which effectively absolved the Jews from action.

Inclusivist philosophies

The *Meditations* conceive of the sacred interdependence of things (VII 9), of tolerance as part of justice (IV 3), and unity of aims to the benefit of mankind (XI 21). Such ideas would have been attractive to Jews struggling inwardly to come to terms with and transcend national defeat. Neither Judaism nor Stoicism was secure at the time of the *Meditations* and the Mishnah. As indicated earlier, Stoicism, for all its popularity, would be supplanted by Platonism a generation or two after the *Meditations*. The authority of the Tannaim was far from universal among the Jews. Part of the purpose of the Mishnah was, no doubt, to strengthen rabbinic authority not only in Palestine but also in the diaspora, to stop the fragmentation and collapse of the Jewish world, and to give new life to the religious tradition of a defeated, humiliated people, in danger of being written off as a fossil. As we have seen, the accommodationist side of rabbinic literature and the rabbinic need for Roman approval is suggested in the fact that the most frequently quoted Tanna is not one of the "big guns" – Rabbi Akiva, Rabbi Meir, or Judah Hanasi – but Judah bar Ilai, a teacher of Judah Hanasi, noted for praising the Romans (*Shabbat* 33b). The evidence of the Dead Sea Scrolls suggests that whereas pre-70 CE Judaism is characterized by its diversity and "scribal creative freedom," post-70 Judaism took on an "orthodoxy," "reducing dangerous multiplicity to a simple, tidy and easily controllable unity" (Vermes 1997, pp. 23–4). The need for unity is memorably expressed in a rabbinic argument soon after the destruction of the Temple (*Bava Metziah* 59b). Rabbi Eliezer ben Hyrkanus opposed the entire school of Yavneh. Though Heaven was on Eliezer's side, and God's sympathy was with the spirit of diversity and individualism represented by Eliezer, he still lost. The need for unity is evident also in the dispute between Rabban Gamaliel II of Yavneh and Rabbi Joshua over the date of the Day of Atonement, which was settled when Rabban Gamaliel ordered Rabbi Joshua to visit him on the date calculated by Rabbi Joshua carrying his money and walking stick (Mishnah *Berachot* II 8–9). Unity was crucial to Jewish survival after 70 CE. Consequently, Judaism shared with Stoicism a fear of schismatics (e.g. *Avot* II 4, *Meditations* IX 23). The cautious conservatism which characterized rabbinic Judaism was a precondition to Roman social policy aiding the Jews' remarkable recovery in the late second century CE. Even but only as ex-revolutionaries, the Jews were part of the empire. The remarkable convergence of Greek and rabbinic ideas in the Antonine era signifies a degree of mutual recognition and interests and helps to explain why hostility between Jews and Rome subsided by the time the Mishnah was edited.

The need for moral action

To Marcus Aurelius, virtuous ideals are barren unless put into communal practice. The rabbinic consensus is that study is more important than good deeds (Mishnah *Peah* I1, *Shabbat* 127a), though Judah Hanasi believed that deeds, not study, are essential (Jerusalem Talmud *Pesahim* 3:7), a view apparently inherited from his father, Simeon ben Gamaliel (*Avot* I 18). According to the *Meditations*: "Let your one delight and refreshment be to pass from one service to the community to another, with God ever in mind" (VI 7); "The aim we should propose to ourselves must be the benefit of our fellows and the community" (XI 21). People are born for deeds of kindness, to promote the welfare of society (IX 42, XI 21). As in the rabbinic dictum "The reward of a *mitzvah* is a *mitzvah*" (*Avot* IV 2), to Marcus Aurelius influenced by Epictetus, an act of goodness is its own reward: "Benefit comes from doing acts that accord with nature. Never tire, then, of receiving such benefits through the very act of conferring them" (VII 74).

Conclusion

This chapter has explored the Jewish psychological adaptation to military defeat and political powerlessness in the Antonine period. It has outlined the basis for a comparison between Stoicism, particularly Marcus Aurelius' *Meditations*, and some rabbinic literature, allowing that questions of dating and attribution are not resolvable. Stoic and rabbinic literature drew on a profound ancient cultural pool, both Jewish and Greek, but specific cultural links might reflect shared conditions in the mid- and late second century CE. Judaism and Stoicism became more compatible after the massive Jewish military defeats of 66–70, 115–17, and 132–35 CE, when a pacifist philosophy became a condition of Jewish survival. The *Meditations* and the Mishnah represent two cultures irretrievably at odds after the Roman–Jewish wars, but seeking a *modus vivendi* based on expedience and similarities in outlook, mutual conservatism, and common social and psychological concerns of the post-Hadrianic period. Stoicized Judaism in effect answered two fundamental questions about the future of Roman–Jewish relations. On the Roman side: What kind of Judaism will not threaten us? On the Jewish side: How can we ensure the survival of Judaism under Rome? The adoption of Stoic ideas in rabbinic Judaism may be seen as a political act, designed to ensure that there would be no further suicidal Jewish revolts against Rome, but also having great psychological value to a defeated people in need of consolation and spiritual direction.

General socio-cultural links have been explored: the contemporaneity of Judah Hanasi and Marcus Aurelius; Judah Hanasi's grief over Jewish catastrophe, which might have inclined him and other Jews in his time to Stoic ideas adapted to Judaism; the emphasis in Judaism and Stoicism on egalitarian education in ethics and moral virtues, in contrast with Roman religion; the Greek cultural milieu in which the Mishnah was edited; mutual disillusionment with military force; and the particular attraction of Stoic ideas to a defeated people, most of whom lived in a Greek environment. There are also literary and ideological parallels: the importance of inner freedom, the universal brotherhood of man, resignation to exile, "loving acceptance" of suffering, and the high value attached to universal law and moral action. Through this comparative approach, Stoic literature, particularly Marcus Aurelius' *Meditations* and rabbinic literature give new perspective on the detente between Jews and Rome by the time of the editing of the Mishnah.

Hellenized Jews, notably Philo and Josephus, might therefore be seen as having considerable influence in the evolution of Roman attitudes and policy toward the Jews during and after the period of the Roman–Jewish wars. Living both in Jewish and Greek worlds, they perhaps best understood that the Jews had to adapt Judaism to achieve cultural integration while preserving their identity and pride (cf. Gruen 1998). At the same time, they witnessed the boomerang effect of assimilation – resentment instead of integration, contempt instead of admiration, hatred instead of acceptance – a phenomenon repeated in much of Europe in the nineteenth and twentieth centuries: "many of the problems of the Jews in the Greek cities arose precisely from their desire to be more assimilated" (de Lange 1991, p. 29). Ideally, no doubt, Rome would at times have liked to do away with Judaism totally. But this was not possible: Judaism was too widespread, well-entrenched, and attractive. Dangerous nationalist elements of Judaism, represented by the Zealots, Jerusalem, the Temple and priestly cult, the ruling class, and overt missionary and militant messianic activity, could be and were eliminated by Rome (Mendels 1992, Aberbach and Aberbach 2000). By 135 CE, it seems that most Jews were cured of excessive desire for assimilation among the people and culture that had so traumatized them. (Part of the attraction of Christianity was that by the time of the Bar-Kokhba war of 132–35 CE it was no longer part of Judaism and therefore, in a sense, free of the stigma of the Jewish defeats; yet, having broken with Judaism it was no longer a *religio licita* and therefore, in a sense, free of the "evil empire" of Rome.) The Stoicizing brand of Judaism promoted by the Hellenized Jews could survive; and perhaps Rome hoped – as in the past, especially in the time of Herod – that Greek culture would absorb the Jewish elements, not the other way round. But now that the Jews no longer had what Rome feared to be an *imperium in imperio*, it no longer mattered: there would be no pressure comparable to that in the time of Caligula, who ordered that a statue of himself should be erected in the Temple in Jerusalem. It may be misleading to say that Hellenistic Judaism withered away in the second century CE; rather, it became absorbed in rabbinic Judaism. Philo's fame as a philosopher helped implant the association of Judaism and Stoicism among the educated Roman upper classes. Josephus' view of Pharisaic Judaism as a form of Stoicism was a further encouragement to post-70 CE tendencies in Roman policy, which tolerated Judaism as a *religio licita* provided it did not threaten Rome. Josephus had some prestige among the Roman upper class and diaspora Jewry as a protégé of the imperial family and author of the official history of the Roman–Jewish war of 66–70 CE. His support for Stoicized Judaism may have encouraged official Roman tolerance toward the Tannaim as representatives of what evidently had to become mainstream Judaism if Judaism was to survive in the Roman empire. It pointed the way to a political settlement in which the Jews would be seen as a religious, not political, group and, harmless to Rome, allowed to survive. They would be represented by the rabbis alone, teaching accommodation to Rome and strictly loyal to non-militant, non-missionary Judaism and, at the same time, acceptable both to inward-looking Jews who sought a form of Judaism whose halakhic intricacies protected them from the Greco-Roman world and also to the more assimilated Jews for whom popular Stoicism was more familiar than rabbinic teachings. Yet, as we have seen, Stoic ideals may have been assimilated into Judaism in the Antonine period also as an expression of collective psychological need, a form of therapy needed to heal a broken people and ensure its survival as a unique people with a culture unbroken by Rome.

War split Judaism from Greek and military culture. Peace allowed a guarded rapprochement with the Gentile world. The Jews again became integrated in the empire. Judaism after 138 CE was restored as a *religio licita*. Long before 212 CE, when all free residents of the empire were granted citizenship (primarily for purposes of taxation), the Jews were evidently seen by Rome as an economic asset. Common ground between Jewish and Greek civilization could be reasserted, often in a disguised or unacknowledged form. By adapting Stoic ideas to Judaism – without necessarily acknowledging influence – the Jews could more easily accept Roman rule, making a virtue of the need to abandon hope of political independence by force.

Stoicized Judaism ensured Jewish acceptance of Roman rule. Jewish adaptation of the Stoic teaching that "we are not to lead events but to follow them" (Epictetus, *Discourses* 3.10.18) implied military, though not spiritual, quiescence. In the proverbial phrase of Cleanthes quoted by Seneca (*Ep.* 107.11) in Cicero's Latin translation: *ducunt volentem fata, nolentem trahunt*. Not until the twentieth century did the Jews rediscover their military instinct as a nation.

In these ways, similarities between the Tannaim and the *Meditations* throw light on the recovery of the Jews in the Roman empire after 138 CE. They reflect a crucial social and psychological turning point in Roman–Jewish relations. The Jews could survive only on Roman terms: they had to give up militant messianism and, officially at any rate, proselytization. Messianic hope lingered, hatred of Rome did not die out, and conversion to Judaism continued through the back door. Yet the defeat of Bar-Kokhba marked the end of Jewish military resistance to Rome and the start of new spiritual resistance, in which dissident strains of Stoicism might have played a part, and which fortified the Jews for what became, perhaps, the hardest struggle for survival in social history (Berlin 1979, p. 253).

Strongly opposed to the evils of power in the most powerful of empires, both rabbinic Judaism and Stoicism gave hope to the underdog. Rome encouraged this hope by retreating from military and cultural imperialism. Both Jews and Romans put their main creative energy into the codification of law. The emphasis on certain values in the *Meditations* and in rabbinic literature – of inner freedom, for example, or universality and inclusiveness, or resignation to exile – had particular resonance in the social and historical circumstances of the mid- and late second century CE. In their forced embrace with powerlessness, the Jews paradoxically gained more lasting power, enabling them to outlast the empire that had crushed them.

Part III
Toward a Secular Culture

5
Secular Hebrew Poetry in Muslim Spain 1031–1140

From the ruined shell of Rome after the empire's fall, most of the world Jewish population came under Islamic rule in the seventh and eighth centuries CE. The main influences on Jewish culture, particularly Spanish Hebrew poetry, for the next half millennium were Arabic. Hebrew poetry in Muslim Spain represents a turning point in Jewish life mainly in its non-theological elements, influenced by contemporaneous Arabic poetry with its various genres: love poetry, including homosexual poetry, poetry of friendship, wine songs, war poetry, and so on.[1] This was the most important Hebrew poetry between the end of the biblical age and modern times. Most of it belongs to the narrow period 1031–1140 when the Umayyad empire fell apart and Christian Europe began to overtake Islam, militarily, economically, and culturally. Hebrew poets not only adopted Arabic versification; they seem to some extent also to have been influenced by a secular lifestyle associated mainly with court culture, while at the same time keeping strictly to Jewish tradition and, in fact, also writing poems for the synagogue liturgy. What did the secularization of Hebrew poetry mean? Was it just literary convention, influenced by Islamic poetry? Or did it reflect a lifestyle anticipatory of the modern era?

The poetry of the age, both Hebrew and Arabic, was stimulated by a decisive historical shift in the global balance of power. The eleventh century was the turning point. By that time, the Islamic empire had split into three caliphates, the Abbasid, Fatimid, and Umayyad, the main unifying feature of which was cultural, in particular the use of Arabic. The eleventh century began with the collapse of the Umayyad caliphate. It ended with the conquest of Muslim-held Sicily and the east Mediterranean, including Palestine, by the Crusaders. By 1099, Jerusalem was in Christian hands, after four and a half centuries under

Islam. The fragmentation of the seemingly stable and powerful Muslim empire in the west Mediterranean into over two dozen city-states (*taifas* = "parts") led to innumerable civil wars in Spain. Fanatical Berber Muslims invaded from North Africa. Gradually, the Christians reconquered Spain from the north. These upheavals were disastrous for the Jews. Yet they created conditions in which Jewish life in Spain, and Hebrew culture, could temporarily flourish.

This age of imperial collapse and failed recovery in Muslim Spain was marked by two distinct periods: (1) civil war among the splinter-kingdoms; (2) Berber invasions from North Africa. The two Hebrew poets who dominated the first period were Samuel Hanagid (993–1056) and Solomon Ibn Gabirol (1021/22–1056?), of whom Gabirol is acknowledged as the greater. In the second period there were also two outstanding Hebrew poets: Moses Ibn Ezra (c. 1055–after 1135) and Judah Halevi (c. 1075–c. 1141). With Halevi, post-biblical Hebrew poetry reached its artistic peak prior to modern times. The poetry of Hanagid and Gabirol is set against the fall of the Cordoba caliphate, while the poetry of Ibn Ezra and Halevi has for its background the Berber invasions of 1090 and 1140. This explosion of creativity came from a society torn apart by internecine war and the spasmodic drive south by the armies of Christian Spain, yet culturally the most advanced in the Middle Ages. Its relatively secular, pluralistic outlook might be seen as a harbinger of the modern age.

Nevertheless, the poets themselves might have wondered to learn that later generations saw theirs as a golden age. Their own experience was war, chaos, instability, and exile, as this brief chronological table shows:

1009–31	Collapse of the Umayyad caliphate.
1013	Fall of Cordoba. Exile of Samuel Hanagid from Cordoba, his birthplace, to Malaga.
1031–91	Over two dozen splinter-kingdoms rule Andalusia, often at war with one another.
1066	Massacre of Jewish community of Granada.
1085	Conquest of Toledo by Christian army of Alfonso VI.
1086	Almoravid invasion and defeat of Christian army at al-Zallaqah, near Badajoz.
1090	Destruction of Jewish community of Granada by Almoravids, witnessed by Ibn Ezra and Halevi.
1091–1145	Almoravid rule of Muslim Spain.
1096–99	First Crusade, culminating in Christian conquest of the Land of Israel from the Muslims.

1135	Capture of Seville by Christian army of Alfonso VII.
1140–50	Almohad invasion and conquest of Muslim Spain.
1147	Capture of Seville by Almohads. Maimonides and his family, resident in Cordoba, are forced into exile.
1147–49	Second Crusade.

How did secular Hebrew poetry blossom in such rocky, dangerous soil? From the time of the Arab conquests of the seventh and early eighth centuries until the thirteenth century, the world Jewish population was still largely concentrated in the Middle East, chiefly in Babylonia under Abbasid rule. Economic decline and political instability, and the shift of the power center of the Arab world from Baghdad to Cairo in the Fatimid empire, led many Jews to emigrate from Babylonia to North Africa or to Spain. Spain, conquered by Muslims in 711, was the frontier not just of Islam but also of the known world. Its large empty spaces and fertile land and its geographical position offered much opportunity within an Arabic culture familiar and congenial to the vast majority of Jews.

The difficulties endured by the Babylonian Jews, driving them to emigrate, are the subject of an undated liturgical poem by the last great religious leader of Babylonian Jewry, Hai Gaon, who died in 1038 having lived for a century. Hai Gaon gives a bitter account of the precarious state of the Jews who, he writes, have survived countless sorrows only to escape no sorrow before death:

> This the people that never were,
> eaten away, scattered, despoiled.
> Babylonia trounced them, Media knocked them out,
> Greece swallowed them, Islam did not vomit them.
> Why make their yoke heavier?
> Why double their misery?
> Powerless, what can they endure?
>
> *Achen sar mar ha-mavet*
> (Carmi 1981, p. 303)

At the start of the golden age, when these lines were written, most Jews spoke Arabic, which had replaced Aramaic as their *lingua franca*. Jewish immigrants to Spain easily fitted in, especially as the country was a frontier with many new immigrants. The similarities between Islam and Judaism also helped: both are monotheisms which hold that salvation is achieved through obedience to divine commandments as revealed to a supreme prophet; both are based on religious jurisprudence interpreted by scholars and judges; both emphasize the importance of dietary laws and communal worship. Throughout the Arab world, the Jews, like the Christians, had the status of a protected religious group (*dhimma*) and were respected as a "people of the book" (*ahl-al-kitab*), a people who possessed holy scriptures recognized by Islam.

With their ancient, sharply defined religious culture, the Jews went on, in fact, to have a disproportionate influence at a time when Spain, with its highly variegated population, was struggling toward national self-definition. In particular, the Jews' stress on their biblical lineage and chosenness, as well as being the bearers of a divine message in a pure and holy literature, was adopted by Christians and Muslims in shaping Spanish culture. Through its impact upon Europe and its empire overseas, this culture later became a seminal force in the making of modern civilization. Judaism, which was nowhere a state religion (except in the land of the Khazars in the ninth to tenth centuries), was the more adaptable under Islamic (and, later, Christian) rule. Psychologically, the Jews' long experience of exile and minority status eased their adaptation within Spanish Muslim society. While the Christians, unused to foreign rule, mostly converted to Islam or fled to Christian Spain, the Jews flourished. Hebrew poetry, their most resplendent cultural monument, is emblematic of the cultural synthesis to which they aspired. But as for daily usage in Jewish life, Arabic went much the same way as Greek in the Roman empire and German in Christian Europe: all were instruments of failed assimilation.Jewish attempts to identify with the culture, however superior, of a hostile people have invariably led to disillusionment.

Hebrew poetry in Muslim Spain owes at least some of its exceptional interest to the tension between the drive for acculturation and the inferior position of the Jews in Muslim society. Until modern times, Bernard Lewis has written (1984, p. 102), the Jews under Islamic rule were generally subjected to countless harassments and petty humiliations, to mockery, insult, and chronic insecurity; they paid higher taxes than Muslims; they suffered severely restrictive laws of inheritance; they could not carry arms; there were limitations on the animals they could ride, the buildings they could build and the places of worship they could use; they were even limited in the clothes they could wear and were obliged to wear a special emblem, the origin of the notorious yellow star.

In the tenth and eleventh centuries, until the Berber invasions, these disabilities were not felt as acutely in Muslim Spain as elsewhere. In fact, there were advantages in being Jewish in Andalusia at this time. Under Abd ar-Rahaman III (912–61), Muslim Spain achieved centralized rule and independence from the Abbasid empire. It quickly became the most powerful, richest, and most culturally advanced country in tenth-century Europe. Its capital, Cordoba, was one of the largest cites of the time with an estimated quarter million inhabitants. Cordoba's central library had some 400000 volumes (Baron 1957, IV, 28). The Spanish Jews at this time may have numbered no more than 60000 (Ashtor 1979, II, 34). Yet they were concentrated in the cities, at the hub of the social, economic, and political life of Muslim Spain. The creation of an independent caliphate in Spain led to the independence of its Jewish population from Babylonian religious authority, which was in decline. Consequently, they were readier than in the past to take part in the life of the wider society, to experiment culturally. A sign of this new freedom was their use, for the first time, of secular forms and genres in Hebrew verse.

The manifest superiority of this rich, elegant, culturally sophisticated society on Islam's toehold on continental Europe drew settlers from the east. At the start of the golden age, most of the Spanish Christian population were recent converts to Islam (Glick 1979).[2] The Muslim rulers were a minority among Christians, Jews, neo-Muslims, and others and, needing their support, were sharply alive to the importance of tolerance and fairness. To ensure their sense of belonging and their loyalty, the Muslim rulers found it expedient to build a universalist Arab culture, rather than a narrow Islamic religious one. The court was the center of this culture. The splendid court of Cordoba and, later, the courts of the splinter-kingdoms, created opportunities for Jewish courtiers. Imitating their Arab colleagues, they became the patrons of Hebrew poets. The importance of courts and of patronage in the golden age may be seen in the fact that when the courts vanished and patronage ceased, Hebrew and Arabic poetry declined. The Jews' alliance with Islamic sovereignty and the concomitant golden age of Hebrew poetry is best understood in the context of the ethnic and religious diversity and conflicts of Hispano-Arab society and its socio-religious problems (Wasserstein 1985, Brann 1991).[3]

The Jews, furthermore, comprised an essential part of the middle class. There was hardly a profession in which Jews were not active. Because of their considerable trading links, their cosmopolitanism and knowledge of languages, the Jews were invaluable as translators, courtiers, and diplomats. Their talents were also a rich source of revenue. The shift of power in Andalusia in the tenth century from the aristocratic elite to the middle class worked to the Jews' advantage, especially in cities such as Granada, where they formed a large part of the population. Hebrew poetry expressed Jewish pride and self-confidence stemming from social and economic success and political power. A point alluded to earlier should be stressed: Spain's geographic position on the frontier of Christian Europe and the great unexplored Atlantic was another factor in breaking down social barriers which prevailed elsewhere among Muslims and Jews. The cooperation and social harmony between them was virtually unique in the Middle Ages and unrepeated in modern times.

The cultural background of the golden age

How did these social conditions make Hebrew poetry blossom? What role did this verse play in the lives of the Spanish Jews? As usual in Jewish cultural history, the forces of change were gradual. Medieval Hebrew poetry had a long, complex socio-linguistic germination. A number of factors in addition to those given earlier were of special importance in promoting literature, stimulating cultural imitation and competition, and in heightening sensitivity to the Hebrew language and sharpening its usage:

1. Christian biblical exegetes often undermined Jewish interpretation. They forced Jewish exegetes, many of whom wrote Hebrew poetry, to study closely the vocabulary and grammar of the Bible in order to refute the Christians and achieve a clear interpretation of the Hebrew text.

2. The Karaites, a fundamentalist Jewish sect, denied the sacred character of the Oral Law and of post-biblical Hebrew, insisting instead that authentic Judaism was confined to the literal truth of the Five Books of Moses. The dispute with the Karaites, who had considerable influence in the ninth and tenth centuries and after, had the effect of forcing their "Rabbanite" opponents to stop their neglect of the Bible and achieve greater awareness of the nuances of the Hebrew text.

3. The proliferation since the late-Roman period of synagogues led to an increasing demand for original Hebrew liturgical poetry which entered the Jewish prayer book (*Siddur*), the earliest editions of which were edited in the eighth or ninth centuries (Reif 1993). All the great medieval Hebrew poets wrote for the synagogue as well as for secular reading.

4. The golden age was part of a flourishing of Jewish literature – legal, homiletical, polemical, exegetical, philological, as well as liturgical – in the years 900–1200 (Baron 1958, VII, 136). This literature was facilitated by the reunification of the majority of the world's Jewish population under Islamic rule and by the intellectual stimulus of the

rise of Islam. It was also part of a great surge in European literary activity resulting from a revolution in book manufacturing. Paper reached the Islamic empire by the end of the eighth century. Within two centuries, Spain became a world center of the manufacture of paper and the production of books.

5. The increasing split between Jews living under Muslim and Christian rule made vital the use of Hebrew in contacts between the two groups.

6. The explosion in the use of Arabic and the growth of Islamic court culture in which Arabic was used in the eighth and ninth centuries led to an enrichment of the Arabic language and a high valuation of correct grammar, stylistic excellence, and beautiful calligraphy:

> Perhaps in no period in human history did preoccupation with the correctness and purity of the spoken and written language become such a deep concern of the educated classes as during the Islamic Renaissance (Baron 1958, VII, 4).

The divine inspiration and truth of the Koran were believed by the Arabs to be proven by its stylistic excellence; the Jews adopted a similar belief about the Hebrew Bible. As the first fully bilingual group of Jewish writers, the Hebrew poets of Muslim Spain were well-acquainted with Arabic and the Koran, though as infidels they were discouraged from writing Arabic. In any case, they were convinced that Hebrew was superior to all languages as it was more ancient and beautiful and, above all, the language in which God had revealed himself in the Bible. They revolted against the eastern style of Hebrew poetry associated with Saadia Gaon, with its over-abundant, enigmatic talmudic and midrashic allusions. Instead, they favored clear biblical language. Their poetry was further influenced by the rediscovery of ancient Greek learning, with its emphasis on philosophy and rhetoric. This resurrection led to a marked increase in the vocabulary and intellectual depth of Arabic language and thought, which Hebrew writers (who were often the translators from Arabic to Latin) adopted in Hebrew.

Poetry, the court, and Islam

The pre-eminent importance attached to poetry in the Islamic empire was the single main catalyst for Hebrew poetry, which was enriched immeasurably in imitation of and competition with Arabic poetry. This influence was not mutual, however: non-Jewish Arabic readers did not usually read Hebrew, and Hebrew poetry was apparently not translated into Arabic. Still, the high status of Hebrew poetry among the Spanish Jews at this time was probably unique in Jewish history. Whole cities, such as Lucena and Seville, were known as "cities of poetry." Court life brought into being the professional Hebrew poet, employed by Jewish courtiers such as the physician and statesman Hasdai Ibn Shaprut (c. 905–c. 970), whose prominent position in the court of the above mentioned Abd ar-Rahaman III made him the natural leader of the Jews in Muslim Spain. Imitating his Arab colleagues, Ibn Shaprut became the patron of scholars and poets. These included the two Hebrew poets who created the artistic basis for the golden age: Menahem Ibn Saruq (c. 910–c. 970) and Dunash ben Labrat (?–c. 970). Neither had outstanding poetic gifts. Yet, ben Labrat revolutionized Hebrew poetry by imitating the quantitative meters and secular themes of Arabic poetry. He was also the first to criticize the artificiality of forcing Hebrew verse into Arabic prosody and the blasphemy of using the Holy Tongue for secular purposes. This criticism reached its bitterest expression in the writings of Judah Halevi. The golden age ironically began and ended with blasts at its own artistic bases. However, the criticism of Hebrew poetry was also imitative, as the Arabs, too, frequently voiced similar complaints against Arabic poetry of the Cordoba caliphate. This poetry was often felt to reflect the artificiality and corruption of court life, the abuse of artists as functionaries flattering their patrons, sycophantically toeing the party line.

Both Hebrew and Arabic poetry were galvanized by the fall of the caliphate and the rise of the splinter-kingdoms in the first half of the eleventh century. The technical and thematic revolution of the tenth century was now harnessed to a radical change in psychological outlook and sensibility. For a brief period, both literatures created poetry of exceptional artistic quality, if not genius.

The Jews had mastered the dominant high culture of the early Middle Ages and gained entree into the highest social and political circles at the zenith of the Umayyad caliphate. Now they realized that their position under Muslim rule in Spain was untenable. Precisely at this moment – in the first half of the eleventh century – the Jews reached the high point of their political power and cultural achievement between the destruction of the Second Temple and modern times. Why was this so? One explanation is that the Jews, as part of a society in chaos, were liberated for a while from the normal social shackles of being Jewish in the medieval world. The Hebrew poet was, to an extent, temporarily free of social constraint and able to use advances in Hebrew poetry to find an original poetic voice. Like Van Gogh's sunflowers, this golden Hebrew culture was dying, and dying in the very poetry which was its brightest sign of life.

The destruction of court society centralized in Cordoba meant the end of "official" court poetry. It freed the individual poet, Muslim and Jew, to explore personal emotion as a subject worthy of poetry (Monroe 1974, p. 21). The social anarchy described in the poetry of Hanagid and Gabirol belongs specifically to the eleventh century. The following lines by Gabirol, though typically they echo a biblical passage (Micah 7:6), could not describe tenth century Andalusia, when the caliphate was strong. They are a grim picture of the chaos, civil strife, and despair which prevailed in Andalusia after the caliphate fell apart:

> Man has no joy on earth:
> Slave murders master.
> Servant girls attack their queen.
> Son strikes parents.
> Daughter does the same.
> Friend, the best remedy I know – madness.
>
> *Ve-lev navuv*

The social stratification in Muslim Spain, already greatly weakened in the course of the tenth century, was largely swept aside. The splinter-kingdoms, battling among themselves, sought allies – Jews and Christians alike – where they could find them. As a result, Jews were allowed to take part in Islamic society to a degree unprecedented in Islamic history and unrepeated since.

In this chaotic state of transition, Arabic poets such as Ibn Hazm (994–1064) and Ibn Zaidun (1003–71) and their contemporary Hebrew poets Hanagid and Gabirol, created a body of poetry extraordinary in its emphasis upon the individual sensibility as well as its technical mastery. The following lines by Ibn Hazm, for example, strike a new note in Arabic poetry:

> I am seen as a youth desperate with love,
> my heart broken, my spirit troubled. By whom?
> Men discern my state and are sure,
> but on closer scrutiny are left in doubt.
> I am like clear handwriting, meaning obscure,
> like a dove cooing every which way
> in its little forest, delighting the ear
> with its melody, its meaning untapped ...

> A girl once loved me, I surprised her with a kiss:
> That kiss was my only life, however long my life is.
> (Monroe 1974, pp. 174–5)[4]

The poetry of Ibn Zaidun, likewise, is animated by a rare sense of real emotion and people. Most of Ibn Zaidun's poems were inspired by his love for an Umayyad princess in the last days of the caliphate and for some time after. His poems of lost love recreate a world that has vanished but are at the same time deeply personal:

> Yes, I remembered you, longed for you, as you were
> in az-Zahara', the sky blue, earth alight,
> the evening breeze languid with pity for me.
> And the garden smiled. A day like the lost pleasure time
> we thieved our nights away as fortune slept.
> Flowers caught our eye, bent with dew as if in tears
> for my sleeplessness.
> (Arberry 1965, pp. 114–15)

In the poetry of Ibn Zaidun, Arabic poetry reached a peak of artistic perfection, described by Albert Hourani as "the last flowering of an original and personal lyrical [Arabic] poetry before modern times" (1991, p. 194).[5] The same is true of Ibn Zaidun's Jewish contemporaries, whose best work is unequalled until modern times.

Hanagid and Gabirol

The new individual tone of Arabic poetry reached Hebrew with lasting impact in the poetry of Hanagid. Hanagid had an exceptionally varied and interesting life and career, though what is known of his life can be summed up in a few lines. As well as being the first major Hebrew poet of the golden age, he was also an important rabbi, the leader of the Granada Jewish community, ultimately first citizen of Granada as vizier (from 1027) and minister of war (from 1038), commander of the Berber Muslim army for nearly two decades of almost constant war. He reportedly never lost a battle.

The complexity of Hanagid's career and the extent of his power are themselves the clearest indication of the new life chances which opened to Jews in Muslim Spain after the fall of the caliphate. The formative trauma of Hanagid's early manhood was, in fact, the end of the caliphate – the horrific siege of Cordoba, his hometown, by the Berbers.

This siege lasted for several years until the Umayyad capital fell in 1013. Exiled from his native city, Hanagid was an eyewitness of the appalling effects of the fall of the caliphate and the civil wars which followed. His rise to power in Granada was, paradoxically, made possible by the very fact of his being Jewish. The Jews, representing the economic strength of the middle class, helped create a precarious stability in the balance of power between the Berber rulers and the Arab aristocratic elite. Hanagid also saw how the neighboring Christian powers began what amounted to a protection racket by which the fragile Muslim kingdoms obtained military aid against their Muslim rivals. He cursed the Christians in impeccable meter and rhyme and called for the renewal of his people:

> Evil queen, cease your reign!
> Reign instead, hated Jews,
> long asleep on bed of pain.
> Wake! There's medicine for you,
> and recompense for being true.
>
> *Malka resha'ah*[6]

The fascination of Hanagid lies in the contradictions of general and poet, leader of an Arab army and head of the Granada Jewish community, public man and tough individualist, religious Jew and secular poet. The toughness and directness of some of his war poetry had not appeared in Hebrew since the Bible and were not to appear again until the twentieth century, when most Hebrew poets have also been soldiers:

> I stationed a regiment in a fortress
> destroyed long ago in war.
> There we slept, below us the dead...
> If they woke to life, they'd kill us
> and take everything we have.
> It's God's own truth, by tomorrow
> we'd all be stone-cold as they.
>
> *Halinoti gedud*

The kingdom of Seville was Granada's main rival. Many of Hanagid's poems describe wars which he fought against Seville. Although Hanagid commanded a Muslim army, he writes as though Jews are at war with the infidel, not Muslims fighting against Muslims. (He never mentions, incidentally, that there were Jews in the armies against which he fought.) Instead, his victories are the victories of the Jewish God:

> In Seville they did evil to the Jews –
> conspiracy, weapons, chains –
> to murder Jewish mothers and babies,
> rich and poor alike.
>
> We laughed when their king spoke arrogantly.
> We crossed the border to avenge our people,
> our warriors savage as lions,
> we swarmed in on them like locusts ...
>
> God tied their hands with rope,
> their hearts too.
> They stumbled over their chariots,
> their horses chains on their feet.
>
> In a word, he broke them
> as a weaver snaps thread.
> Famous warriors in chains,
> dragged before the king –
> at his will they lived or died.
>
> I was faint at the bloody torture,
> the pampered foot stabbed with thorns,
> warriors' corpses tossed on a pile.
>
> > *Ha-li ta'as bekhol shanah*[7]

The Arabs led by Hanagid were not so secular as to overcome their prejudice against him as an infidel Jew, damned to perdition; neither were they so devout as to shirk from the leadership of an inordinately gifted Jew. As a prominent figure in the Granada court, Hanagid had his Jewish retinue, including the young Gabirol who seems to have admired Hanagid's poetry as well as his statesmanship. In one of his panegyrics for Hanagid, Gabirol compares him with his namesake, the prophet Samuel:

> Wisdom-seeker, delver into her mysteries
> to gather her from exile,
> making her treasures his,
> her silver and gold.
>
> > *Mi zot ke-mo shahar*

To Gabirol, Hanagid was a model of the synthesis to which he aspired between Arab culture and the Jewish tradition. As a poet, however,

Gabirol went much further than Hanagid in using the new-found freedom of Andalusian poetry. Whereas much of Hanagid's poetry is outgoing and public, Gabirol's is deeply personal. The sadness and loneliness in Gabirol's poetry is unparalleled in any other medieval Hebrew poet. His works reflect not only his physical illnesses and mental tortures but also his awareness that the hoped for cultural synthesis between Jews and Muslims in Spain was a pipe dream:

> I am buried – not in a desert but in my house,
> my coffin.   I agonize, orphaned of mother and father,
> brotherless.   Young, alone, poor.   Thought
> is my only friend.   My tears are stirred in blood and wine,
> thirsting for a friend –
> I will die before that thirst is quenched.
> The heavens block my yearning.
> Alien am I to all.
>
> *Nihar be-kor'i groni*

> Should you want to join the man forever young,
> as your soul gutters by the underworld's flame –
> mock worldly things, be not the fool
> of wealth and honor, a son to have your name.
>
> Value poverty and humility, then die
> as Seled did, with no son.
> Try to know your soul well. It alone
> will live when skin and flesh are gone.
>
> *Im te'ehav lihyot be-anshe Heled* [8]

The execution of his patron, Yekutiel ben Isaac ibn Hassan, in 1039 confirmed his apprehensions about the future. It is recorded in the following lyric:[9]

> See the sun red-cloaked at dusk,
> stripping itself of north and south,
> dressing itself crimson,
> leaving the land naked, to sleep
> in night's dark shelter.
>
> Then the sky went black as a sack
> for the death of Yekutiel.
>
> *Re'eh shemesh*

In the face of outrage to his body, his soul, and his social world, Gabirol retreats to his infinitely gentle, suffering spirit, to a dialogue with soul or Creator. The poet is trapped in a shifting no-man's land in the long religious war between Muslims and Christians, in which the Jews are losers. Terrified, he calls to God, the beloved in rabbinic interpretations of the Song of Songs:[10]

> Open the gate, my love!
> Get up, open the gate!
> I tremble in terror.   Mother's slave,
> Hagar, mocked me in her arrogance,
> for God heard her son Ishmael's cry.
> In the dead of night
> the wild-ass Muslims chased me,
> the wild-boar Christians trampled me.
> When my exile's end was fixed
> my heartache grew worse.
> No one can explain – and I am dumb.
>
> *Sha'ar petah*

Social breakdown in Andalusia and Hebrew creativity

The pessimism of Gabirol's poetry foreshadowed the end of Andalusian Jews under Muslim rule. In 1066, Hanagid's son, Joseph, who had succeeded him as vizier of Granada, was murdered. In one of the earliest pogroms in European history, about 3000 Jews of Granada were massacred. An Arabic poem by Abu Ishaq helped to trigger off the pogrom. It incited Badis ibn Habbus, king of Granada, to wipe out Jewish influence in the Granada government:

> This was Badis' fatal mistake, making our enemy rejoice:
> Not Muslim but Jew he made his minister.
> Now the Jews are not just low-down:
> They're arrogant, insolent too.
> They got more than they ever dreamed of,
> ignoring Muslims dying in misery.
> How many noble Muslims are brought low
> before this wretched monkey-Jew!
>
> (Monroe 1974, pp. 206–7)

It is possible to see this poem and the pogrom which followed as a turning point in the history of the Andalusian Jews, a warning that they lived on a live volcano:

The slaughter in Granada showed them the tenuousness of their position in alien lands. Over the generations they had come to believe [*sic*] that they were as much citizens of Spain as were the Muslims and Christians, the Andalusians and Arabs, the Berbers and Slavs – now it was clear: Spain was a land of exile as were all the other diasporas (Ashtor 1979, II 191).

As in Russia 700 years later, anti-Jewish violence in Muslim Spain was a gauge of general political and social instability, not only in the splinter-kingdoms that had inherited the Umayyad empire but in the Islamic world as a whole as the balance of power between Muslims and Christians shifted to the clear advantage of the Christians. The lack of strong central authority in the Arab empire led to political breakdown and to Christian military success, in Spain and the Holy Land. The Christians won control of trade in the Mediterranean. The Muslims lost economic power in lands controlled by Islam. The defeats in Spain and the Holy Land at the end of the eleventh century were not just military blows. They were also unprecedented religious and psychological set-backs to Islam. They led to growing fanaticism among the Muslims, which increasingly soured relations between Muslims and Jews. To devout Muslims, the integration of the Jews within Spanish Muslim society was a sign of defeat, even of moral decline and corruption. After the fall of Toledo in 1085, the splinter-kingdoms invited the Almoravid Berbers to cross the straits of Gibraltar to save them from the Christian infidel. In 1086 the Berbers defeated the Christian army of Alfonso VI of Castile at Sagrajas. Between 1090 and 1102 they ended the disunity which had prevailed since 1031. They seized Andalusia and made it a province of their North African empire. This military feat led to the migration of most Andalusian Jews to Christian Spain. Unexpectedly, it heralded an Indian summer of Hebrew poetry.

Ibn Ezra and Judah Halevi

Hanagid and Gabirol were wholly Andalusian poets in the time of the splinter-kingdoms and civil wars. Ibn Ezra and Halevi were born in Andalusia but after the Almoravid invasion were exiled to Christian Spain. Despite maltreatment by the Andalusian Muslims, Ibn Ezra remained nostalgic for the Andalusia of his youth. No other Hebrew poet applied so expertly Arabic metrics, themes, and images to Hebrew.[11] The following poem, for example, bears an Arabic imprint in its meter (in the Hebrew ABCBDB), its imagery, and feeling:

> Let man always know
> unto death he moves.
> As day to night creeps past
> he may think he is at rest –
> at rest on a boat
> flying in the wind.
>
> *Yizkor gever*

Ibn Ezra's affection for Andalusia evidently grew as he discovered the pains of being a stranger and a Jew in Christian Spain. In one of his poems, *Pnei he-El levad*, the world is a mother with a stillborn child in her belly and a dying child on her back. He might have been thinking of his own life. To Ibn Ezra as to Gabirol, poetry consoled the poet and his readers:

> You who are heartsick and cry bitterly –
> do not grieve.
> Come into the garden of my poems
> to find medicine, sung aloud.
> Compared to them honey is bitter
> incense stinks: these poems make the deaf hear
> the stammerer speak, the blind see,
> the lame run.   The grieving, the heartsick,
> those who cry bitterly find joy in them.
>
> *Kol ish deveh levav*

In poems written to Halevi, his protege, he poured out his heart:

> Even my enemies
> take pity, while my obstinate brother refuses
> to admit his folly has stripped me
> of everything precious.   My children
> too betray me; strangers hurry to dress
> the wound my flesh and blood inflicted.
> Will I ever again find the strength
> to take up the wanderer's staff fate

thrust into my hands? Mornings I chew
twigs for my hunger, at dusk
stagnant water quenches my thirst.
I sink deeper and deeper
into a pit of depression, and barely
pull myself out. My eyes are glazed
with wandering, my innards
rumble like the sea, my nerves are on edge.
I dwell among wolves for whom
the word human means nothing.

(Levin 1992, pp. 35–6)

Halevi, whose own unhappiness in Spain led him to a fervent nationalist longing to return to Zion, vainly entreated Ibn Ezra in verse to return to his native land:

How can I find peace with you gone?
My heart beats after you.
If I left off waiting for your return
I'd die. Look, the mountains of our separation
testify: clouds are cheap with rain. I cry buckets.
Come back to Muslim Spain, lamp of Muslim Spain.
Make your mark on every heart and hand.
Pure of speech among the stammerers:
Why spread Hermon's dew on cursed Gilead?

Ech aharecha emtza margo'a

Halevi was born in Tudela, then under Muslim rule, near the Christian Border. As a young man, he came south to Granada where he met Ibn Ezra. The Almoravid invasion drove him to Toledo, only recently captured by the Christians, where he worked as a doctor. After the Toledo Jews were set on by a bloodthirsty mob in 1109 and his patron was murdered, Halevi came back to Andalusia. He lived in Cordoba for some thirty years. When the Almohads invaded southern Spain, he set out for the Holy Land. It is not known if he reached his destination.

The two decisive events in Halevi's life were the Almoravid invasion of Andalusia in 1090 and the Christian conquest of the Holy Land in 1099. The first aroused his disillusionment with Muslim Spain – indeed, with any form of gentile rule – and the second his yearning for messianic redemption and the return to the Land of Israel. To the North African scholar, Rabbi Habib, Halevi confessed in a letter that "Greece and its wisdom have drowned me in thick black grease; Islam and Arabic have blackened me; Christianity has torn me apart, destroyed me" (Brann 1991, p. 90). In poetic dialogues between the Congregation of Israel and God (the Lover), again based on the Midrash on the Song of Songs, Halevi conveys with intense passion the torment of being trapped between two rival religions:

> Friend – suffering forces me to live
> with viper and scorpion, captive.
> Pity me!
>
> I despair of sunrise.
> Day by day I cannot hope.
>
> What can I say, lover?
>
> Crusaders, freeborn, in Jerusalem, my palace,
> while I slave for Arab and Christian –
> a dog in their tormenting hands.
> > *Yodi, hefitzuni yeme oni*

> Lover, have you forgot how you lay between my breasts?
> Why have you sold me for all time?
> Did I not follow you in the wilderness?
> Let the mountains be my witnesses –
> Seir and Paran, Sinai and Sin!
> My love was yours, you wanted just me –
> how can you share yourself with others?
> I am crushed by the Persians,
> scorched by the Greeks,
> thrust among Christians, driven among Muslims:
> Is there a saviour but you?
> A prisoner of hope but me?
> Give me your power, I'll give you my love!
> > *Yedidi, hashakhahta*

The suffering of the people of Israel is seen by the poet as a punishment and a means of expiation for sin. Israel takes almost masochistic pleasure in its persecution – this is God's will, but it is also God's will to free his people as he did in the past:

> Since you became love's home,
> my loves are pitched by you.

My enemies' curse makes me glad.
Let them curse me – as you did.
They learned to hate from you
and I love them – they hound the one you hurt.
The day you scorned me I felt the same.
How can I love the one you hate?
Till your fury goes and you free again
your people whom you freed from Egypt.

Me'az me'on ahavah

The conquest of the Holy Land by the Crusaders after four and a half centuries of Muslim rule was a disaster to the Jewish communities of Palestine (as of those in Europe). Yet it also awakened the Jewish hope of return to the land of Israel at a time when the majority of the world's Jewish population was still in the Middle East. The memory of Hanagid's military accomplishments was still green: if Jerusalem could be captured by Christians, could it not someday fall to the Jews?

A further stimulus in Halevi's poetry was the rise of the Almohads in the second and third decades of the twelfth century. The Almohads, as mentioned previously, were a fanatical North African Berber tribe. Unlike the Almoravids, they were also a messianic movement whose founder was believed to be the messiah, destined to restore Islam to the true path and create a kingdom of heaven on earth. The Almohads were, in fact, the last gasp of the Islamic empire which had ruled Andalusia since 711. They ended Andalusian Jewish life under Islam when they invaded in 1140, but they might also have stirred up parallel Jewish messianic hopes, such as those expressed in Halevi's writings. Such hopes are often a sign of social trouble. Halevi's decision to go to the Holy Land, to which his poetry points as inevitable, may be seen as part of a more general religious phenomenon involving Muslims and Christians as well as Jews.

Halevi's poems of longing for Zion are among the best-known Hebrew poems outside the Bible. Yet they belong to no genre or tradition. Rather they are the response of one unusually gifted poet to a decisive crisis in medieval Jewish life. They express nostalgia not just for a Zion that Halevi had never seen – and which had never existed except in the world of Jewish legend – but also, implicitly, for a lost, once powerful and splendid Andalusia in which great hopes and illusions had died.[12] In these poems, a western voice speaks at a time when the demographic process that was to bring the most Jews westward was not yet completed. For brief moments, Hebrew, in engaging the obsession closest to its heart, breaks out of the shackles of Arabic ornamentation and speaks with real individuality and passion:

> My heart is in the east and I –
> on the end of the west: how can I enjoy,
> how taste my food, how keep my vows
> while Zion is in Christian hands
> and I in Arab chains.
> I'd lightly leave the good of Spain
> to see the Temple's dust again.
>
> *Libi be-mizrah*

> Zion, will you not ask about your captives?
> They ask for you, the last of your flock.
> Accept their greeting, west and east, north and south,
> far and near on every side; my greeting too,
> lust-locked to weep Hermon's dew across your hills:
> A jackal I am, wailing out your grief,
> a harp for the dream-song of your exiles' homecoming.
>
> *Zion, ha-lo tishali*

The longing and searching of the Zion poems were not literary conventions. They were the true feelings of the poet, driving him in his old age to leave Spain for Palestine. The plangent, questing mood of the Zion poems pervades Halevi's work, the secular love poems as well as the liturgical ones.

> Ofra washes her clothes in my tears.
> She spreads them in the sunshine of her life.
> She has no need of fountains,
> nor sun to beautify her light.
>
> *Ofra tekhabes*

> Time's slaves – slaves of slaves,
> but God's servant is free.
> For his part in life man prays:
> My part in you I see.
>
> *Avdei zeman*

> God, where can I find you,
> hidden in heaven on high?
> And where can I not find you –
> you fill the universe with glory!
>
> *Yah, ana emtza'akha*

Conclusion

With Halevi's departure forever from Spain in 1140 – he died a year or two later – and the Almohad conquest of Andalusia, the Jews of Muslim Spain and Hebrew poetry were exiled. By the start of the thirteenth century, the Almohads were themselves defeated by Christian armies. The empire of Islam was squeezed out of Europe. And so, the flowering of Hebrew poetry in the years 1031–1140 was the final creation of a dying empire that had made Spain the cultural center of the Western world. It was a long goodbye of a minority once integrally a part of this empire, whose alienation and demise marked the empire's fall.

The merits of medieval Hebrew poetry should not be exaggerated. Its influence was hardly decisive in Jewish life as biblical and talmudic literature was. Few individual poems stand out as incontestable works of genius. To unsympathetic readers, Hanagid is emotionally shallow and repetitive, Gabirol melancholy and obscure, Ibn Ezra unoriginal, Halevi sentimental. Furthermore, Hebrew poets forced on themselves a crippling prosody: Arabic metrics and techniques, rhetoric and thematic conventions. This, too, was part of Jewish assimilation into Arabic culture. The creation of standard Arabic and the establishment of clear readings of the Koran for a diverse and growing Muslim population had affected the Arabic language adversely:

> When the philologists received wide-spread recognition from the upper strata of society it was difficult for the would-be poet not to adhere to the canons of language and style they established. This led to artificiality, with the emphasis on the manner of saying a thing rather than on the meaningful content (Watt 1984, p. 48).

Medieval Hebrew literature was a step down from a more glorious literary past. True, each of the major poets of the golden age brought a revolutionary new quality to Hebrew: the confident, aggressive voice of Hanagid; psychological anguish bound up with a philosophical system in Gabirol; the dedication to poetry as a world in its own right, for its own sake, in Ibn Ezra; romantic longing for a distant time and a faraway land in Halevi. Yet, Hebrew poetry had never served just as ornamental prose, as was common in Arabic. It was, after all, the language in which God had created the universe, in which he had given the Ten Commandments at Sinai. Now, cliché-ridden and prettily artificial, it was largely sapped of its power, its natural beauty, and emotional depth. The overwhelming influence of the Bible was also detrimental, leading to slavish adherence to biblical language and imagery – partly in imitation of Arabic poetry's emulation of the Koran, partly because the brilliance of the Bible overshadowed medieval Hebrew – and a perverse, illusory ideal of biblical "purity" of language. Detachment from living, spoken Hebrew also contributed to the excessively literary approach to poetry, which was to pervade Hebrew literature until the time of Bialik, in which clever linguistic pyrotechnics were more highly valued than clear, direct speech. As shown previously, some Hebrew poets, notably Halevi, actually confessed their bitter awareness that they had worked their way into an artistic straightjacket.

Still, medieval Hebrew poetry marks a major turning point in Jewish socio-cultural history. Hebrew became for the first time a vehicle for the expression of a way of life alien to traditional Judaism. Influenced by the Andalusian Arab aristocracy, with their love of beauty and pursuit of fleeting pleasure, it betrayed the religious ideals of Judaism, its stress on self-discipline, divine judgement and life in the hereafter. The revolutionary nature of their poetry is suggested in the fact that Hebrew poets often expressed severe guilt at the very act of creating secular poetry; only Hanagid seems to have been free of such guilt. Yet none of them abandoned traditional Jewish faith and practice. To the contrary. Unlike their Arabic contemporaries, the Hebrew poets were often rabbis, religious judges, scholars and biblical exegetes, or a combination of these. (Isaac Ibn Ghiyyat, the innovative eleventh century *paytan*, was head of a yeshiva in Lucena.) They kept Muslim society at arm's length in a number of ways: by writing in a language which Arabs generally did not know; by expressing in these writings a stern loyalty to Judaism and a conviction of the inferiority of other religions, including Islam; by championing the Hebrew Bible as the model of stylistic excellence; and by making a vast contribution to synagogue liturgy.

Their poetry certainly suggests all sorts of behavior not normally associated with rabbis. Imagine an important contemporary orthodox rabbi discovered to have written the following lines:

> Plunge into pleasure, have a good time!
> Raise the flask, down the wine!
> Dance ecstatic to birdsong and lyre!
> Clap hands, drunk by the riverside!
> Bang at the door of that good-looking girl!
> *Dadei yefat to'ar*

The author of these lines, Moses Ibn Ezra, understandably came to be embarassed by such poetry especially as in his later years he was famous for his penitential poems (*selihot*) – so much so that he was known as *ha-salah* (the penitential poet). Yet his secular poetry is typical of Arabic poetry in Andalusia and can be read to express nothing more than wine-song conventions.

The question arises: since they were the first fully bilingual Hebrew poets, why did they not write Arabic poetry? Their works on philosophy and linguistics – for example, Hanagid's *Sefer ha-Osher*, Gabirol's *Mekor Hayim*, Ibn Ezra's *Sefer Shirat Yisrael*, and Halevi's *Kuzari* were all written in Arabic. Why not Hebrew poetry as well? To attempt to answer this question is, in effect, to probe the nature of Jewish acculturation within the empire of Islam.

It seems that however radical their poetry in its time, however much influenced by secular Arabic poetry and lifestyle, the Hebrew poets wanted to assert firm loyalty to the Jewish faith. They wrote Hebrew poetry because, despite the inherent artificiality of its adopted poetics, it was best capable of expressing their strongest feelings. At the same time, this poetry was an act of cultural synthesis, of alliance and mimicry, of assimilation and competition, aimed though it was exclusively at Jews – medieval Hebrew poetry was apparently not translated into Arabic for the benefit of Arabic readers. Enthusiasm for this assimilation ideal was such that it might have led some Hebrew poets to adopt at times a secular voice alien to them. Symptomatic of the twisted state of Jewish–Muslim relations in the latter part of the "golden age" is the fact that the most famous Jewish philosophical work of this period, Halevi's *Kuzari*, written in Arabic, was a defense of the allegedly inferior religion, Judaism. More than this, "The *Kuzari* was a glorification of rabbinic Judaism and an unabashed statement of nationalism, very much in the modern sense of the word" (Stillman 1979, p. 60). Such a work would, of course, have been unlikely if the Jews had been accepted as equals in Arab society. Especially after the pogrom in Granada in 1066, it was clear that the Jews were not tolerated in positions of power under Muslim rule.

The artificiality of Hebrew poetry might be seen in this light as an inadvertent enactment of the artificiality and awkwardness of Jewish life under Muslim rule in medieval Spain.

In this Hebrew poetry, bitter despondency toward Arab society was implicitly far greater than that toward any aspect of Judaism. Jewish acculturation in Muslim Spain was based on the assumption of a realizable parity within a tolerant, essentially secular Arabic civilization. The fall of the Umayyad empire led, instead, to a failure of Arab universalism and a resurgence of Islamic religious militancy in which the Jews were seen as part of the problem of the empire's decline. The nationalist undercurrent in Hebrew poetry may be seen as a reaction to this exclusivist zealotry.

In the *Kuzari*, Halevi argues that the Jews are distinguished above all other peoples through their capacity to receive divine prophecy. Only in the Land of Israel could they fulfil their prophetic destiny. Such views are not found among the earlier poets of the golden age, such as Hanagid and Gabirol. They betray the poet's disillusionment with Muslim Spain. The strongest thrust of Hebrew poetry in the years immediately prior to the Almohad invasion was a nagging unease and, at times, despair with the host country. Consequently, the medieval Hebrew poets created an ideal alternative world in their poetry. In so doing, they anticipate an independent modern Hebrew literature, part of the resurgence of Jewish nationalism and the return to Zion.

Part IV
From Theology to Sociology

6
The Baal Shem Tov, Mystical Union, and Individualism

The Hasidic movement is a major turning point in Judaism, the most important and influential Jewish religious phenomenon since the destruction of the Temple in Jerusalem in 70 CE. The movement was founded in the Ukraine by the legendary Rabbi Israel ben Eliezer, known as the Baal Shem Tov ('Master of the Good Name [of God], 1700?–60, also known by his acronym as the Besht). It began in reaction to the dry melancholy scholasticism which prevailed in European communities following the 1648–49 massacres and the crushing of popular messianic hopes after Shabbetai Zvi (1627–76), who was widely believed by the Jews to be the Messiah, converted to Islam in 1670. This failure created widespread grief and disillusionment among European Jews for several generations after. Hasidism drew much of its inspiration and ideas from Jewish mysticism, or Kabbalah. It attached the highest importance to joyful prayer, rather than study, in the attempt to attain unity (*devekut*) with God (Scholem 1955, Dan 1983, Idel 1988). While Hasidism continued traditional messianic hope, it did not teach that the messianic age was necessarily imminent.

The idea of mystical union with God or with a higher being is universal in theological systems. It may take many forms, metaphorical and moral as well as metaphysical. In Hinduism this concept is expressed in the saying *Tat twm asi* ("This is thou"); a human being, by finding his or her true immortal self (*atman*), becomes united with Brahman and, in so doing, achieves *nirvana*. In Buddhism, similarly, humans must strive to recognize the unity of all within the eternal Buddha, the *dharmakaya*, the absolute truth or reality that transcends human perception. Jewish mysticism teaches *devekut*, commonly translated as adhesion, cleaving, union with God. Christian mysticism refers to Jesus' words "Abide in me and I in you" (John 15:4) as pertaining to divine union, which has its concrete expression in baptism and the Eucharist. Even Islam, which insists on the absolute transcendence of God, has developed the mystical doctrine of *tawhid* (union).

In *Surviving Trauma: Loss, Literature and Psychoanalysis* (1989), I argued that a remarkable correspondence exists between the process leading to mystical union and the process of grief following a bereavement;[1] and I developed this idea in later work, notably *Charisma in Politics, Religion and the Media* (1996). While mysticism cannot be equated with grief – like other forms of creativity, it transcends its origins and enters a system of religious faith with meaning and value of its own – it can, in some cases at least, provide an effective outlet for the expression of grief, a means by which the bereaved might struggle to work through the process of grief. Withdrawal after loss might become the withdrawal needed for mystical contemplation. Yearning and searching for the lost person might evolve into the yearning and searching for a spiritual being. The anger, confusion, and depression which often emerge in grief might be expressed in the mystical "dark night of the soul." "Finding" the lost person might have its parallel in mystical "finding" and illumination. The transformation undergone by the bereaved in the process of mourning might have its counterpart in spiritual rebirth. And finally, union with the lost person might become union with the divine being. These phenomena might underlie all sorts of creativity, in social life and politics as well as literature and the arts. Among the Jews, as we have seen in previous chapters, the experience of defeat, exile, and loss is fixed in the national character, and Jewish survival has depended on creative responses to it; otherwise the Jews would have vanished from history.

Grief might incline the bereaved to mystical union or similar phenomena, as this tendency is already inherent in him or her as a result of loss. In their yearning for reunion, bereaved persons commonly seek to identify themselves with, and at times even incorporate themselves into, the lost person (Rees 1971). This quest may translate itself into an expression of mystical union or communion with a divine being, or a social organism or nation. For this reason, apparently, the language often used by widows to describe a temporary sensation of union with their lost husbands, of resembling or "containing" them, is not dissimilar from the language of mystics. One widow described the following experience: "At dawn four days after my husband's death, something suddenly moved in me – a presence almost pushed me out of bed – terribly overwhelming" (Parkes 1986, p. 120). From then on, this woman had a strong sense of her husband's presence, either near or inside her.

Another widow spoke of her happiness at having her late husband within her: "It's not a sense of his presence. He is here inside me. That's why I'm happy all the time. It's as if two people were one" (*ibid.*, p.121). Such language is comparable with that describing mystical union, except that the mystic speaks not of a lost person but of a divine being. In normal grief, however, the mystic's belief in the reality of this union or communion is far stronger and more persistent than that of the bereaved. The mourner is likely to be aware of the irrationality of such reactions to loss. Clinical studies treat such phenomena, when transient, as a normal coping mechanism; these studies maintain, however, that when such phenomena are persistent, they can become a pathological means by which the bereaved denies the loss and strives to recover the lost person (Bowlby 1980, p. 289).

The foregoing sketches ideas that I have developed more fully in *Surviving Trauma* and *Charisma in Politics, Religion and the Media*. What is the relationship between Hasidism as a turning point in Jewish history with the Baal Shem Tov's inner life? In this chapter, I propose to link the Baal Shem Tov's influence as a teacher of mystical union with his experience of childhood loss. The correspondence between private and public, inner reality and social and political reality, is fundamental in charismatic relationships (Aberbach 1995, 1996). The idea of an intersection between a "public" quest for mystical union and the "private" quest for a lost person may be explained with specific reference to influential mystics whose emphasis upon the importance of mystical union may be linked with their childhood experiences of bereavement: the Besht and Jiddu Krishnamurti (1895–1986), perhaps the best-known of twentieth century mystics. Illustrations of mystical union in creative literature – by Edgar Allan Poe, Emily Bronte, John Clare, D.H. Lawrence, Forrest Reid, and Martin Buber – corroborate the idea that bereavement, mostly in childhood, may be a causative factor in the need for mystical union.

The Baal Shem Tov

The doyen of the academic study of Jewish mysticism, Gershom Scholem, discovered (1955), that the concept of *devekut* had an important place in kabbalistic mysticism long before the rise of the Hasidic movement. The Besht, however, attached far greater importance to *devekut* than his mystical predecessors, making it central to Hasidic theology and, as Scholem put it, "the ultimate goal of religious perfection" (p. 123).[2] Although reliable information on the theology of the Besht and the degree to which it was amplified or altered by his followers is scarce, there is little doubt that the increase in the importance of *devekut* among eighteenth-century East European Jews derives largely from his influence. To the Besht, *devekut* was not just the highest attainment of religious life, as the kabbalists had taught. It *was* faith. It was also the first rung of mystical ascent, which everyone, in theory, could climb. In this way, esoteric mystical concepts became more accepted as part of Torah and entered the mainstream of Jewish life. The Besht taught that through the *mitzvoth* – the daily acts of kindness and love – through communion with the inner light of prayer and study, and through communion with the spirit that animates the holy letters of the Hebrew alphabet humans can make contact with the divine worlds and attain *devekut*.

The only extant first-person account of the Besht's mystical practices appears in a letter dating from 1751 and addressed to his brother-in-law in the land of Israel. In this letter, he described his method of concentration on the letters of the Hebrew alphabet as his means of attaining *devekut*. "Whenever you offer your prayers and whenever you study," he exhorted, "have the intention of unifying a divine name in every word and with every utterance of your lips. For there are worlds, souls and divinity in every letter" (Jacobs 1977, p. 151).[3] To the Besht, the ultimate aim of *devekut* was messianic redemption. He told his brother-in-law of a vision of an "ascent" to the palace of the messiah. There, the sages and holy men "took great delight on high when, through their Torah, I perform unifications here below" (p. 150). The Besht wondered how long humankind must wait before the messiah comes. This is the messiah's reply:

> You will know of it in this way; it will be when your teaching becomes famous and revealed to the world, and when that which I have taught you and you have comprehended will spread abroad so that others, too, will be capable of performing unifications and having soul ascents as you do. Then will all the *qelippot* [impurities] be consumed and it will be a time of grace and salvation (pp. 150–1).

The imagery and aims of *devekut* in the Besht's teachings and even the concentration on the letters of the tetragrammaton, are familiar from kabbalistic literature; the emphasis on *devekut*, however, appears to be original to the Besht. Why did he attach such importance to *devekut*? What did *devekut* mean to him? Why did previously esoteric mysticism become part of the popular culture of East European Jews in the late eighteenth and nineteenth centuries? These questions have never been fully answered.

Indisputable facts about the Besht are scanty and any analysis of the possible meaning of *devekut* to him is speculative. Even the allegation in Hasidic literature that he was orphaned in early childhood has never been documented, although there seems to be no reason to question it.

Whatever *devekut* meant to the Besht, it is necessary to set aside the image of the man as founder of the Hasidic movement. The Besht was evidently not the leader of a significant movement in his lifetime. Nor, for that matter, does it seem that he aimed to start a movement.[4] Scholars have argued that many social, religious, and political forces underlie the rise of Hasidism: the turmoil of eighteenth-century Polish-Jewish life, the impact of the Sabbatean heresy and Frankism upon East European Jews, the decline of Jewish communal organization, the increasing gap between rich and poor, educated and ignorant, the reaction against the excessive intellectualism of Talmudic study and against Rationalism and the Enlightenment. These forces pertain more, perhaps, to the development of Hasidism among the Besht's disciples, though they might have affected the Besht personally to some extent, directly or indirectly. His emphasis upon *devekut* might be seen as a reaction against the extreme social, cultural, and political pressures of the age through intense focus upon the spiritual. Like the ideas of other great religious leaders, however, the concept of *devekut* was probably not propounded by the Besht purely in order to meet the spiritual needs of his age. It is more likely that – as in the case of charismatic leadership generally[5] – there was an intersection between external social realities and the inner world of the Besht: *devekut*, satisfying a private spiritual need, could also have had a wider application in the East European Jewish world, an unexpected stimulus to radical change.

It is unlikely that this alleged correspondence of inner and outer reality will ever be fully understood or a definite answer given to the question of why the Besht emphasized *devekut* to such an extent. An understanding of the personal motives can explain the appeal of Hasidism to the Jewish masses. In light of grief studies, the Besht's unprecedented emphasis upon *devekut* may be linked with his alleged experience of childhood loss. For in the tales gathered from various sources in *Shivhe ha-Besht* (1815), he is described as a child of his parents' old age and orphaned early on. Like Alyosha in Dostoyevsky's *The Brothers*

Karamazov, the Besht received his calling in early childhood from a parent on the point of death:

> He took his son in his arms and he said, "I see that you will light my [memorial] candle, and I will not enjoy the pleasure of raising you. My beloved son, remember this all your days: God is with you. Do not fear anything" (1970, p. 11).

The Besht's childhood tendency to wildness, solitude and wandering in childhood is linked to his orphanhood: "It was his way to study for a few days and then to run away from school. They would search for him and find him sitting alone in the forest. They would attribute this to his being an orphan. There was no one to look after him and he was a footloose child" (p. 12).

Traces of bereavement may be found in many of the Besht's teachings. In an often-recorded parable of the Besht's, the symbolic function of *devekut* to the child bereaved of his father may be inferred:

> A king had built a glorious palace full of corridors and partitions, but he himself lived in the innermost room. When the palace was completed and his servants came to pay him homage, they found that they could not approach the king because of the devious maze. While they stood and wondered, the king's son came and showed them that those were not partitions, but only magical illusions, and that the king, in truth, was easily accessible (in Hundert, ed., pp. 295–6).

Although this parable is susceptible to many interpretations, the message that nothing separates the son from his father – that the son's feelings of loss and alienation can be overcome – might have special attraction to one who has lost his father in early childhood and who yearns for reunion with his father or, failing that, with a fatherlike God.

In another of the Besht's parables of a prince estranged from his father, the prince, after a long exile, receives a letter from his father. Seeking to avoid ridicule at the extremity of his joy, he gives a public party in which he can unobtrusively give free rein to his delight at being once again in touch with his father (*ibid.*, p. 303). This parable, too, may have poignant meaning to one who has lost his father in childhood and thus suffers estrangement and a futile longing for the celebration of reunion. A similar interpretation might also be attached to the following homily, attributed to the Besht, in which the sense of separation between humans and God is illusory and easily overcome:

> He who cleaves to one part of the unity cleaves to the whole. And the same applies to the opposite condition: "I sought him whom my soul loveth, I sought him, but I found him not" [Song of Songs 3:1]. The meaning is that the Holy One Blessed be He disguises himself behind several garments and partitions, such as straying thoughts or the cessation of study and prayer... But for the men of knowledge, who know that no place is empty of Him, these are not true disguises (*ibid.*, p. 302).

At the same time, such parables will have significance also to a people in mourning after large-scale massacres and a messianic debacle.

Jiddu Krishnamurti

The foregoing discussion suggests that bereavement might have been one of many factors predisposing the Besht to conceive of *devekut* not simply as an aspect of religious life but as its very essence. In considering this possibility, it is interesting to compare him with Krishnamurti. Krishnamurti is unusual among mystics in allowing a critical, documented biography to be written. The biography, by Mary Lutyens (1975, 1983), makes clear that his mystical leanings, his role as the messiah of the theosophists and his later role as an independent religious teacher had much to do with childhood bereavements, particularly the loss of his mother when he was nine. His disciple and confidante, Lady Emily Lutyens (the mother of his biographer), recalled: "His mother having died when he was very young, he was always yearning to be back in her arms" (1975, p. 82).

From an early age, Krishnamurti was inclined to "spiritual" experiences owing to unresolved grief. Like many others who have illusions or hallucinations of the lost person, he had visions of his dead mother, which apparently signified his denial of her death and his yearning to be reunited with her. In Hindu society and the pre-modern world in general, such "visions" were more likely to be regarded as evidence of contact with higher beings than as signs of grief. In addition, five of his 11 siblings died in childhood or as young adults. He was deeply affected by some of these losses, and his sense of being "chosen" and "protected" by the higher beings may have derived in part from his survival. In the year before his mother's death, he lost his eldest sister and discovered that he, like his mother, could occasionally "see" the girl (1975, p. 5).

For much of his adult life, Krishnamurti was periodically afflicted with immense unexplained physical pain during which he would behave like a small child in need of his or her mother and would address the women around him as "Amma" or "Mother." Mary Lutyens was present on a number of these occasions in the 1920s and recalled that "He had behaved to me at times as if I were his mother and he a child of about four" (1983, p. 69n). Furthermore, she wrote,

> It seemed that only when he became a child again was he able to relax and thereby obtain some relief from the pain, which was with him all day now as a dull ache as well as intensely in the evenings. But he could not become a child without a "mother" to look after the body (1975, p. 184).

At one point, he had recurrent visions of his dead mother (*ibid.*, pp. 165–6), as he had also experienced in childhood. As part of this "process," as he called it, he would have hallucinations of union not only with his mother but also with the entire world; this may be regarded as the basis of his mystical-charismatic identity. In 1922 in California he had a hallucination that can be understood as foreshadowing his later role as an international spiritual teacher, since it shows the depth of his need to identify himself with all animate and inanimate things:

> There was a man mending the road; that man was myself; the pickaxe he held was myself; the very stone which he was breaking up was a part of me; the tender blade of grass was my very being, and the tree beside the man was myself. I could almost feel and think like the roadmender, and I could feel the wind passing through the tree, and the little ant on the blade of grass I could feel. The birds, the dust, and the very noise were a part of me. Just then there was a car passing by at some distance; I was the driver, the engine, and the tyres; as the car went further away from me, I was going away from myself. I was in everything, or rather everything was in me, inanimate and animate, the mountains, the worm, and all breathing things (p. 158).

Krishnamurti's desire to "belong to the world" may have resulted from his mother's death, since this marked the point after which he no longer belonged to a secure family. The craving for reunion with the mother – "to be back in her arms," as Emily Lutyens reported – could not be satisfied. The craving evolved, however, into a need that could be satisfied: to be one with the public, with the whole world and with the higher ideal or beings, which he called his "Beloved" and described as "the open skies, the flower, every human being" and which could be found "in every animal, in every blade of grass, in every person that is suffering, in every individual" (p. 250). In one of his most Christ-like pronouncements, he declared:

> I belong to all people, to all who really love, to all who are suffering. And if you would walk, you must walk with me. If you would understand you must look through my mind. If you would feel, you must look through my heart. And because I really love, I want you to love (p. 233).

His renunciation of the role of messiah in 1929 was accompanied by a new sense of union, self-annihilation, and renewal. It is of great psychological interest that this spiritual turning point involved the conviction that "henceforth there will be no separation":

> If I say, and I will say, that I am one with the Beloved, it is because I feel and know it. I have found what I longed for, I have become united, so that henceforth there will be no separation, because my thoughts, my desires, my longings – those of the individual self – have been destroyed ... I have been united with my Beloved, and my Beloved and I will wander together the face of the earth (*ibid.*, p. 250).

In the case of Krishnamurti, as of the Besht, the quest for union – in whatever sense this union is used – may have derived in part from childhood loss and constituted a mystical expression of delayed grief. Although loss is no prerequisite for mysticism, and mysticism is far more than a symptom of bereavement, the potential healing qualities of such teachings to the bereaved and the alienated, for whatever reason, are clear. The empowerment given by mysticism, with its potential for social change, also links Krishnamurti with the Besht: for Krishnamurti believed that human beings are capable of radically transforming themselves and their world.

Mystical union in other literature

The creative uses of grief in the transformation of Jewish life have analogies in creativity in all forms. In particular, there are many literary examples of union – not just with lost persons but also with objects and abstractions – which may be regarded as transcendent forms of delayed grief. The function of identification with the lost person is well expressed by Proust in *Remembrance of Things Past* (1913–27) through the use of imagery of "grafting" that is reminiscent of the concept of union or cleaving in *devekut*. After his mistress, Albertine, died in a riding accident, Proust observed that just as an artist lives on in his work, so also a lost person may remain alive within the mourner, who grafts the memory, as it were, onto his heart:

> It is often said that something may survive of a person after his death, if that person was an artist and put a little of himself into his work. It is perhaps in the same way that a sort of cutting taken from one person and grafted on to the heart of another continues to carry on its existence even when the person from whom it had been detached has perished (1981, III 534).

The theory that identification with the lost person may represent an attempt to prevent further losses by becoming one with the dead (Krupp 1965) together with the idea that absorptive mysticism may in some cases have the same origin, finds support in Proust's comment and in other literary illustrations. Creative literature often describes a feeling of connection, if not actual union with a lost person in the animate or inanimate world through language that recalls mystical union. In Edgar Allan Poe's story "Ligeia" (1838), for example, a man bereaved of his wife feels her presence within himself as in a shrine, in which her memory is constantly reflected in his contemplation of the natural world (1975, p. 113).[6] Similarly, in Emily Bronte's *Wuthering Heights* (1847), Heathcliff's impassioned outburst over the dead Catherine expresses yearning for union with the lost person in language not dissimilar from that of the longing for the mystical union:

> …what is not connected with her to me? and what does not recall her? I cannot look down to this floor, but her features are shaped on the flags! In every cloud, in every tree – filling the air at night, and caught by glimpses in every object by day – I am surrounded with her image! (ch. 33).

Experiences such as that expressed by Heathcliff are not, strictly speaking, "mystical"; when directed toward a divine being, however, they could form the basis of a striving for mystical union.

The poetry of John Clare expresses similar yearning for the dead in terms reminiscent of the quest for mystical union. Clare, born in Northamptonshire in 1793, had a twin sister, Elizabeth, who died a month after birth. The son of a farm labourer, Clare worked on a farm from about age 12, attending school in the evenings. At 16, he fell deeply in love with Mary Joyce, the daughter of a wealthy farmer who apparently forbade her to meet her lover. Clare never forgot his first love and in periods of insanity long after Mary's death in 1838, he held conversations with her, under the delusion that she still lived and was his wife and had borne his children. In fact, she never married. Clare's chronic grief for Mary suggests a deeper level of unconscious grief for his lost sister, for at times he writes of Mary as if she were a part of him, his twin. This feeling of union is, again, reminiscent of a mystical experience of union. In the poem beginning "Lovely Mary, when we parted," he declared, "The past hath made us both as one"; in "Child Harold," he wrote, "Mary, thy name loved long still keeps me free / Till my lost life becomes a part of thee."

The urge for union with the dead appears also in the writings of D.H. Lawrence after his mother's death in 1910. In the poem "The End," written shortly after her death, he expresses the desire for union: "If I could have put you in my heart, / If I could have wrapped you in myself / How glad I should have been!"

Such sensations of incorporation with the lost person appear to be especially frequent and intense among those bereaved or severely deprived, especially in childhood.[7] Again, the language with which this phenomenon is described frequently recalls mystical union. The autobiographical novelist Forrest Reid, for example, described the period during and after his father's death when he was five; he wrote of times

when I could pass *into* nature, and feel the grass growing, and float with the clouds through the transparent air; when I could hear the low breathing of the earth, when the colour and the smell of it were so close to me that I seemed to lose consciousness of my separate existence. Then, one single emotion animated all things, one heart beat throughout the universe, and the mother and all her children were united (1926, p. 208).

One final example, from the writings of Martin Buber, is especially apt as Buber's philosophy was strongly influenced by the Besht and the Hasidic movement. This experience of union, described in *Daniel* (1913), Buber's book of dialogues, might again be connected with childhood loss:

> On a gloomy morning I walked upon the highway, saw a piece of mica lying, picked it up and looked at it for a long time; the day was no longer gloomy, so much light was caught in the stone. And suddenly as I raised my eyes from it, I realized that while I had looked I had not been conscious of "object" and "subject"; in my looking the mica and I had been one; in my looking I had tasted unity (1964, p. 140).

According to Buber's biographer, Maurice Friedman, Buber's mother "disappeared without leaving a trace" when the child was three (1981, I, 4). He saw her only once afterwards, over 20 years later. This loss, writes Friedman, "was the decisive experience of Martin Buber's life, the one without which neither his early seeking for unity nor his later focus on dialogue and on the meeting with the 'eternal Thou' is understandable" (*ibid.*, p. 13). The abandoned child was raised by his grandparents who, he recalled, never discussed with him the circumstances of his loss or his feelings, and whom he was frankly afraid to ask about his mother's departure. In an autobiographical fragment (1973, pp. 18–19), Buber describes his first apprehension that his mother would not return as the possible origin of his philosophy of meeting and dialogue. His unusual attraction to the teachings of the Besht may have been linked to his discovering in the founder of Hasidism a kindred spirit who had found a spiritual solution in Judaism to emotional quandaries stemming, as his did, from childhood loss. For the bereaved individual, as for the bereaved nation, grief can be a stimulus to creative renewal.

In conclusion, although the concept of mystical union has many shades of meaning, religious and social as well as psychological, its potential importance as a force for individual creativity and social change should not be ignored. A comparison between the Besht, Krishnamurti, and others who had parallel mystical or semi-mystical experiences, such as Martin Buber, leads to the conclusion that mystical union might at times be linked to the yearning for union which a bereaved person often feels toward the dead. It might act as a way of compensation, a defense against depression, a form of restitution toward the dead; or, by asserting the alleged harmony which underpins existence, it may act as a stay against anger and the horrifying apprehension of the random, chaotic nature of existence. Mystical union might have served the Besht and Krishnamurti (and, by implication, other mystics with comparable backgrounds) as a sublimated expression of the craving for reunion with the lost person. This unresolved grief was harnessed to the wider social aim of comforting, healing, and transforming their followers, reuniting them with their spiritual roots in an age of crisis. A potential socio-psychological attraction of mystical union is the cleaving of charismatic leader and followers in a community in which an intimate sense of family, which through childhood loss or disruption has been lost or never experienced, can be achieved. Through this union, solitude, estrangement, and the sluggishness of grief can be overcome, and the will can be galvanized for action and renewal. For the Jews, Hasidism provided both a spiritual basis for Jewish continuity and also, by reaffirming human power to influence the divine order, the potential for radical social change.

7

Marx and Freud

Emancipation and the End of Rabbinic Dominance

From ancient times until the nineteenth century, Jewish life was primarily characterized by the absence of political power and an exceptional emphasis on religious learning. At the highest echelons of Jewish society was a rabbinic elite, which, building on the biblical and talmudic tradition, created one of the most powerful and profound of civilizations. Memory, analytic ability, and originality were prized above all as tools for bringing human beings closer to God. The rabbinical class was often a family affair, with fathers handing down their office to their most talented sons. Neither wealth nor family mattered to the intellectually egalitarian East European Jews when it came to rabbinic scholarship. The scholar might be dressed in rags but remained an aristocrat. A great scholar had something of the prestige of a nuclear scientist in the 1940s: someone with the uncommon brain power to open up the secrets of learning and the ability to reveal its power to the world. The dream of Jewish parents was to marry their daughters to scholars:

The dowry of a girl was proportional to the scholarship of the prospective bridegroom. Very rich fathers used to go to the yeshiva and ask the director for the best student, whom they would then seek as a son-in-law. An outstanding student would receive not only a rich dowry, but also a given number of years of *kest* – that is, of board at the home of his parents-in-law while he continued his studies. In this way, the son of the *prost* [common] family may marry into a family with *yichus* [distinction]; and in this way learning served as a potent instrument of social mobility – perhaps the most potent in the shtetl society (Zborowski and Herzog 1969, p. 82).

The secular enlightenment, by weakening religion, undermined this elite and forced it to use its enormous cultural capital in other areas, usually by means of secular schooling, which expanded enormously in the nineteenth century. This unleashing of rabbinic intellectuals into secular life "was an event of shattering importance in world history" (Johnson 1994, p. 341).

This chapter discusses the life and work of two representatives of this erstwhile rabbinical class at the turning point of modern Jewish and general intellectual history: Karl Marx (1818–83) and Sigmund Freud (1856–1939). In which ways can their rabbinical origins be detected in their most determinedly secular lives and thought?

Marx and his tormented vision

Marx left little to indicate the psychological roots of his ideas and creative motivation. Hardly anything is known of his childhood and family. Like Freud, he destroyed most of the documents pertaining to his early years. Judging from his writings, Marx was motivated primarily by the social inequities of his age, by the poverty and suffering brought on by the rise of industrialism. This may be so. Yet Marx's personality – described by acquaintances, and even disciples, as dictatorial, intolerant of rivalry and criticism, hot-tempered, destructive, vain, ruthless, conspiratorial, power-hungry – cannot be explained purely in terms of his anguished response to the plight and the needs of the workers in nineteenth-century Europe. Isaiah Berlin suggests that Marx's depiction of the workers as outcasts, discriminated against, exploited, deprived of their freedom, debased by forces beyond their control, is also a portrait of the Jews, and a reflection of Marx's personal torment and alienation despite his baptism:

> When Marx speaks for the proletariat, in particular when he alters the history of socialism (and of mankind) by asserting that there is no common interest between the proletarians and the capitalists, and therefore no possibility of reconciliation; when he insists that there is no common ground, and therefore no possibility of converting the opponents of mankind by appeals to common principles of jus-tice, or common reason or common desire for happiness, for there are no such things; when, by the same token, he denounces appeals to the humanity or sense of duty of the bourgeois as mere pathetic delu-sion on the part of their victims, and declares a war of extermination against capitalism, and prophesies the triumph of the proletariat as

the inexorable verdict of history itself, of the triumph of human reason over human irrationality – when he says all that (and is virtually the first to say it, for the Puritans and Jacobins did, at least in theory, allow the possibility of persuasion and agreement), it is difficult not to think that the voice is that of a proud and defiant pariah, not so much the friend of the proletariat as of a member of a long humiliated race (Berlin 1979, pp. 282–3).

The theme of alienation which came to dominate Marx's later writings is expressed most powerfully in his poetry, written at a time when he knew next to nothing about the working conditions of the poor. These lines from his verse tragedy *Oulanem* were written before Marx was 20:

> ... we are chained, shattered, empty, frightened,
> Eternally chained to this marble block of Being,
> Chained, eternally chained, eternally.
> And the worlds drag us with them on their rounds,
> Howling their songs of death, and we –
> We are the apes of a cold God.
>
> (Payne 1968, p. 71)

The bitterness and rage aroused by Marx's conviction of being an outcast are certainly inexplicable in the light of his economic conditions, though during his first years in London (1849–56) he and his family occasionally lived in appalling poverty, and he gained shocking firsthand knowledge of the life of the poor. What is striking about Marx's poverty is the extent to which it was self-inflicted. Marx was raised in comfortable circumstances in Trier, where his father was a lawyer. He married into a wealthy, aristocratic Prussian family. He could easily have avoided poverty. In 1848, for example, he inherited 6000 gold francs – a fortune at the time – from his father's estate. He gave 5000 of it to a fund for arming Belgian workmen (*ibid.*, pp. 175–6). After being expelled from Prussia, France, and Belgium for revolutionary activities during the upheavals of 1848, he arrived in London almost penniless. Even so, he never took a job. When his daughter Franziska was born in March 1851, the family did not have the money to buy a cradle; when she died the following year they did not have enough for a coffin. Marx lived mostly on gifts, legacies and, finally, on Engels' annual stipend, which provided for him and his family for the rest of his life. This might be seen as a secularized expression of an attitude and a lifestyle which, as we have seen, were pronounced among the East European Jews (and still found among some Orthodox Jews): his mind was proof of royalty, the world owed him a living. Nor can Marx's sense of alienation be explained simply by his personal frustrations and failings, though these were real enough. In view of his ambition, his prodigious intellectual gifts and his personal charisma (though he was a clumsy public speaker), Marx gained astonishingly little power and influence in his lifetime. His career effectively began with his death. Today he is honoured as a founder of modern economic history and sociology; and even after the fall of the Soviet empire much of the world's population still lives under the spectre of his ideas (or what pass as his ideas). Yet in his lifetime he was, by and large, a failure. Except for a brief period in 1842–43, when he was editor of the liberal newspaper *Rheinische Zeitung*, and his chairmanship of the International Working Men's Association (1864–72), he held no position of authority. His books were hardly read. The frustration of being ignored and the threat of being forgotten gave an acerbic edge to his character. But this, too, was only part of what made Marx. Marx's physical sufferings also left their imprint on his character and work. His ailments were severe and included chronic liver trouble and stomach disorder, headaches and insomnia, and the well-known boils. For most of the 30-odd years which he spent in London, Marx was afflicted with boils, some the size of a fist, which covered his body, festered and stank, and for which no proper treatment was known. (While completing *Das Kapital* in 1867, he hinted endearingly to Engels that his concern with the working class, though genuine, was infused with a heavy dose of personal anguish: "I hope the bourgeoisie will remember my carbuncles until their dying day.") Yet again, Marx's ailments do not fully account for his sense of being an outcast and for the demonic creative drive underlying his thought.

More serious than Marx's poverty and illnesses was a heavy burden of loss, in adolescence and in manhood. His daughter, Eleanor, wrote that he was deeply grieved by the death of his younger brother, Edouard, in 1837 and of his father in 1838. (He had a daguerrotype photograph of his father in his pocket when he died.) In addition, during his early years in London, Marx lost three of his children. Two died in infancy, but the third, his eldest son, Edgar, lived to the age of eight and was Marx's favorite. His death in 1865 was a shattering blow. Tragic though they were, and although they undoubtedly left their imprint on Marx's character and work, these misfortunes occurred mostly in later life, after Marx's personality and his main ideas had already been formed.

In considering possible childhood roots of Marx's sense of alienation, his social and religious background and his position in his family are of outstanding importance. "The tradition of all the dead generations," wrote Marx in *The Eighteenth Brumaire of Louis Bonaparte* (1852) "weighs like a nightmare on the brain of the living" (1969, p. 15). Both of Marx's parents were children of rabbis and descended from long lines of rabbinical ancestors, some of them quite eminent. The French Revolution and the Napoleonic wars had brought a measure of civil rights to the Jews, freeing them from the ghettoes and opening up to them various professions which had previously been closed. In this tumultuous age, Marx's father, in common with many young Jews, turned to rationalism. He became a lawyer and gradually abandoned his Jewish traditions to the extent of breaking with his family. However, after Napoleon's fall in 1815, many of the civil rights which had been granted to the Jews were revoked. Marx's father converted to Protestantism in 1816 because otherwise, as a Jew living in Prussia, he would have been barred from the legal profession. His wife and children were converted several years later (Marx was six at the time). Though some biographers believe that the Marx family most likely felt relief at being freed from the burden of Jewishness, it is highly unlikely that the baptism was attended by an entirely clear conscience. To a rationalist like Marx's father, Judaism was an insular tradition, fraught with superstition, a millstone round his neck in his professional life. Yet he personally turned to baptism only under duress, in response to anti-Semitic legislation. Was the society in which such legislation was possible any more enlightened than the narrow, almost medieval Jewish society in which he had been raised? And considering the gradual break with his family, of which baptism was the final severance, it is impossible to believe that Marx's father was entirely free of inner conflict over his Jewish origins or that he failed to transmit this conflict to his son.

In common with Disraeli, Marx in a lifetime of writing left no account of the psychological effects of baptism on him and his family. Also like Disraeli, he put forward the view that Christianity is the sublime form of Judaism. But in contrast with Disraeli, Marx hated Judaism with the passionate intensity of a rabid anti-Semite. Though Marx was not unsympathetic to the problems of the Jewish working class, he knew little of Jewish history or religion. In the *Eighteenth Brumaire*, he argues that "Cromwell and the English people had borrowed speech, passions and illusions from the Old Testament for their bourgeois revolution. When the real aim had been achieved, when the bourgeois transformation of society had been accomplished, Locke supplanted Habakkuk"

(1969, p. 17). Yet nowhere does Marx acknowledge 'the revolutionary nature of prophetic Judaism on its own terms: the whole idea of "the forcible overthrow of the entire existing social order," as he puts it at the end of the *Communist Manifesto*, was not dissimilar from the furious idealism of the prophets who insisted on the spiritual values of monotheism, particularly social justice, in opposition to a polytheistic, materialistic world. (Marx did, however, lament his "prophet's" beard when he had to have it cut off in his last sickness.) The idea that the nation-state will be transcended by an international order based on justice comes ultimately from the prophets. At times, Marx's imagery recalls his personal obsessions as one who could be accepted neither as a Jew nor a Christian but was forced, as it were, to recreate the world to suit himself. For example in the *Communist Manifesto*, Marx writes, virtually as an indirect confession of his own aims, how the aristocracy, succumbing to the upstart bourgeoisie, is obliged to lose sight of its own interests by supporting the exploited working class and in so doing attacking the bourgeoisie: "the aristocracy took revenge [on the bourgeoisie] by singing lampoons on their new master and whispering in his ears sinister prophecies of coming catastrophe" (1971, p. 56). The paradoxically scientific, yet messianic, inevitable violent revolution of the working class leading to a New Age of conflictless society was, on one level, the age-old Jewish messianic longing, when hatred and prejudice would be no more. To Marx, the "real conditions of life" would replace ancient prejudice:

> All fixed, fast-frozen relations, with their train of ancient and venerable prejudices and opinions, are swept away, all new-formed ones become antiquated before they can ossify. All that is solid melts into air, all that is holy is profaned, and man is at last compelled to face, with sober senses, his real conditions of life, and his relations with his kind (*ibid.*, p. 35).

In *Das Kapital*, Marx revealingly associates the working class with the ancient Israelites:

> Just as it was written upon the brow of the chosen people that they were Jehovah's property, so does the division of labour brand the manufacturing worker as the property of capital (1934, I 382).

Though it might be argued that *Das Kapital* could only have been written by a Jew disillusioned by emancipation, Marx abhorred Judaism as a social illness, a cancer which would be cured only by the rise of a socialist state. Marx had incalculable influence on socialist and communist movements. His hatred of the Jews, a sign of recoil against his Jewish background, did enormous damage by encouraging Marxists to hate Jews and feel contempt for Judaism – even after anti-Semitism was officially outlawed by the Soviet Union. Marx could be described as a link between Luther and Hitler: "Luther wanted to convert Jews; Marx wanted to abolish them; Hitler wanted to expel and subsequently to exterminate them" (Carlebach 1978, p. 352).

Anti-Semites (including Hitler) quoted Marx on the Jews with relish. Marx, largely ignorant of Judaism, felt himself to be stigmatized by his Jewish origins. He identified Judaism with the hated capitalist system, an antisocial force of alienation. Real emancipation meant doing away with Judaism, he wrote in "On the Jewish Question":

> What is the worldly basis of Judaism? Practical necessity, selfishness. What is the worldly culture of the Jew? Commerce. What is his worldly God? Money. All right! The emancipation from commerce and from money, from the practical real Judaism, would be the self-emancipation of our age (Mendes-Flohr and Reinharz 1980, p. 266).

It is psychologically significant that this condemnation (which was at the same time a sincere attempt to solve the Jewish question) was the first thing Marx wrote after his marriage in 1843. It is an extraordinary topic for a man on honeymoon to be thinking about. Marx and his bride were staying with his mother-in-law, the Baroness von Westphalen at Kreuznach. Marx had married only after much struggle. His engagement had lasted seven years and was opposed by his wife's family partly because of Marx's Jewish origins: "To marry a Jew was shocking enough, but to marry a jobless, penniless Jew who had already achieved national notoriety [as editor of the radical *Rheinische Zeitung*] was quite intolerable" (Wheen 2000, p. 51). "On the Jewish Question" was followed by "A Contribution to the Critique of Hegel's Philosophy of Law," which consigns religion in general to the scrapheap of history ("Religion is the opium of the people") and introduces the proletariat whose revolution will bring about an atheist world in which people are treated equally. The chief psychological elements of Marx's later life and thought coalesce in these juxtapositions: rejection of Judaism, marriage to the Christian world, overthrow of this world by the proletariat.

Marx's prejudices against the Jews were essentially adopted from Christian beliefs: the Jew is associated with materialism, with capital, and greed. In giving away his money and behaving improvidently, even recklessly when it came to his and his family's needs, Marx was declaring in effect that he was not a Jew. Like Raskolnikov, he could give away his last coppers in a gesture of true Christian kindness – forgetting, or never knowing, that charity (*tzedakah*) is in any case originally a Jewish concept, and highly developed in Jewish life (Zborowski and Herzog 1969, pp. 191–213). Being careless or foolish with money meant that the imputation of capitalist did not apply to him. His baptism had "cured" him of all that. Such thoughts might have been especially pressing at the time of his marriage, which while marking a further breach with Judaism also brought home the degree to which emancipation was illusory: clearly his wife's family thought of him as a Jew still, and disapproved. Ironically, Marx broke out of the Christian stereotype of the Jew only to land himself in the classic economic position of the Jewish intellectual: he studied, and others (particularly Engels) provided for him.

Marx's relationships with Jews were invariably fraught with prejudice and defamation. Distaste for Judaism and for Jews was, of course, not uncommon among converted Jews, many of whom were well-educated and had reacted against what they saw rather too exclusively as a persecuted, irrational, backward, and impoverished way of life. The downgrading of their origins might in some cases have been a tactic for dealing with guilt over the betrayal of their faith. Self-hate was their patriotism. Though often defamed as a Jew, Marx, a fighter drawn to - controversy, a brilliant debater, with a gift for invective, never responded (Carlebach 1978, p. 337). The dictatorship of the proletariat would deal with Marx's anti-Semitic enemies. Also, Marx seems to have ignored evidence showing that the association of Jews with capital was sheer prejudice: the European Jewish masses in fact constituted a downtrodden proletariat, and they had a growing sense of national identity. When it came to the Jews, Marx discarded his favorite motto, *De omnibus dubitandum* (Doubt everything) (Wheen 2000, p. 388): he *knew* that Judaism and capitalism were one and the same.

The virulence of Marx's anti-Semitism – together with other distorted aspects of his personality – indicates a psychopathological origin, possibly in Marx's early relationships with his parents and siblings. His position in his family may have inclined him to a sense of alienation, to bitter hatred, to a dictatorial intolerance of rivalry, as well as to an obsession with social justice. Marx's birth was followed in rapid succession by six siblings. As in the case of Freud, whose family structure was similar, these multiple births may have led to a certain deprivation or distortion of consistent maternal love and care in infancy and early childhood.

Marx seems to have felt little warmth toward his mother. The animosity aroused by being displaced from the mother's affection may have found a later scapegoat in capital and in the Judaism which Marx prejudicially associated with capitalism, which he mistakenly imagined was in its death-throes. The fact that Marx's mother controlled the family's purse-strings after the father's death – and that she was extremely wary of helping her wayward son – would have reinforced these associations.

Marx's tormented vision of man as an outcast derived much of its force from his own sufferings – his poverty, failures, illnesses, bereavements – but more especially from his sense of being alienated from his family, from the religion into which he was born and that to which he was converted, from the society in which he lived. Marx's struggle for social justice, admirable as it was in itself, was colored by personal conflicts and torments. Marx in effect attempted to detach the prophetic fervor and moral ideology from Judaism and, adopting the stance of an anti-Semite, to recycle this fervor and ideology in a socialist system. Though he tried to create a universalist system transcending religion, nationality, and prejudice, Marx also represented many of the conflicts of emancipated European Jewry as Jewish life and Judaism were transformed in the modern period.

"Infidel Jew": Freud, Jewish ritual, and psychoanalysis

Marx's intellectual outlook was formed by the liberal environment, and the reaction against it, in the first half of the nineteenth century. In contrast, Freud, born a generation later, grew up in an atmosphere of political and economic anxiety, nascent racist anti-Semitism and Jewish nationalism. Yet, as in the case of Marx, from the standpoint of traditional Judaism – Judaism, that is, as a religious way of life – Freud was a heretic and a self-confessed one at that: he was concerned less with providence than with secular enlightenment, less with Jewish religious–national consciousness than with psychoanalytic insight, less with the continuation and growth of the Jewish religious tradition than with the universal brotherhood of man governed by reason.

Freud was the first in his family to have the choice of how to define himself as a Jew. Unlike his rabbinic ancestors, Freud devoted his life not to the idea that the Jews are divinely chosen as "a light to the nations" but to the principle that all people, the Jews included, are driven by the same fundamental instincts. Freud was raised in an assimilated Jewish environment which extolled the virtues of enlightenment (or Haskalah in Hebrew) and, while retaining some traditional practices, rejected rabbinic Judaism with its emphasis on talmudic law as being narrow, backward and largely antithetical to the modern world and to scientific progress. Judging from Freud's own writings, anti-Semitism and the attraction of secular enlightenment, far more than the healthy, vibrant side of the rabbinic tradition, drove him to succeed in the non-Jewish world.

At the time of Freud's birth, Judaism was defined largely in religious terms. Most Jews, particularly in Eastern Europe, expressed their Jewishness through ritual observance. Freud's generation had access as never before to higher education which at the time did not sit well with Jewish religious practices. These maintain family and communal cohesion but set the Jews apart from the Christian world. These practices include: regular prayer and study in Hebrew and Aramaic, the observance of the Sabbath, festivals and dietary laws, and the maintenance of customs such as circumcision, the bar mitzvah, rabbinic weddings, and funerals. As a result, tension, conflict and guilt were at an especially high pitch, and this was true in Freud's case as revealed most strikingly in *The Interpretation of Dreams*.

Freud's family background – both his parents came from orthodox Jewish homes in East European towns – was a source of strength, energy, and conflict, particularly with his father. Freud's troubled bond with his father had a specifically Jewish side and deeply colored his psychoanalytic theories (Robert 1976). Jakob Freud, like many other Jewish fathers at the time, "was too much of a Jew to break with a bloodless tradition in which his children saw nothing but the empty aping of ritual, but not enough of a Jew to hand down a possibility of authentic self-contained and self-justifying existence" (*ibid.*, pp. 9–10). Freud regarded being Jewish as a training in embattled minority views (Freud 1926, p. 274), and it may be that as founder of a new tradition he had to play down the virtues of the old. Yet the evidence seems to be that Freud knew precious little about these virtues, for religious Judaism as he saw it at home was a thing of shreds and patches, abhorrent in its hypocrisy (Aberbach 1980). Freud might have been referring to himself when he wrote that a religion "must be hard and unloving to those who do not belong to it" (Freud 1921, p. 98). Absent in Freud's conception of Jewish ritual and learning is its warm, healthy, lifegiving side, enabling the Jews to survive hatred and persecution through the ages. His sense of what it meant to be a practicing Jew was inauthentic and confused and led in the end to his notorious dismissal of Judaism in *Moses and Monotheism*.

What is known of Freud's religious background? Revealingly little.[1] Jones (1957, p. 350) writes of Freud's parents: "Whatever may have been their custom previously, after coming to Vienna [in 1859] they dispensed with the Jewish dietary observances and with most of the customary rituals." The family continued to celebrate Passover and Jakob Freud conducted the *seder* by heart. To the end of his life he studied the Talmud and read a great deal of Hebrew literature (Heller 1956, p. 419). Freud himself mentions none of this in his surviving writings, nor that he himself in his youth was "conversant with all Jewish customs and festivals [and] had of course been taught Hebrew" (Jones 1953, pp. 19, 21). What is clear is his almost total non-observance already as a young man and his general failure to recognize the life-affirming role of religious ritual, which he dismissed as "antiquated nuisance" (*ibid.*, p. 351). His dominant view was that religion is a form of immaturity (Freud 1927, p. 53), and he describes neurosis as "an individual religiosity and religion as a universal obsessional neurosis" (Freud 1907, pp. 126–7). While his father might have fasted on Tisha B'Av (the anniversary of the destruction of the Temple in Jerusalem) and Yom Kippur, Freud himself did not. He wrote to his fiancee on 8 September 1883, a few weeks before Yom Kippur: "Am I to fast at Yom Kippur ... ? Surely not" (E. Freud, ed. 1960, p. 55). The idea of being married under a *chupa* (canopy) by a rabbi was "anathema" to Freud (Jones 1953, p.140). The rite of circumcision is denigrated by Freud as a relic of castration, a possible cause of anti-Semitism (Freud 1939, pp. 91, 123). Freud's cremation in London was a final act of defiance against Jewish ritual as cremation is against Jewish law.

Freud's family life was devoid of Jewish ritual. His wife, who came from a very religious home, would have liked to observe some of the rituals: "In 1938 Martha and Freud were still carrying on a longstanding humorous (and yet serious) argument over the issue of lighting candles on Friday evenings; Martha joked at Freud's monstrous stubbornness which prevented her from performing the ritual, while he firmly maintained that the practice was foolish and superstitious" (Roazen 1975, p. 48). Jones writes that after Freud's death "she would find interest in discussing Jewish customs and festivals with anyone of a similar cast of thought" (Jones 1953, p. 152). Freud's children consequently knew very little about Judaism. Freud's son Martin tells of his maternal grandmother, Emmeline: "She stayed with us occasionally and on Saturdays we used to hear her singing Jewish prayers in a small but firm and melodious voice. All of this, strangely enough in a Jewish family, seemed alien to us children who had been brought up without any instruction in Jewish ritual" (M. Freud 1957, p. 14).

In this way, the Freud family, in common with many Western European Jewish families at the time, abandoned Jewish tradition. It may be that psychoanalysis, with its own ritual and dogma, its stress upon the inner life, its faith in the potential improvability of man, in some ways represents the return of the repressed tradition in altered, secular form. Freud's theories themselves alert us to the potential significance of the abandoned religious way of life which, perhaps like early memories, cannot be forgotten without trace or substitute. "It is typically Jewish," wrote Freud to his son Ernst on 17 January 1938, "not to renounce anything and to replace what is lost" (E.L. Freud, ed. 1960, p. 440). In view of the massive literature on Freud, it is extraordinary that the most basic information pertaining to his Jewish practices and education is almost totally lacking. The fragments which have survived usually contradict one another. For example, there is Freud's self-description as "godless" (Gay 1987, pp. 37, 38), an "infidel Jew" (Freud 1927, p. 170); yet, Roazen (1975) points out, he could still argue the existence of God and see religion as having a positive function:

> Despite his scepticism, with individual patients in treatment Freud felt that religion might serve as a constructive resolution of inner conflicts. He even sometimes regretted the increasing inability of modern men to believe in God (p. 48).

"Un-Jewish" was Freud's description of his education (E.L. Freud, ed. 1960, p. 394); how does this square with the fact that he was sent to synagogue classes (Jones 1957, p. 350) and that the closest adult friend of his youth was Samuel Hammerschlag, who taught him Hebrew and Bible at school? "He has been touchingly fond of me for years," said Freud of Hammerschlag, "there is such a secret sympathy between us that we can talk intimately together. He always regards me as his son" (Jones 1953, p. 163). If his education was truly as "un-Jewish" as he alleges, how was it that for his thirty-fifth birthday his father presented him with a Bible with a Hebrew inscription: "Thou hast seen in this Book the vision of the Almighty, thou hast heard willingly, thou hast done and hast tried to fly high on the wings of the Holy Spirit" (*ibid.*, p. 19). Was Freud being a touch disingenuous in claiming to be uncertain of the meaning of the word Menorah (Jones 1957, p. 350), yet able to allude with brilliant aptness on the eve of his departure from Nazi-occupied Vienna in 1938 to the rabbinic legend of Rabbi Yohanan ben Zakkai (*ibid.*, p. 221)?

As for change in Freud's religious observances and spiritual life, there is virtually no information. How did Freud pass from the stage at which, he admits with no explanation in *The Interpretation of Dreams*, he was "content with *spiritual* food" (Freud 1899, p. 208) to become absolutely and profoundly irreligious and critical of religion in old age?

How did he come to express such diametrically opposite views toward Judaism as those in a letter to his fiancee of 23 July 1882 and in *Moses and Monotheism*? In the letter, he praises his betrothed's grandfather, Chief Rabbi of Hamburg, and expresses sympathy for the life-affirming practice of ritual blessing: "the law commands the Jew ... to say grace over every fruit which makes him aware of the beautiful world in which it is grown. The Jew is made for joy and joy for the Jew" (E.L. Freud, ed. 1960, p. 21). In *Moses and Monotheism*, in contrast, Freud dismisses religion as a compulsive neurosis and Judaism as a "father-religion" killed by Christianity, the "son-religion", making Judaism a "fossil":

> Judaism had become a religion of the father; Christianity became a religion of the son. The old God, the Father, fell back behind Christ; Christ, the Son, took his place just as every son had hoped to do in primeval times ... and from that time on the Jewish religion was, to some extent, a fossil" (Freud 1939, p. 88).

And how does one account for the extremes in Freud's attitudes toward his Jewish origins, veering as he did between desiring baptism to Christianity and martyrdom for the Jewish cause? Jewish religious ritual as he saw it in Vienna of the late nineteenth century was so repugnant to him that he actually discussed with his friend and colleague Josef Breuer the possibility of conversion to Christianity rather than undergo the ordeal of a traditional Jewish wedding (Jones 1953, p. 167). (When Freud's friend, the Swiss pastor Oskar Pfister declared to him in 1918 that his work showed that he was the best of Christians, Freud did not object, though his daughter, Anna, found this idea incomprehensible.) At the other extreme is his remarkable declaration to his fiancee on 2 February 1886: "I have often felt as though I had inherited all the defiance and all the passion with which our ancestors defended their Temple and could gladly sacrifice my life for one great moment in history" (E.L. Freud, ed. 1960, p. 202).

Among Freud's reasons for destroying his own early letters, diaries and other memorabilia of childhood – Gay's biography of Freud (1988) covers Freud's childhood and youth in under 20 pages – was a not-unjustified fear that public knowledge of his personal background and motives might undermine the credibility of his new "science," which he did not want to be dismissed as a "Jewish national affair" (Abraham and Freud, eds 1965, p. 34). Freud's father belonged to a transitional generation in that he was born into a strictly orthodox Jewish East European environment, abandoning his orthodoxy as a young man and marrying Freud's mother (his third wife) in a reform synagogue, but never totally turning away from Jewish religious life. He never went as far as some who, like Heine, saw Judaism less as a religion than as a misfortune and won their "entrance ticket" to European civilization through baptism. But the emotional and cultural upheaval caused by his move from a largely rural Hasidic world, wholly Jewish and dominated by rabbinic authority, to a secular, sceptical, enlightened, anti-religious existence in one of the great European cities, seething with chauvinism and anti-Semitism, was inherited by Freud.[2] Uprooted from Jewish orthodoxy, yet not accepted in the Gentile world, Freud created an intellectual territory of his own which transcended and implicitly rejected both religious parochialism and racism.

The poisonous anti-Semitism of his environment, a strong dose of Jewish self-hate, and revulsion at Jewish religious ritual were all important factors both in Freud's neglect of his religious heritage and, presumably, in his creation of psychoanalysis[3]. As we have seen, he rarely acknowledged the normative, healthy aspects of the religious tradition he rejected as a collective neurosis, or publicized his enormous debt to it. In particular, Freud was a product of an educational tradition sustained by the Jewish religion, which for hundreds of years had made the Jews the only large group among whom literacy and learning was a religious duty. The psychoanalytic role which Freud created for himself was in some ways similar to that of East European rabbis, who often advised members of their congregations in their personal lives, and had close circles of adherents. While he had probably inherited his prodigious memory and analytic ability from his rabbinic ancestors, Freud ignored the practical importance of the talmudic background to his way of thinking (Frieden 1990). Kafka once wrote that Freud's works are a continuation of the Talmud, though there is not a single reference to the Talmud in the 23 volumes of Freud's *Collected Works*. (Freud does incidentally refer to the Holy Ghost.) The intellectual milieu in which Freud lived was hostile to the Talmud as the source of rabbinic authority, associated not so much with family and social stability as with Jew-hatred as well as with superstition and the unscientific, which had been rejected in favor of rationalism and secular enlightenment.

These are, of course, only some of the possible reasons why Freud's religious background was important in his creation of psychoanalysis.[4]

It may be that, especially as in the case of other Jewish thinkers with a rabbinic family background, such as Marx or Durkheim, the phantom way of life was transformed into a universal system of thought in which the alienation and the disabilities involved in being Jewish could be overcome and the causes of all forms of social malaise, including racial hatred, be subjected to rational enquiry and, like illnesses, be treated and cured.

Still, what is unusual about Freud in the context of his time is not the denial but the extent to which he asserts his Jewish origins – in a social rather than religious sense – especially in response to anti-Semitism.[5] Among Freud's interpretations of his own dreams, the clearest and most moving are often those reflecting his Jewishness. Freud connects some of them, particularly those concerning Rome, with his father's humiliation by an anti-Semite. Anti-Semitism, far more than anything positive in the Jewish religious tradition, gave Freud a sense of identity as a Jew (see Aberbach 1980). This point cannot be overstressed as psychoanalysis is an implicit attack on anti-Semitism, and on human prejudice in general; Freud's central assumption is that all human beings are driven by the same instincts and are, in a sense, equally wicked. Therefore, it is ludicrous for any set of people to regard themselves as racially superior.

Once actually in Rome (which he visited many times after completing *The Interpretation of Dreams*), Freud seems to have felt most acutely the extent of his break with his rabbinic ancestors, as he stood in front of Michelangelo's Moses in the church of San Pietro in Vincoli.[6] Here, as he revealed in a startling confession, he saw himself not in the role of the biblical lawgiver or creator of a new Torah, but as part of the rabble who abandon the true God and his eternal Word:

> Sometimes I have crept cautiously out of the half-gloom of the interior as though I myself belonged to the mob upon whom his eye is turned – the mob which can hold fast no conviction, which has neither faith nor patience, and which rejoices when it has regained its illusory idols (Freud 1914, p. 213).

However bold and fearless Freud was in defending his people against anti-Semitic onslaughts, he saw himself as an "infidel Jew," a heretical conformist in joining the mutiny against Jewish tradition. In a different age, he might have been a new Moses, continuer of a great religious tradition. Instead, like Marx, he founded a breakaway system of thought which, ultimately perhaps, could best survive and flourish within the very tradition which it set out to undermine.

8
Conflicting Images of Hebrew in Western Civilization

The secularization of Hebrew since the eighteenth century represents a major cultural turning point in Jewish history. The uses of Hebrew until the modern period were largely determined by the identity of the Jews as the only religious minority tolerated in Christian Europe and by the theocratic character of the countries where most Jews lived. Hebrew served Judaism primarily as the Holy Tongue (*leshon ha-Kodesh*) until the late nineteenth century. The fragmentation and conflicts of identity which have come to characterize the Jewish people are expressed in their Hebrew culture since the time of the French Enlightenment: in orthodox rabbinic Judaism, which preserved Hebrew in a unique educational system for two thousand years, against which assimilated Jews rebelled from the eighteenth century onward; as a stimulus toward assimilation itself, for which increasingly modernized Hebrew came to serve as a tool in the Haskalah (Enlightenment) movement, only to become obsolete (as did Yiddish, the main daily language of the European Jews prior to the Holocaust) as emancipated Jews mastered European languages and began to function primarily in them; as part of the foundation of the Western civilization – via Christianity and translations of the Hebrew Bible in the vernacular – into which most European Jews assimilated; as the ideological basis of secular nationalism in the idea, rooted in the Hebrew Bible, of a "chosen people" and a national community united by ancient, sacred cultural bonds; and Zionism and the re-establishment of a Jewish state whose living culture was modern Hebrew, uniting the European (Ashkenazic) and Oriental (Sephardic) Jews.[1] This is the sole instance of an ancient minority language and political entity restored in the modern period.

Not least significant in this highly varied and complex picture are negative perceptions of Hebrew on the part of Jewish creative writers and thinkers. Such views begin among nineteenth- and early twentieth-century European, particularly German, writers such as Marx, Freud, and Kafka; they become prevalent among American writers born prior to the Second World War, such as Henry Roth, Charles Reznikoff, Arthur Miller, Saul Bellow, Woody Allen, and Philip Roth; and they diminish after the war. This is evidently an unusual, if not unique, sociological phenomenon, the significance of which has not been sufficiently appreciated.

Modern Hebrew has had mercurial value in comparison with its more iron-clad pre-modern identity. It has mostly withered in a variety of majority cultures, involved multiple meanings and cultural cross-currents, and reflected many aspects of individual and collective social psychology. Hebrew is a majority culture only in Israel, where it has flourished since 1948, though many of the great modern Hebrew writers were born in Europe. In the diaspora, Hebrew often appears less a living culture than a sociological phenomenon, a site of the clash between Jewish tradition and assimilation in modern societies. This chapter begins by considering the traditional Jewish perception of Hebrew as the Holy Tongue; then Hebrew as the basis of Western civilization, particularly in England; the ambiguously stimulating and deadening effects of emancipation on Hebrew, converting the sacred tongue into a dispensable educational tool; consequent ambivalence toward Hebrew among modern Jewish writers; anti-Semitism as a cause both of the revival of Hebrew among Jewish nationalists and the suppression of Hebrew among assimilationists.

Traditional views of Hebrew

For most of Jewish history, the rabbinic view of Hebrew has predominated: it is the sacred language of humanity, the language in which God created the world and gave the Law to the Jewish people (Epstein 1959, de Lange 1987). It is the language of the three most influential books in Jewish history – the Bible, the Mishnah, and Siddur (prayer book). The Hebrew Bible was the defining characteristic of the Jews – the "People of the Book" – the ancient pagan world. It was "something to which none of the other ethnic groups in the Near East possessed any equivalent" (Millar 1993, p. 337). As a minority language in an often-hostile environment, Hebrew was a weapon of resistance. Particularly after the failure of the three Jewish revolts against Rome, in 66–70, 115–17, and 132–35 CE, Hebrew became vital to Jewish survival:

> The struggle of the Jewish people against Greek and Roman domination was accompanied by a literature which encouraged and

intensified resistance. After military defeat it became frequently the only weapon, an important instrument of hope and survival (Fischel 1971, col. 301).[2]

As we have seen in previous chapters, the Jewish educational system sustained by the rabbis, which was the single most important factor in Jewish survival, was founded on the study of Hebrew, the Hebrew Bible and the Mishnah, the Hebrew legal code which is the basis of the Talmud, edited in the Galilee, c. 200 CE. Hebrew literature was unique in its monotheist moral teaching and intolerance of idolatry. Belief in its sacred origin was enhanced by its literary quality. Also, unlike much religious literature, the Hebrew Bible is mostly suitable for children. Few people in history have attached such importance to children's education as the Jews, or have needed to. In talmudic literature, a man who fails to teach his children Hebrew is considered as though he has murdered them (*Sifre* on Deut. 11:19).

Until the eighteenth century, the view of Hebrew as the Holy Tongue was taken for granted, not only by Jews but also by the Christian and Muslim majority. Emancipation and assimilation posed the greatest cultural threat in Jewish history. In reaction, some Jewish writers, mostly in Eastern Europe, made renewed assertions of the importance of Hebrew in Jewish survival. S. Ansky (1863–1920) sums up the value of Hebrew among pre-modern Jews in his Yiddish and Hebrew play *The Dybbuk* (1917–20):

> There are seventy languages in the world, and the holiest among them is Hebrew. And the holiest work in the Hebrew language is the Torah, and its holiest part is the Ten Commandments, and the holiest word in the Ten Commandments is the name of God (1992, p. 32).

Ansky and other East European Hebrew and Yiddish writers such as Peretz Smolenskin (1842?–85), M.Z. Feierberg (1875–99), C.N. Bialik (1873–1934), and S.J. Agnon (1888?–1970) created a positive value for Hebrew as a secular language capable of being restored and of restoring its speakers in the Land of Israel. Smolenskin describes Hebrew as integral in Jewish survival:

> We are secure if we hold fast to the ancient language which has accompanied us from country to country, to the tongue in which our poets and prophets spoke, in which our forefathers cried aloud with their dying breath ... Our language is our national fortress; if it

disappears into oblivion the memory of our people will vanish from the face of the earth (Mendes-Flohr and Reinharz 1980, p. 325).

The Hebrew poet and critic, Simon Halkin, rightly contrasts Hebrew with the many other languages in which Jews have written:

> ... only the Hebrew language has spanned the vastness of Jewish history in time and space. Hebrew, therefore, has proved the single repository of Jewish existence as a whole; and its literature – including the productivity of the last two hundred years – holds the only continuous record of Jewish vitality (1950, pp. 211–12).

Hebrew and Yiddish writers, though often highly critical of the Jewish educational system, tend to express veneration for Hebrew and, in general, for Jewish learning. Typical in this regard was Mendele Mocher Sefarim (pen name of S.J. Abramowitz, 1835?–1917), in his classic autobiography, *Of Bygone Days*, written both in Hebrew and Yiddish (1894–1915) and set in Lithuania in the 1830s and 1840s. Mendele recalls that in Kopyl, his hometown, practically all the men studied, mostly in Hebrew. Scholarship was more highly esteemed than wealth: "No one could gain honor except through being a scholar and God-fearing" (1947, p. 264).

The valuation of learning produced a virtually unparalleled sociological phenomenon: wealthy Jews would not only seek to marry their daughters to poor but brilliant scholars but would feel that *they* had got the better bargain! Hobsbawm observes: "It was right that the poor Jewish scholar should marry the daughter of the richest local merchant because it was unthinkable that a community which respected learning should reward its luminaries with nothing more tangible than praise" (1997, pp. 272–3).[3]

Even when the memory of learning Hebrew in childhood involved corporal punishment – as education generally did – Hebrew was not something to abandon but part of an uncontested way of life, in some ways rich, beautiful, and immensely satisfying. This was the case, for example, in Feierberg's Hebrew story "In the Evening," published in 1897, which communicates powerfully the sense of being in exile in a hostile world, prefigured in the biblical texts:

> The rabbi dealt out blows, shouted, and taught us the Bible on one side of the table, while his assistants did the same on the other. The third reading from the Book of Genesis flowed forth in a frightful

lament, each word ripping with misery and the dread fear of God: "Get thee from thy land, and from thy kindred, and from thy father's house, to the land that I will show thee" [12:1] (1973, p. 86).

The child's lack of critical perspective is an asset here, and the atrocious teaching "method" does not stifle his imaginative response to the power of the narrative. At times, however, Hebrew opened a world of great charm and insight. Bialik, for example, in his mystical autobiography (1903–23) recalled a two-week convalescence after a beating by a teacher in the Ukrainian village where he was born; but then in another local school, he studied the 23rd Psalm:

> The translation of the words became superfluous, almost detrimental. The words flowed and flowed from the heart with the meaning bound up inside them. The gate of understanding was opened of its own accord, "like a tree planted" – quite literally, that was the tree under whose shade we were sitting. "By streams of water" – plainly, this was the water channel below. "The valley of the shadow of death" – that was the ruin, where evil spirits lurked, and the teacher had forbidden us to enter it. "You prepare a table before me" – this was surely the table that we were sitting at now, engaged in "God's Torah." "In the presence of my enemies" – who are these enemies if not the "hooligans," the young shepherds, a curse upon them, who sometimes appear with their staffs and packs on top of the hill, showing us from the distance "pig's ears" and mocking us with their "*geer, geer, geer*"? ... Surely they are those very same "wicked" in the psalm, who are destined, God willing, to be "like chaff which the wind drives away," one puff – and they are gone ... (1999, pp. 49–50).

The stories of the Hebrew Nobel laureate Agnon represent a summing up of the value of Hebrew through the ages and its capacity to function both as a Holy Tongue and also as a language of a modern secular state. To the child in Agnon's fiction, however, Hebrew is holy and capable of redeeming the Jews from exile. The child in the story "The Kerchief" (1932) associates a local beggar with the Messiah, as in the Talmud (*Sanhedrin* 98a), and imagines that he is waiting to save the Jews. The image of the beggar-Messiah is parallel to the image of Hebrew itself prior to the twentieth century, impoverished but capable of uniting and transforming a downtrodden people:

> Yesterday he sat among the beggars and they did not recognize him, but sometimes even abused him and treated him with disrespect; and

now suddenly the Holy One, blessed be He, has remembered the oath He swore to redeem Israel, and given him permission to reveal himself to the world (1970, p. 47).

It is possible to see modern Hebrew as a revolt against tradition, but linguistically it has a firm base in biblical Hebrew (Saénz-Badillos 1993). Modern Hebrew represents a dialectic of tradition and change. The poet Yehuda Amichai writes of the intricate relationship of modern to biblical Hebrew in "National Thoughts":

> Caught in a homeland trap:
> to speak now in this tired language,
> torn blinded from biblical sleep
> shuttling from mouth to mouth
> in words that spoke of miracles and God
> to say now: car, bomb, God.
>
> (1975, p. 38)

The Hebrew Bible, Western civilization, and nationalism

The image of Hebrew as Holy Tongue was shared by orthodox Jews and Christians and Muslims, though knowledge of Hebrew was widespread only among Jews. Both Jesus and Mohammed regarded the Hebrew prophets as their ancestors, whom they aimed to emulate. But to Christian Europe, especially after the Reformation, the Hebrew Bible also had vast political influence, even when Christianity declined. The central biblical image of the Jews (in the Five Books of Moses) as slaves who rebelled, gained freedom, created their own laws and sacred scripture and, having emerged as a nation, established their own state, is an archetype of modern nationalism.

The Church already in the early Christian era assumed the identity of the "true Israel" in the Hebrew Bible. The Greek Bible, because of its missionary internationalism spurred by the conviction that the Second Coming was imminent, could not satisfy the nationalist instincts of peoples trawled into the net of Christianity. The survival of ancient nations that translated the Hebrew Bible into the vernacular – notably Armenia in the fifth century and Ethiopia around the same time (Hastings 1997, p. 198) – is evidence of the power of the cultural nationalism of the Bible among non-Jews.

Translations of the Bible into the vernacular throughout Europe in the century after the invention of printing by Gutenberg in the 1450s – in

German, English, French, Spanish, Portuguese, Swedish, Danish, Finnish, Hungarian, and Polish, among others – became the central tool for nation building: "Of all the works published, translations of the Bible were the most important, not only in the history of the Reformation but also in the history of languages" (Elton 1971, p. 289). Luther's German translation (1521–34) ran into 377 editions by the time of his death in 1546 (*ibid*.)! Between 1560 and 1611, there were over 100 editions of the Bible in English, and between 1611 and 1640 about 140 editions of the King James Authorized Version (Hastings 1997, p. 58).

Evolving nation-states in Europe tended to identify with ancient Israel. Especially in the age of nationalism during and after the American and French revolutions, European nations struggling for independence were often compared with the Jews (even, ironically, when these nations were known for anti-Semitism). The Puritans and, later, revolutionaries in America, France, Italy and elsewhere, including Washington, Robespierre, and Garibaldi, carried the torch of the prophets. They brought increasingly secularized ideals of liberty, human rights, and equality into the forefront of what was to become Western democracy (Kohn 1946). Even as religion lost its predominance to secular enlightenment, the ideological influence of the Hebrew Bible persisted.

Biblical influence was central in the German poetry of Klopstock (notably *The Messiah*, 1748–73), whose conception of the poet was that of prophet, teacher, and patriot. Goethe saw the Hebrew Bible not just as the book of one nation but also as the archetype for all nations. In Hungary, translations of the Psalms and Karolyi's Bible translation "influenced the development of Hungarian literary language for centuries" (Szakaly 1990, p. 94). Biblical language of the emergence from slavery, prophetic denunciations of the wicked and hopes for freedom not only for Hungary but for the world, are frequent in Petofi's poetry. Andrusyshen, in his introduction to the poems of Shevchenko, draws attention to the profound influence of the Bible and the Jewish people on the Ukrainian poet, an identification based on perceived similarities between Jews and Ukrainians:

> ...a people mighty in spirit but deprived of effectual means of defence; a people who, in spite of almost interminable suppression of their rights and privileges as a nation, like the Jews of the ancient and recent past, succeeded in preserving their identity intact (Shevchenko 1964, p. *l*).

Shevchenko as a child would read from the Psalms at vigils of dead serfs, and those he later translated into Ukrainian (nos 1, 12, 43, 52, 53, 81, 93, 132, 137, 149) were ones he felt would be most inspiring to Ukrainian nationalists. On being freed from prison in Siberia in 1859, he translated Isaiah 35:7

> And the Lord's ransomed will return to Zion
> with song and eternal joy,
> and sorrow and sighs will flee.
>
> (10)

Biblical influences are plentiful, too, in the poetry of Mickiewicz, whose Polish nationalism has likewise been described as "Judaic": "that of a conquered, humiliated and oppressed nation dreaming of resurrection" (Talmon 1967, p. 96).

In a world of evolving nation-states in which the secular culture had not yet taken full hold and *the* Book was still the Bible, such influences were perhaps inevitable. Verdi's "Chorus of Hebrew Slaves" (*Va pensiero*) in the opera *Nabucco* (1842), written two decades before Italy's independence, is a patchwork of biblical texts, particularly from Psalms (48:5, 137:2–2), Isaiah (22:4, 51:17), and Song of Songs (8:14). In its longing for freedom, *Va pensiero* became Italy's unofficial national anthem, illustrating the degree to which the Hebrew Bible permeated European culture:

> Go, my thoughts and longings quickly
> to the sweet-scented mountain and valley,
> to our home long ago!
>
> To the Jordan river bring greetings,
> to the ruined Temple of Zion.
>
> My country, so lovely and wretched,
> memory of joy and despair!
>
> Golden harps of the prophets,
> tell me: why do you hang mute
> on the willows?
>
> Sing again songs of our homeland,
> of the past.

We have drunk the cup of sorrow,
and repented in bitter tears.

Inspire us, God, with courage
to endure to the end.

The overwhelming influence of the Hebrew Bible on European nationalism has a twofold irony: (a) that some of the countries whose culture
derived largely from Judaism engaged or collaborated in genocide
against the Jews; (b) that the religious culture of the Jews, adopted in
Christianity, was ultimately transformed into a secular national ideology which, in turn, led to the renewal of Jewish political life and the
recreation of a Jewish state. The two prime literary creators of modern
national Jewish identity in Hebrew literature were the neo-prophetic
poets C.N. Bialik (1873–1934) and U.Z. Greenberg (1896–1981)
(cf. Aberbach 1988, Leoussi and Aberbach 2002). To these and
other Hebrew writers, the Hebrew language, however secularized, retains
its power to transform people and society. In contrast, among Jewish
writers in languages other than Hebrew, the pressures of assimilation
often led to a polarized view of Hebrew as a foreign, intrusive, and
unwanted "Other."

Hebrew and ambivalent emancipation

Prior to the nineteenth century, the authority of the Hebrew Bible was
largely uncontested in Europe. The rise of secular enlightenment and
the decline of religion led to a critical revaluation of the Hebrew Bible as
of all religious texts. The French Enlightenment and the Revolution
forced onto the agenda the issue of Jewish emancipation and civil rights:
could the secular ideology of liberty, equality, and fraternity be applied
also to the Jews? The French National Assembly debated this question
for over two years before deciding, reluctantly, in the affirmative, in
1791. Emancipation from the start was a deeply ambivalent and flawed
process, summed up by the French advocate of emancipation, Count
Stanislas de Clermont-Tonnerre: "Jews should be denied everything as a
nation, but granted everything as individuals" (*Encyclopedia Judaica*
vol. 5, col. 606). This idea that French citizenship was conditional upon
Jewish renunciation of their Jewish nationality had sinister implications
for the future of the European Jews and their culture, including Hebrew.
When in 1807 Napoleon convened the Jewish Sanhedrin, he insisted
that its members make the so-called National Affirmation, declaring

allegiance to France and renouncing Jewish national identity. The preservation of Hebrew could thus be seen as unpatriotic. Jews in later generation "would reinterpret the Sanhedrin's solemn assurances in such a way as to divest Jewish identification of all but its narrowest religious connotation" (Sachar 1981, p. 63). Ambivalence toward Jewish emancipation was shared by most important eighteenth- and nineteenth-century thinkers, for example, Diderot, Voltaire, Michelet, Proudhon in France; and von Dohm, Fichte, Hegel, Treitschke, Dühring, de Lagarde in Germany. These thinkers prepared the way not for the integration of the European Jews but for the rise of racial anti-Semitism and ultimate genocide. By the end of the nineteenth century, anti-Semitism figured prominently in European politics (Vital 1999).

Among Western and Central European Jews, confusion about Jewish culture became a virtually psychopathological feature of emancipation, reflecting the ambivalence of emancipation itself. From the time of Moses Mendelssohn (1729–86), Hebrew was seen as a bridge between traditional Judaism and non-Jewish culture. As the language of Holy Scripture, Hebrew was blessed by the German academic world with status not inferior to Latin and Greek and, therefore, suitable as a vehicle for Jewish assimilation. Some nineteenth-century Jews, especially in Germany, dazzled by the hope of emancipation, and dismayed by the anti-Semitism pervading the culture into which they longed to assimilate, felt that they could assert patriotism by denigrating their Jewish culture and suppressing Hebrew. For even liberal enlightened thinkers who supported emancipation, such as Voltaire and von Dohm, often attacked Jews for being an insular backward people with an inferior culture (Hertzberg 1959). Herder sang the praises of cultural pluralism and called himself a friend of the Jews; yet he labeled the Jews as "parasites" and opposed emancipation (Katz 1980, p. 60). The only solution for such a people was baptism. The demand for total Jewish assimilation recurred ominously even in the most liberal European states. At the same time, European (and to a lesser extent also American) Jews were often confronted with the accusation that they were incapable of integration into Christian society.

Hebrew was stripped by the Enlightenment of its aura of reverence and reduced to a didactic tool by which Jews ignorant of European languages and learning could gain secular education. This was a revolutionary transformation: Hebrew, originally in Germany, but increasingly elsewhere, could be used somewhat like baptism in Heine's quip, as an "entrance ticket" to European civilization. In the nineteenth century many educational works were written in or translated into Hebrew.

But Hebrew could also be seen as a best discarded symbol of religious insularity and educational backwardness, a bar to emancipation, to desired assimilation, acceptance, and worldly success.

A consequent recoil from Hebrew is evident, for example, among German rabbis who eliminated Hebrew prayers as an anachronism; Jewish communities which failed to establish schools in which their children learned Hebrew, or who provided a second-rate education which put the children off; in the massive insecurity leading to grotesque patriotism, above all among German Jews, for countries harboring genocidal impulses toward the Jews, and exaggerated attachment to their cultures in preference to Jewish culture; and in the ignorance of Hebrew, most strikingly among the Jewish or baptized Jewish intelligentsia.

The nineteenth- and early twentieth-century German-speaking Jews were in the forefront of a socio-psychological revolution among the Jews: for the first time they revered non-Jewish culture as superior to their own. Marx's school report has favorable comments on his knowledge of Greek and Latin but the entry on Hebrew is blank. Freud, who as a young man kept a diary in Greek, professed ignorance of Hebrew although this was extremely unlikely. As we have seen (page 124), Freud gave his children no Jewish education whatsoever, while the founder of political Zionism, Theodor Herzl (1860–1904), was largely ignorant of Hebrew and envisaged German as the language of high culture among the Palestinian Jews. He only slightly exaggerated when he asked his colleagues in the Zionist movement, "Who among us can ask for a railway ticket in Hebrew?" He needed special coaching to undergo the ordeal of reciting the short blessings when called to the Torah in Basel in 1897: "When he was called up to the Torah, he found that the few Hebrew words of the benediction were causing him more anxiety than all the speeches he had delivered, more than the entire direction of the congress" (Elon 1975, p. 237). Kafka was even more frightened of Hebrew than Herzl. In his 1919 "Letter to His Father," he tells that for years he was terrified that he would be called to recite the blessing as his father had not troubled to have him taught Hebrew (1978, pp. 56–7). Shortly before his death in 1924, Kafka began studying Hebrew. His last writings include lists of Hebrew vocabulary. Here was one of the greatest masters of language struggling with the language that Jewish children have traditionally been taught as their birthright. The examples of Freud, Herzl, and Kafka are somewhat atypical among German-speaking Jews as they came to identify strongly with Jewish life and culture. As we shall see, Jewish authors writing in English were infected with devaluatory views of Hebrew similar to those pioneered by German-speaking Jews.

Anti-Semitism and the revival of Hebrew

Fundamental to modern Jewish nationalism and the revival of Hebrew is the question: how was it that the Bible was assimilated into Christian Europe, but ultimately not the Jews? Europeans identified with the world of the Bible and thought of themselves as the "new Israel." In Christian dogma, Judaism was a corrupt and fossilized rabbinic culture which the coming of Jesus Christ had made obsolete. The Jews were not partners with Christians in the same biblical culture, though they zealously preserved and studied the Bible in the original Hebrew as a living daily presence. In considering the impact of the Hebrew Bible in translation, it becomes clear how powerful a force the original Hebrew has been, and is, to the people whom Hastings calls "the true proto-nation" (1997, p. 186). Modern Zionism was not a new creation but a resurrection and adaptation to modern conditions of the same nationalism that gripped Christian Europe. The Christian nations of Europe, deriving their national identity as chosen peoples from the Jews, adopted the doctrine that they were the elect heir to Judaism. The Jews could live on with their fossilized Judaism purely as a tolerated token of the supremacy of the Church, damned in the eyes of God as murderers of the Savior, identified with contemptible material existence devoid of spirituality, with no original cultural development of their own, subject to ceaseless hatred and persecution. Two seemingly conflicting phenomena – the adoption in Christian Europe of the Hebrew Bible in translation and hatred for the people who created and preserved the Bible in the original Hebrew – might therefore be seen as part of the same phenomenon. The perversion in the name of Christianity of the Jewish concept of chosenness, which in the Hebrew Bible is dependent entirely on moral behavior, contributed to national conflicts and to the Holocaust:

> ... the more powerfully one identified one's own nation as chosen, the more one might want to eliminate the first chosen nation, the Jews, from the face of the earth (*ibid.*, p. 198).

Christian genocidal hatred culminating in genocide forced the European Jews away from unrequited patriotism toward the countries in which they lived to rediscover their own ancient nationalism based on the Hebrew Bible and the Land of Israel. The most remarkable fact about modern Hebrew is that in 1881 – the crucial date in modern Jewish history, when the Russian pogroms broke out after the assassination of Tsar Alexander II and the first modern *aliyah* (emigration to the Land of Israel) began – there were no native speakers of Hebrew. Within a century, there were several million. There could be no clearer proof of the latent power of cultural nationalism: "the people who gave the world the model of nationhood, and even nation-statehood, lost it for itself for nearly two millennia and yet survived" (*ibid.*, p. 186). The Jews in exile (*galut*) had kept a sense of nationhood, not alone as a memory of the past but as a living, ever growing presence, in words deemed eternally holy. If the Bible in translation could give the English, Americans, Germans, Scandinavians, Poles, Hungarians, Italians, and many others a sense of chosenness in their "new Jerusalem," how much more could the Bible in the original Hebrew give the Jews ineradicable nationhood.

Equally remarkable in the continuous life of Jewish nationalism, for nearly 2000 years Jews might have evaded hatred, persecution, discrimination, and violence by converting to Christianity or, in the case of the Oriental Jews, Islam. For the most part they did not do so. The living sense of nationhood nourished by the Hebrew Bible, which they carried with them and which transcended territory – though the Land of Israel was daily present to them – was more powerful than the persecution and allure of rival religions. Only in the late nineteenth century did conversion to Christianity especially in Western Europe, become increasingly widespread. Ironically, baptism was counterproductive, for it stimulated a new, insidious criterion of discrimination: race. Emancipation failed in most of Europe. Only in English-speaking countries did it succeed, though not without anguish and struggle.

The Bible and British national identity

Britain was virtually the only European country with a sizeable Jewish population where emancipation worked, mostly; among the reasons was that perhaps no people, apart from the Jews themselves, have so totally absorbed the Bible as the British.[4] The Bible was the main unifying force of the different, often warring groups in the British isles long before the Norman Conquest in 1066; and in the distinctiveness and cohesion of its national identity, England was centuries ahead of other West European societies (Hastings 1997). As early as the Anglo-Saxon poem on the battle of Maldon of 991, the nation is exhorted to stand firm as Israel did against invasion:

> ... the principal message is simply that of the heroic defence by a mixed band of Englishmen of "their land, the land of Ethelred the King, the place and the people"... England is seen in biblical terms, a nation to be defended as the Israel of the Old Testament was defended (*ibid.*, p. 42).

The Welsh in particular came to identify themselves with ancient Israel: "The Welsh myth of election pictured the community as the lost tribes of Israel, a latterday chosen people" (Smith 1999, pp. 136–7), and the translation of the Bible into Welsh in 1563 rejuvenated Welsh national consciousness. (The decision of John Knox and the Scottish reformers to adopt the English Geneva Bible of 1560 and the King James Authorized Version of 1611 and not translate the Bible into Scots was an important factor in weakening the Scots language and Scottish national identity, leading to increasing cultural and political union with England.) The poetry of Chaucer, Shakespeare, Spenser, Milton is packed with biblical themes and allusions. The English translations of the Hebrew Bible in the sixteenth and seventeenth centuries were revolutionary milestones in British (and European) history and in English literature. The translations, culminating in the Authorized Version of 1611, removed the Bible from a Church-based elite of Latin readers and made it accessible to the much larger numbers who knew English (Dickens 1970). On the centenary of the Authorized Version, Jonathan Swift (1712) acknowledged the debt of English to the Bible in translation:

> ... if it were not for the *Bible* and *Common Prayer Book* in the vulgar Tongue, we should hardly be able to understand any Thing that was written among us an hundred Years ago: Which is certainly true: for those Books being perpetually read in Churches, have proved a kind of Standard for Language, especially to the common People. And I doubt whether the alterations since introduced, have added much to the Beauty or Strength of the *English* Tongue, though they have taken off a great deal from that *Simplicity*, which is one of the greatest Perfections in any Language (Boulton 1966, p. 117).

Steiner sums up the importance of Tyndale, the great pioneer of Bible translation into English:

> Beyond Shakespeare, it is William Tyndale who [as translator of the Hebrew Bible into English in the 1530s] is begettor of the English

language as we know it ... It is Tyndale's cadences, sonorities, amplitudes and concisions (he is a master of both) which, via his commanding effect on the Authorized Version, characterize global English as it is spoken and written today. No translation-act, save Luther's has been as generative of a whole language (1996, p. 49).

Bible-based Jewish nationalism had vast influence on the Elizabethans and on the English revolution in the seventeenth century, in some ways a model for later revolutionary nationalism. The imperialism of the Elizabethans – the "ancestor of modern nationalism" (Kermode 1965, p. 12) – is reflected in their literature, notably Spenser's *The Fairie Queene* (1590, 1596) in which corrupt Catholic Spain and Ireland are set allegorically against the "true Israel" of the Protestant Church. Spenser is described by Hastings as "an out-and-out English Protestant nationalist" and *The Fairy Queene* as "the quintessence of Elizabethan nationalism," celebrating the union of England and true religion under the sovereignty of Elizabeth; it is "a work of reconciliation between old Englishness and new Englishness, a closing of ranks between the 'Merrie England' which Catholics claimed had been lost with the Reformation and the Protestant gospel" (1997, pp. 82–4). Spenser transforms the war between Protestant England and Catholic Spain into myth, the divine Una, the true universal English Church and its virgin empress, Elizabeth I, opposed to Duessa, the satanic Roman Church. In Book I, after his struggle with moral impurity, the saintly Red Cross Knight – St George the dragon killer, symbol of England, defender and future husband of Una – arrives Moses-like at the top of a holy mountain where he glimpses the heavenly Jerusalem and the likeness of its earthly counterpart, Cleopolis (London):

> The new *Hierusalem*, that God has built
> For those to dwell in, that are chosen his ...
>
> X 57

England's identification with Israel reached its height during the mid-seventeenth-century Puritan revolution, whose outstanding poet was Milton. The revolution was driven by the religious–nationalist ideology and fervour of the prophets; by self-identification as a chosen people with a divine covenant and messianic hopes, a love of liberty and opposition to overweening monarchic rule. Milton read the Bible in Hebrew. Among Milton's earliest writings were translations from Hebrew psalms pertaining to Israel's escape from slavery to freedom:

> When the blest seed of Terah's faithful son [Abraham]
> After long toil their liberty had won,
> And passed from Pharian [Egyptian] field to Canaan land,
> Led by the strength of the Almighty's hand,
> Jehovah's wonders were in Israel shown,
> His praise and glory was in Israel known.
>
> from Psalm 114

> ... in despite of Pharaoh fell,
> He brought from thence his Israel ...

> His chosen people he did bless
> In the wasteful wilderness ...

> And to his servant Israel,
> He gave their land therein to dwell.
>
> from Psalm 136

The motif of freedom would later become central in Milton's poetry, including *Paradise Lost*, and in his political works supporting Cromwell and the revolution.[5] Milton's English patriotism derives primarily from the Hebrew Bible:

> For Milton, the sacred community is above all the English People marvellously chosen to be the heralds of salvation for the human race. There is nothing in Calvinism to warrant this, nor indeed does it spring from any of the accepted orthodoxies of the Reformation; it is rather a conjunction of the Covenant-idea with Renaissance nationalism, and it is one for which Milton found his warrant above all in the Old Testament Scripture, which pointed to a national community bound by Covenant-bonds to its divine king. "Why else was this nation chosen before any other," he asks [*Aeropagitica* IV 340], "that out of her, *as out of Sion*, should be proclam'd and sounded forth the first tidings and trumpet of Reformation to all *Europe*?" Here in his religious patriotism is Milton's most intimate link with the Hebraic notion of a sacred community (Fisch 1964, pp. 123–4).

Paradise Lost ends with the prophecy of the birth of the nation of Israel, to which England would be heir:

> ... to sojourn in that land
> He comes invited by a younger son

In time of dearth, a son whose worthy deeds
Raise his to be the second in that realm
Of Pharao: there he dies, and leaves his race
Growing into a nation …

XII 159–64

Though strongest in the seventeenth century, the predominant influence of the Bible on the English language and on British nationalism continued until the twentieth century. In his translation of the Psalms in 1719, Isaac Watts was moved to replace "Israel" with "Great Britain" (Hastings 1997, p. 62). Burns was taught to read mainly from the Bible. Byron's *Hebrew Melodies* (1815) reflect similar identification with the world of the Bible. Coleridge, in the *Biographia Literaria* (1817), points out that fine English is less likely to come from scholars, whose style is artificial and burdened with their linguistic knowledge, than from men who regularly read the Bible. To Blake, immersed in biblical prophetic imagery, the visionary ideal of England is a "new Jerusalem":

I will not cease from mental fight,
Nor shall my sword sleep in my hand
Till we have built Jerusalem
In England's green and pleasant land.
"Jerusalem" (1804)

The influence of the Authorized Version continues in more recent English literature. For example, in Lawrence's *Sons and Lovers* (1913), Paul Morel, a loose self-portrait of Lawrence as a young man in Nottingham at the beginning of the twentieth century, is raised on the Bible, which has associations everywhere:

Paul never forgot … seeing a big red moon lift itself up, slowly, between the waste road over the hill-top, steadily, like a great bird. And he thought of the Bible [Joshua 10:11–12] that the moon should be turned to blood (1974, pp. 98–9).

In James Joyce's *Ulysses* (1922), similarly, the Hebrew Bible is constantly alluded to, for example, in the parodic account of Bloom's Elijah-like theophany (cf. II Kings 2:11) at the end of the "Cyclops" episode:

When lo, there came about them all a great brightness and they beheld the chariot wherein He stood ascend to heaven … And they beheld Him even Him, ben Bloom Elijah, amid clouds of angels ascend to the glory of brightness at an angle of fortyfive degrees over Donohoe's in Little Green Street like a shot off a shovel (1973, p. 343)

Finally, the fragments collected by T.S. Eliot to shore against the ruined religious civilization of Europe, in *The Waste Land* (1922), include the Hebrew Bible, specifically Ezekiel (2:1, 6:6), Ecclesiastes (12:5), and Isaiah (32:2):

> What are the roots that clutch, what branches grow
> Out of this stony rubbish? Son of man,
> You cannot say, or guess, for you know only
> A heap of broken images, where the sun beats,
> And the dead tree gives no shelter, the cricket no relief,
> And the dry stone no sound of water. Only
> There is shadow under this red rock,
> (Come in under the shadow of this red rock),
> and I will show you something different from either
> your shadow at morning striding behind you
> or your shadow at evening rising to meet you;
> I will show you fear in a handful of dust.

In short, if one wants to understand English national identity and English literature, a knowledge of the Hebrew Bible is essential.

Ambivalence toward Hebrew among Jewish writers

One might have thought then that Jewish authors writing in English would have an especial sensitivity to and appreciation of Hebrew, if only as an entree to English literature. Up to a point, reverence and affection for Hebrew survived the Jewish migrations westward. The literary scholar David Daiches, for example, recalls his Edinburgh childhood in the 1920s, when he studied Old Testament history at George Watson's Boys' College:

> I would lay my Hebrew Bible conspicuously on the desk before me. "What does the Hebrew say, Daiches?" the teacher would ask when he came to some obscure incident, and sometimes after class the boys would crowd round and ask me for the true meaning of one of the franker sexual references ... (1997, p. 14).

Louis Jacobs, founder of the Masorti movement in England, describes methods for studying the Hebrew Bible in a Manchester *cheder* in the 1920s:

> When we arrived in the portion in Exodus dealing with the ox that falls into a pit [21:33–4] we would be led outside into the earthen yard where some of us would actually dig the pit while others would act out the part of the ox (1989, p. 14).

˘ However, much of the creative Jewish writing in English, following the lead of German-Jewish writers, is scarred with undisguised ambivalence toward Hebrew. This is evidently a new phenomenon both in Jewish social psychology and in English literature, for although English literature is not lacking in anti-Semitic caricature, it treats Hebrew with utmost respect. Among Jews, ignorance of Hebrew was traditionally regarded as little short of national suicide: "Loss of Hebrew has always been a long step toward loss of law, custom, and knowledge, and toward oblivion by absorption" (Wouk 1992, p. 102). A Jew ignorant of Hebrew generally felt incomplete and ashamed, tried to learn or, if unable, kept his ignorance to himself. However, among Jewish writers writing in languages other than Hebrew – above all, in English – this attitude is frequently reversed. There are remarkable, often gratuitous, assertions of ignorance of Hebrew, not with contrition and shame, but at times actual pride, virtually as a badge of belonging to another culture.

Among Jewish writers, split attitudes to Hebrew became apparent in the nineteenth century: East European Jews were attached to it while the rest were mostly ignorant, indifferent, or hostile. The East European Jews who preserved Hebrew lived in a socio-cultural world substantially different from that of West European Jews: they were far more numerous and were persecuted to a far greater extent; surrounded by mostly illiterate peasants, they tended to be highly observant and subject to rabbinic authority; their secular education was limited while their Jewish religious education was vast, in contrast with West European Jews, who became increasingly urbanized and professionally trained in the course of the nineteenth century. The revival of Hebrew is primarily the achievement of the East European Jews. Most important Jewish authors writing in English have roots in Eastern Europe, but their attitude to Hebrew is mainly that of the West. An analysis of these writers gives valuable sociological insight into the self-image of a minority under pressure both from within and without to assimilate. With notable exceptions, such as A.N. Klein and Cynthia Ozick, they tend to criticize, denigrate, or caricature Hebrew and generally give a limited and distorted picture of Hebrew language and Jewish culture. Non-Jewish writers do not do this. Even writers such as Charles Reznikoff, with considerable warmth toward Jewish tradition, are alienated by Hebrew. These lines are from *Five Groups of Verse* (1927):

> How difficult for me is Hebrew:
> even the Hebrew for *mother*, for *bread*, for *sun*
> is foreign. How far have I been exiled, Zion.
>
> (1976, p. 72)

True, the negative images of Hebrew in some English literature are actually not so different from accounts of Jewish education in Hebrew and Yiddish literature, for example, the passage from Feierberg quoted earlier. Consider, for example, Henry Roth's classic novel of American-Jewish immigrant life, *Call It Sleep* (1934), in which David Schearl in his first day in *cheder* learns to associate Hebrew with ignorance and cruelty:

> The boy fumbled on. As far as David could tell, he seemed to be making the same error over and over again, for the rabbi kept repeating the same sound. At last, the rabbi's patience gave out. He dropped the pointer; the boy ducked, but not soon enough. The speeding plane of the rabbi's palm rang against his ear like a clapper on a gong.
> "You plaster dunce!" he roared, "when will you learn a byse is a byse and not a vyse. Head of filth, where are your eyes?" He shook a menacing hand at the cringing boy and picked up the pointer (1960, p. 215).

Similar associations of caricature and menace, though not unmixed with affection, are found in Saul Bellow's novel *Herzog* (1964). The university professor Moses Herzog remembers his time in a Montreal *cheder* in the 1920s, when he was taught the story of the attempted seduction of Joseph by Potiphar's wife (an appropriate flashback in view of Herzog's troubled relationships with women):

> The pages of the Pentateuch smelled of mildew, the boys' sweaters were damp. The rabbi, short-bearded, his soft big nose violently pitted with black, scolding them. "You, Rozavitch, you slacker. What does it say here about Potiphar's wife, *V'tispeseyu b'vigdo...*"
> "And she took hold of..."
> "Of what? *Beged.*"

"*Beged*. A coat."

"A garment, you little thief. *Mamzer*! I'm sorry for your father. Some heir he's got! Some *Kaddish*! Ham and pork you'll be eating, before his body is in the grave. And you, Herzog, with those behemoth eyes – *V'yaizov bigdo b'yodo*."

"And he left it in her hands."

"Left what?"

"*Bigdo*, the garment."

"You watch your step, Herzog, Moses. Your mother thinks you'll be a great *lamden* – a rabbi. But I know you, how lazy you are. Mothers' hearts are broken by *mamzeirim* like you! Eh! Do I know you, Herzog? Through and through" (1976, p. 131).

The Canadian novelist, Mordecai Richler in his autobiographical *The Street* (1969) had similarly jaundiced memories of Hebrew in Montreal:

> The old underpaid men who taught us Hebrew tended to be surly, impatient. Ear-twisters and knuckle-rappers. They didn't like children (1985, p. 4).

Arthur Miller describes learning Hebrew as a child, again as an alien culture learned by rote. The one Hebrew word he remembers – a *tsadik*, a righteous man – he translates incorrectly:

> This bearded ancient taught purely by rote, pronouncing the Hebrew words and leading us to repeat after him. In the book, the English translations of the passages from Genesis faced the Hebrew, but there were no English translations of the English: what did *firmament* mean? The worst of it was that when I spoke a passage correctly, the old man would kiss me, which was like being embraced by a rose-bush. Once he leaned over and, laughing, gave my cheek a painful pinch and called me *tsadik*, wise man, a compliment I understood neither then nor later (1987, p. 25).

More negative in its caricature of Hebrew is Bruce Jay Friedman's novel *Stern* (1962) whose central character recalls going to synagogue as a child and thinking it marvellous that the old men knew, as he puts it, when to bow and when to groan:

> He went to Hebrew School, but there seemed to be no time at all devoted to the theatrical bows and groans, and even with three years

of Hebrew School under his belt Stern still felt a loner among the chanting sufferers at synagogues. After a while he began to think you could never get to be one of the groaners through mere attendance at Hebrew School. You probably had to pick it all up in Europe. At the school, Stern learned to read Hebrew at a mile-a-minute clip. He was the fastest reader in the class, and when called upon he would race across the jagged words as though he were a long-distance track star. The meaning of the words was dealt with in advanced classes, and since Stern never got to them, he remained only a swift reader who might have been performing in Swahili or Urdu (54–5).

In many American writers, the characterization of Hebrew is not devoid of affection; in the case of Roth's David Schearl, in fact, the Hebrew text of Isaiah chapter 6 becomes a source of unbearable awe and in a scene unparalleled in all the literature on *cheder* education the boy actually breaks *into* the *cheder* in order to read the Hebrew story of Isaiah's theophany: "Holy, Holy Holy is the Lord of Hosts." Other writers such as Norman Mailer or Harold Pinter volunteer little more than that their Hebrew education stopped mercifully at age 13. In contrast, Philip Roth's caricature in "The Conversion of the Jews" (1957) is hostile and lacking any redeeming empathy. It describes an intelligent boy in Hebrew class whose authoritarian teacher forces him to read so fast from a Hebrew text that he cannot understand what he is reading. (In his autobiographical memoir, *The Facts*, Roth mentions that at his bar mitzvah he read the Hebrew text "at breakneck speed" [1989, p. 120].) So disgusted is he with his teacher that in the end he runs from the classroom and onto the roof where he threatens to jump unless the crowd below declares their belief in Jesus Christ. This is the extent of Roth's portrayal of Jewish education in his early writings.

The South African novelist, Dan Jacobson, describes how as a child he was dragged by his father to synagogue and Hebrew classes (1985, p. 28). Failure to learn Hebrew is a theme also in his semi-biographical story, "Through the Wilderness":

All the attempts that had been made in my childhood to teach me Hebrew had ended in failure. I had been determined that they should. For all the usual, obvious reasons. I had associated the Hebrew language with being alien, set apart; exposed; implicated in what I was convinced at an early age was a continuing, unendurable history of suffering and impotence; involved with a religion in whose rituals I could find no grace, no power, no meaning… (1977, p. 160).

Hebrew in Woody Allen's writings is also part of the problem of alienation; it is not a source of cultural richness and insight. His film *Zelig* (1983) explores the issues of identity, assimilation, and the wish to belong in which Hebrew is an impediment. Zelig has an extraordinary gift (or curse) of assimilation – with Irish he becomes Irish, with Chinese he becomes Chinese, with Blacks he actually turns Black, and so on. Under hypnosis he confronts some of the causes of his alienation from society and his longing to be accepted:

> I'm twelve years old ... I run into a synagogue ... I ask the rabbi the meaning of life ... He tells me the meaning of life ... but he tells it to me in Hebrew ... I don't understand Hebrew ... Then he wants to charge me six hundred dollars for Hebrew lessons (1990, p. 77).

Clive Sinclair in "Scriptophobia" (later to become the opening of his novel *Blood Libels*) alludes further to the low standing of Hebrew. The narrator Jake Silkstone, a writer, recalls his Hebrew education in London as a disaster prefiguring his later life. He has studied 'with all the enthusiasm of a Philistine':

> "Why do I need to learn Hebrew?" I asked my melamed.
> "Because you are a Jew," she replied.
> "But all the Jews I know talk English," I protested.
> "God doesn't," she replied, "He only listens to Hebrew."
> "But I never speak to God," I said, "I don't believe in Him."
> Instead of trying to convert me with ontological, cosmoligical, or teleological arguments, the defender of our benevolent deity slapped me around the face.
> "I'll teach you to say such things," she screamed.
> True to her word, though ignoring that on the door, she dragged me into the Ladies' lavatory, where she violently washed out my mouth with soap and water (Sinclair 1991, p. 261).

Jewish critics, too, seem at times unable to resist the admission of ignorance of Hebrew. Lionel Trilling, in an essay on Wordsworth and the Mishnaic tractate Ethics of the Father, makes an unexpected detour to his childhood, when he first became acquainted with the rabbinic work in English translation, clandestinely, presumably in synagogue, for he was meant to be saying his prayers "in the Hebrew language, which I never mastered" (in Abrams, ed. 1972, p. 49).

Another critic, John Gross, recalls in his autobiography how at the time of the establishment of Israel in 1948 he was discouraged from learning Hebrew:

> I was even slightly put out by the fact that the textbook from which I tried, not very successfully, to learn modern Hebrew was called Hebrew for All in English, but Ivri, L'mud Ivrit – "Hebrew, Learn Hebrew!", which sounded so very much more peremptory – in Hebrew itself (2001, p. 164).

Similarly, in his book on *Enthusiasms* (1983), Bernard Levin pointedly omits Hebrew: "I went to Sunday school, though that was almost entirely a matter of learning Hebrew (at which I proved a singularly poor scholar)" (p. 58).

The sense of the oppressive foreignness of Hebrew is scathingly exposed by John Diamond (2001). Diamond tells how he took his malfunctioning computer to a repair shop in the East End of London. The repair man is a Hasidic Jew who offers to do the job for nothing if Diamond will recite the *Shema* (the Jewish credo beginning "Hear O Israel, the Lord is God the Lord is One" [Deuteronomy 6:4–9]) in Hebrew. Diamond confesses that he does not know Hebrew and has not been in a synagogue since age 11. The Hasid, undaunted, persuades Diamond to put on *tefillin* (phylacteries). He recites the Hebrew words and Diamond repeats them as best as he can. In a guilty swirl of stereotypes, Diamond finally escapes with his newly repaired computer.

Conclusion

Hebrew as a minority language under pressure of assimilation is a rich and vivid subject for sociological analysis, reflecting a complex religious and socio-psychological turning point in Jewish life. Some modern Jewish writers have regarded their assimilation and acceptance in the majority culture to be jeopardized by their Jewish origins. They declare ignorance of and distance from "foreign" Hebrew culture. How do we interpret the recoil at Hebrew by a Jewish intellectual elite? What accounts for the split in the value of Hebrew among East European Jews who looked and went east and East European Jews who looked and went west? The Lithuanian social origins of Dan Jacobson are similar to those of Mendele; Woody Allen came from the same German-Jewish background as Yehuda Amichai; Arthur Miller and Philip Roth are sons of Galician Jews and derive, therefore, from the same world as Agnon and Greenberg; Norman Mailer comes from a Russian rabbinical family whose social status was somewhat higher than that of the families of Bialik and Feierberg. The attachment to the Hebrew Bible which characterizes much of Middle America is largely absent among the American Jews.

In a broad sociological perspective, Jewish writers committed to Hebrew cultural nationalism retained their love for Hebrew. Those who assimilated largely lost that love. In English literature, for the first time, Hebrew ceased to be an object of veneration. Hebrew teachers were denigrated, caricatured, or dismissed, Hebrew was seen as a relic of the past; it was associated with the damp basement, the sadistic ignorant teacher, the world of the fathers to be escaped into a brave new world of English. Some of this literature might be condemned as anti-Semitic if the authors were not Jewish. Certainly, there are few parallels in English literature: Joseph Conrad, whose native language was Polish, does not denigrate Polish; Vladimir Nabokov does not attack Russian; Kazuo Ishiguro does not run Japanese down.

Hostility to and denigration of Hebrew is sometimes caused by its association with religious backwardness compounded by poor teaching and the allure of a dominant secular culture. But these criticisms are valid to a greater or lesser extent also among East European Hebrew writers, most of whom had a similarly deficient education. Why do English-language Jewish writers present such a narrow and distorted image of Hebrew as having little or no value? One answer lies in the desperate hopes aroused by Jewish emancipation in Continental Europe, fatally undermined by Jew-hatred. The ideal of emancipation was realized primarily in English-speaking countries, above all America. As a society of immigrants, America offered the Jews more freedom and opportunity than anywhere else. The American Jews could not only assimilate into American culture with relative ease, they could also contribute in making this culture as one minority among many (Sachar 1993). However great Kafka was as a German writer, he could not be authentically German in his Jewishness; Bellow, in contrast, could be American in his Jewishness. America gave the Jews their best chance of removing the ancient stigma of Jewish identity in Christian society and escaping religious–social discrimination. If in countries such as Germany or France, which ultimately betrayed the Jews, the tradition of National Affirmation – the renunciation of Jewish nationhood and of cultural distinctiveness, including Hebrew – was carried out by the Jews as a quid pro quo for specious emancipation, in English-speaking countries, where emancipation was mostly genuine, how much more the Jewish instinct to suppress Jewish culture and Hebrew.

At the same time, especially in the climate of hatred and discrimination which existed in the United States until the Second World War and was not fully overcome until the 1960s, Jewish assimilation inevitably created ambivalence to Jewish culture.

The American assertiveness of some Jewish writers such as Bellow – a phenomenon with clear European parallels, especially in Germany – derived partly from insecurity. Bellow was made to feel that his Jewishness was an impediment, according to Philip Roth:

> Bellow once told me that "somewhere in my Jewish and immigrant blood there were conspicuous traces of doubt as to whether I had the right to practice the writer's trade." He suggested that, at least in part, this doubt permeated his blood because "our own Wasp establishment, represented mainly by Harvard-trained professors," considered a son of immigrant Jews unfit to write books in English. These guys infuriated him (2001, p. 142).

The negative value of Hebrew among Jewish writers reflects coolness toward Judaism and Jewish culture among the first and second generations of Jewish immigrants to English-speaking countries under the pressure of assimilation and anti-Semitism. We have explored some signs of ambivalence: Hebrew may be an interesting fragment of a writer's makeup but belongs to childhood. It is not a living culture but an outmoded one, in an impoverished, even cruel educational system from which the writer feels alienated. It contrasts unfavorably with non-Jewish education. It is associated with a religion which is no longer observed or even respected from a distance. It is not part of a collection of mixed memories or kept up in adult life; neither is it seen in the context of Jewish history or even of specifically English literature. It stands on its own as a definitive statement of a problematic situation. The portrayal of Hebrew in English literature illustrates what has been lost in the warm medievally insular religious culture of the East European Jews. Haunted by the failure of emancipation in Europe and by the Holocaust, Jews were and to some extent still are vulnerable to uncertainty as to the genuineness of their assimilation into the dominant culture. The rejection of Hebrew is evidence of painful self-consciousness and perhaps even cultural self-hate. The image of Hebrew in the diaspora has improved in recent years partly owing to the strength of Hebrew in the State of Israel and the expansion of Jewish education in many Jewish communities. Still, within most of these communities, however wealthy and highly educated, the general standard of Jewish education is mediocre and Hebrew is practically a foreign language.

The low valuation of Hebrew as a minority culture illustrates what other minorities in Britain and elsewhere in the West do well to avoid: mixed feelings toward their own culture, ignorance and denigration of their native languages and traditions, and a tendency to see Western culture as superior. The Jewish example highlights the cultural cost of assimilation, even in a pluralistic society uniquely alert to the dangers of racism.

Lost to most diaspora Jews is the deep empathy for Hebrew culture illustrated in an anecdote told by Michael Ignatieff in his biography of Isaiah Berlin. Isaiah recalled his first lessons in Hebrew in Tsarist Russia before the Revolution and how his rabbi once paused to say: "Dear children, when you get older, you will realize how in every one of these letters there is Jewish blood and Jewish tears." To which Ignatieff added, "When Berlin told me this story eighty years later...for a split second his composure deserted him and he stared out across the garden. Then he looked back at me, equanimity restored, and said, 'That is the history of the Jews'" (1998, p. 21).

Part V

From Assimilation to Nationalism

9
The Renascence of Hebrew and Jewish Nationalism in the Tsarist Empire 1881–1917

In previous chapters, we have explored the secularization of Hebrew in a long-term framework including medieval Spain and the French Enlightenment. This chapter considers in greater detail a narrower and in some ways more striking change: the point at which modern Hebrew literature emerged as art, between the outbreak of the pogroms in 1881 and the 1917 revolution. This renascence is arguably the most important development in Jewish culture since the Bible. Hebrew literature was the main cultural spur to the rise of modern Jewish nationalism. The Russian Jewish population prior to 1881 had been moving toward increased acculturation within the Tsarist empire and had hopes of emancipation and civil rights. They were deeply wounded, psychologically as well as economically, by Russian government policies legislated in a futile reactionary struggle to adapt to major changes in socio-economic conditions and the international balance of power.

In common with other creative groups of Hebrew artists prior to 1948 – the prophets, the Tannaim, the poets of the "golden age" in medieval Muslim Spain – artistic breakthrough in the 1881–1917 may be shown to coincide and to be connected with a turning point in the dominant empire. The literature of 1881–1917 continued the pattern of these earlier periods. Crisis in the Tsarist empire led to heightened Jewish national identity. As in the earlier periods, Hebrew literature is, among other things, a record of imperial upheaval, social and cultural metamorphosis, and wanton violence. The very fact of writing Hebrew itself expressed, or implied, a strong current of religious–nationalist feeling. The main difference between Hebrew literature in the Tsarist empire and its antecedents is its predominantly secular character.

159

This chapter sets out the historical and literary background to Hebrew literature of 1881–1917, describes some of its salient qualities and influences, particularly in Russian literature, and interprets reasons for its artistic distinctiveness. It will be argued that this literature, in common with contemporary Russian literature of the pre-1881 era, might be interpreted *ipso facto* as an act of subversion. It represents on one level a rejection of Tsarist authority, an assertion of Jewish national feeling and a declaration of independence from the empire. In doing so, it engaged in a dynamic relationship with the dominant literary culture, adapting and assimilating many of its features while aiming at a distinctively Jewish mode of expression. Hebrew grew both as an ethnic branch of Russian literature and as a counterculture.[1]

Historians are generally agreed that the Jewish problem in Tsarist Russia was inseparable from the general weaknesses of the empire. In a psychological sense, furthermore, the image of the Jew in Russian society and culture betrayed Russia's distorted self-image under the pressure of the need for rapid change. For to see the pogroms as isolated anti-Semitic outbursts is historically incorrect. They were, in fact, only a small fraction of the general unrest in Russia during the period, a symptom of the breakdown of Tsarist authority (Fuller 1985, Klier and Lambroza 1992). Challenged by the intelligentsia and the working masses alike, the government created the first modern police state, with extensive use of spying, repression, and terror. In its dying days, despite an improving economy, the Tsarist empire had trouble feeding its large and growing population. It had the largest standing army in the world – about two and a half million – but to a degree unprecedented in history, the army was used to control and crush the internal opposition. In 1903, when the second wave of pogroms began, about one-third of its infantry and two-thirds of its cavalry were used against its own citizens (Fuller 1985).

Nevertheless, the Jews more than most other ethnic groups suffered under Tsarist rule. Even prior to 1881 the Russian Jews were burdened with countless laws and restrictions. Most prominent was their confinement within the so-called Pale of Settlement on the western frontier of the empire. The pogroms brought about an "ideological metamorphosis" away from adaptation and merging with Russia and in favor of mass emigration: "spontaneously in almost every town of any size societies were founded for the colonization of Palestine" (Frankel 1981, p. 49). The May Laws, passed in May 1882, which officially blamed the Jews for bringing the pogroms on their own heads, accentuated further their exclusion from Russian society. From then on, they were subjected to escalating waves of anti-Semitic violence and official discrimination. They left the territory of the empire in exceptionally large numbers. The majority – about two million in all – went to America, but two waves of these emigrants, totalling about 65 000, comprised the first *aliyot* (migrations to Palestine). The number of Jews who left Russia during this time comprised two-thirds of the total rate of emigration, though the Jews were less than 5 percent of the empire's population. For these reasons, 1881 is often regarded as the great turning point in modern Jewish history. Most significantly, 1881 roughly marks a point of *artistic* departure in modern Hebrew literature (Alter 1988, Aberbach 1993). The structural innovation in Russian Jewish politics after 1881 – its autonomy not only in relation to the state but also to the established Jewish leadership, which it now opposed (Frankel 1981, Lederhandler 1989) – was reflected in Hebrew literature. Prior to 1881, Russian Hebrew writers did not for the most part create works of enduring aesthetic value; after 1881 they did.

From the time of the freeing of the serfs in 1861 until 1917, the Russian Jews produced three different generations of writers and bodies of literature (though there was some overlapping), each representing a different mode of Jewish adaptation to the crumbling Tsarist empire. The first, in Yiddish, was led by Mendele Mocher Sefarim (Mendele the Book Peddlar, pen name of S.J. Abramowitz, 1835?–1917)[2] and by his younger contemporaries Sholom Aleichem ("How do you do?", pen name of Sholom Rabinowitz, 1859–1916), and I.L. Peretz (1852–1915). Yiddish literature became to a large extent – unsuccessfully as it turned out – a vehicle for the survival of the Russian Jews as an ethnic minority within a clearly defined territory. A second, younger group consisted of assimilated Russian Jews – such as Isaac Babel, Osip Mandelstam, Boris Pasternak, Ilya Ehrenberg. These writers were born in the last years of the Pale of Settlement, abolished by the 1917 revolution. They rejected Yiddish and Hebrew in favor of Russian. Eventually they came to prominence as major Russian writers under Soviet rule.

The third group – the subject of this chapter – had the most far-reaching influence. It included such figures as C.N. Bialik (1873–1934), Saul Tchernichowsky (1875–1943), M.J. Berdichevsky (1865–1921), M.Z. Feierberg (1875–99), and J.H. Brenner (1881–1921). These writers created a literary culture that acted as midwife to the birth of Zionism and the State of Israel. Hebrew literature of 1881–1917 was inseparable from the rise of political Zionism. Yet, the nationalism of this literature was Herderian in its primary concern with Jewish culture rather than with politics. Characteristic of this literary movement is the fact that

Mendele, its outstanding artist in fictional prose, was contemptuous of political Zionism (Aberbach 1993, pp. 45–6); Bialik, though hailed as the poet laureate of the Jewish national renaissance, persisted in writing deeply personal lyrics and neglected national themes (Aberbach 1981, 1988); and Ahad Ha'am ("One of the people," pen name of Asher Ginzburg, 1856–1927),[3] its outstanding theoretician, was locked in fierce debate with political Zionists in the years after 1897, when the World Zionist Organization was founded by Theodor Herzl (1860–1904). Other important Hebrew writers of the period, including David Frischmann (1859–1922), Zalman Schneour (1886–1959), Gershom Shoffman (1880–1970) and, above all, Uri Nissan Gnessin (1879–1913), were primarily interested in the creation of art rather than in having educational or political influence. This literature, in contrast with much pre-1881 Hebrew literature, attached great importance to childhood and to aggadah (Aberbach 1995), to the exploration of the inner life of the individual, and to the creation of a distinct Jewish aesthetic as part of the developing national consciousness. Bialik and M.Y. Berdichevsky (1865–1921), who in many ways were ideological opponents, were agreed in their high valuation of aggadah: each produced anthologies of aggadah. Bialik's, edited jointly with J.H. Ravnitzky (1908–11), has become a modern Hebrew classic. Berdichevsky's work has been undeservedly forgotten. The crucial spur in the Jewish national awakening was cultural. In this regard, it may be compared with other cultural nationalisms, including those of the Slovaks, the Greeks, and the Irish (Hutchinson 1987).

Historical and literary background

During the nineteenth century, the Jewish population of Russia rose to nearly five million. It made up the largest, most homogeneous and dynamic, and most persecuted Jewish community of the time. The collapse of the Tsarist empire was by no means inevitable. Yet its weaknesses became clear with the fiasco of the Crimean War (1853–56). The freeing of the serfs in 1861 weakened the empire further by exacerbating its main problems: backwardness, social inequality, chronic poverty, unemployment, and overcrowding in the cities. At the same time, autocratic rule was undermined by a new and growing university-educated intelligentsia and the limited introduction of capitalist-based industry. The failure of the Polish revolt of 1863 and the Russian–Turkish war of 1877–78 set off waves of Russian nationalism which, in turn, led to violent anti-Semitism. It may be that the use of Jew-hatred was not sanctioned officially as a diversion from revolutionary unrest within the empire (Rogger 1986, Löwe 1995); yet there is little doubt that the pogroms had this effect up to a point. Russian Judeophobia came by the end of the Reform Era, in 1881, "to incorporate literally all of the fears and obsessions of a society in the midst of traumatic social change" (Klier 1995, p. 455). There were two major waves of pogroms, in 1881–84 and 1903–06, in the Pale of Settlement. From the outbreak of pogroms in 1881 until the 1917 revolution, these circumstances stirred up a new Jewish national self-consciousness, with profound cultural and political consequences.

Hebrew literature prior to 1881 was a vital part of the background to the cultural nationalism of post-1881 Hebrew literature. The Odessa pogrom of 1871 was a significant turning point (Zipperstein 1985, Haberer 1995). Jewish intellectuals such as Mendele and Peretz Smolenskin (1842?–84) began at this time to question Haskalah ideals, and elements of Jewish nationalism entered Hebrew literature (Patterson 1985). The leading Hebrew poet of the pre-1881 era, Judah Leib Gordon (1830–92) – not Bialik – is cited by Kedourie (1960 pp. 100–1) as communicating in his poetry the alienation and the violent revolt against authority and restraints which are characteristic of national movements. The lexicographer Eliezer Ben-Yehuda tells in his autobiography (1917–18) that he conceived of Hebrew as a vehicle for Jewish nationalism in Palestine already in the late 1870s under the impact of the Russian nationalism stirred up by the Russian–Turkish war of 1877–78.

Nevertheless, prior to 1881 Hebrew literature was, for the most part, non-nationalistic, heavily didactic, artistically clumsy, and linguistically shallow. The rise of Jewish nationalism after 1881 was a critical force galvanizing both the language and the literature. It brought the latter within a span of two generations into the front ranks of Western literature. (Samuel Joseph Agnon, the leading Hebrew novelist after Mendele's death in 1917, went on to win the Nobel Prize for literature in 1966.) Hebrew in the Tsarist empire prior to 1881 had been used mainly as a catalyst for educational reform among the Jews and their assimilation (or "russification") into Russian society. The eighteenth century Age of Enlightenment and the liberal ideals promulgated by the French Revolution and spread by the Napoleonic wars had their Hebrew offshoot in the Haskalah (Enlightenment) movement. As in Germany and Galicia in the late eighteenth and early nineteenth centuries, Hebrew was adapted as the language by which the largely uneducated Jews could be introduced to the arts and sciences, particularly the latter. As long as Hebrew writers believed that emancipation and civil rights – above all the abolition of the Pale – were possible under Tsarist rule, they used Hebrew to promote secular education.

The Russian Haskalah, lasting from the 1820s to 1881, was the springboard for post-1881 Hebrew literature. It inspired much translation of educational works as well as experiments in poetry, drama, autobiography, and fiction, including the earliest Hebrew novels, starting with Abraham Mapu's *Ahavat Zion* (*The Love of Zion*, 1853) and included influential works by Gordon (Stanislawski 1988), Smolenskin, Mendele, Braudes, and others (Patterson 1964). Though this work has scant artistic merit, its historical importance is vast. Its relationship with post-1881 Hebrew literature brings to mind Saltykov-Shchedrin's fable of the ram troubled by a word (freedom) which it cannot clearly remember. The Jews in the same way were dimly aware of a viable national identity beyond Russia's borders: the pogroms were the main trauma bringing it to consciousness.

The pogroms and Hebrew literature

The pogroms which broke out after the assassination of Tsar Alexander II in 1881 were the death-blow to Haskalah ideology and the hope of Jewish emancipation under Tsarist rule. After 1881, Hebrew literature was inseparably part of a critical mass of national feeling, of will and creativity liberated by trauma and the new realism which followed. Hebrew writers no longer used Hebrew literature primarily to teach the ideology of assimilation and Russian patriotism. They aimed instead to depict Jewish life as they saw it, for its own sake and with empathy. Apart from the already-mentioned fiction of Mendele, poems of Bialik and essays of Ahad Ha'am, the high points of their achievement include: four short novels by Gnessin; a group of semi-fictional autobiographies by Mendele, Bialik, Feierberg, Brenner, and Berdichevsky; poems by Tchernichowsky; and the Hebrew translations of Sholom Aleichem's stories by I.D. Berkowitz (1885–1973) and the Hebrew translations (by Peretz and others) of Peretz's stories. The chief literary characters in Hebrew at the turn of the century, Mendele the Bookpeddler and Sholom Aleichem's Tevye the Dairyman – both tragi-comic creations – are without precedent or parallel in Jewish or any other literature. Interestingly, these characters are based on Yiddish originals, but they became inseparably a part of Hebrew literature. The bulk of this work, comprising a dozen or so volumes in all, was published in the 15 years between 1896 and 1911. Rarely in literary history have a literature and language undergone such massive change as Hebrew did in this short time.

This literature has a unique socio-linguistic character. Its writers were all native Yiddish speakers. Their leader was Mendele who had a seminal role as the "grandfather" both of modern Yiddish and Hebrew fiction. His novels, most of which were written twice, first in Yiddish and then in Hebrew, were the principal achievement in Hebrew prose fiction prior to 1939. Two of these Yiddish works, *Die Kliatsche* (*The Mare*, 1873) and *Masos Binyomin ha-Shlishi* (*The Travels of Benjamin the Third*, 1878), predate 1881; the latter, published in 1896, became the first classic in modern Hebrew. Mendele was the first to recognize in Yiddish a catalyst for the creation of lasting art in Hebrew. Mendele's novels are mostly set during the reign of Nicholas I, and the Hebrew drafts post-date the Yiddish ones by as much as 30 years and more (e.g. *The Mare*); yet, the basic conditions of the Russian Jews in the time of Nicholas II, when all the Hebrew drafts were written, were little better than they had been a half-century previously. Consequently, they largely retained their social relevance after 1881.

Unlike post-1948 Hebrew writers, Hebrew writers of 1881–1917 were self-taught intellectuals, mostly without even a high school diploma. Almost all were lapsed from a religious background and had intensive experience of rabbinical seminaries (*yeshivot*), where they were for the most part outstanding scholars. Their alienation from traditional Judaism and their struggle to adapt to a new, secular world are central motifs in their autobiographical works (Mintz 1989). The richness of their style, at its best, reflects years of study. They brought a religious fervor and reverence for the Hebrew language in adapting its classical idioms to modern secular art. Perhaps the closest literary analogue to this aspect of their achievement is James Joyce's *Ulysses*. They denied through mock-heroic satire the sacred authority of the sources but implicitly accepted their imperishable value and their power to inspire (Aberbach 1993).

Hebrew and Jewish liberation

The metamorphosis of Hebrew after the pogroms of 1881–82 helped to bring about political metamorphosis via the Zionist Organization in which the Russian Jews soon became the largest and most influential group. Zionism promoted Hebrew as the national language of all Jews and the growth of creative literature in Hebrew as an integral part of the national renaissance. The sudden, steep rise in the status and artistic value of Hebrew literature would have been highly unlikely had the Russian empire been stronger and less gripped by Jew-hatred. Jewish literature became a vehicle for a form of emigration into a private national domain, the full dimensions of which would soon be mapped out. While there was and could be no open call for revolution, a number of new features of Hebrew literature were revolutionary: Bialik's revival of the biblical prophetic style, bitter, angry, and critical of the status quo, striking in imagery and rhythmic power, demanding truth and justice; Berdichevsky's call for the Nietzschean release of the instinctual power of the individual; Tchernichowsky's idealization of the Greek way of life, its heroes and mythology, whose healthy, democratic nature implicitly contrasted with the repression of Tsarist rule and the stifling narrowness of Russian Jewish life; the introduction of the heretic as a sympathetic character in the writings of Feierberg, Brenner, Berdichevsky, and others. The defiant spirit of the age is, perhaps, best captured in Bialik's poems, such as *En zot ki rabat tzerartunu* (*Nothing but your fierce hounding, 1899*):

> Nothing but your fierce hounding
> has turned us into beasts of prey!
> With cruel fury
> we'll drink your blood.
> We'll have no pity
> when the whole nation rises, cries –
> "Revenge!"

Not least, the elevation of the common Jew as a subject of serious Hebrew literary art, rather than to promote an educational message, was revolutionary. It began with Mendele's act of introducing the character of Mendele the Bookpeddler into a Hebrew story in 1886, after over two decades of depicting this character exclusively in Yiddish fiction (Aberbach 1993a, 2001). This act implicitly rejected the idea of inborn superiority, for even ordinary Yiddish-speaking Jews – a bookseller, a bathhouse attendant, or beggar – could be presented artistically and with human significance. This literature counteracted the dehumanization of the Jews resulting from anti-Semitic violence, poverty, and discrimination.

The disdain which Russian-Jewish intellectuals previously felt for the ignorant, superstitious Jewish masses now largely disappeared. It was replaced by warm and curious, though not uncritical, sympathy. The populist movement in Russia in the late 1870s, with its idealization of the Russian peasant, also left its mark on Jewish literary self-perceptions.

Even the ultra-Orthodox pious Jews, the Hasidim, who throughout the nineteenth century had served as the chief satiric target in Hebrew (Davidson 1966), were now described far more seriously (in Peretz's collection of stories, *Hasidut*, with glowing empathy), as repositories of profound folk wisdom.

The waves of pogroms of 1881–84 and 1903–06 liberated the Hebrew language and literature in specific practical ways. Emigration to Palestine triggered off by the pogroms brought about the creation of hundreds of Hebrew-speaking groups in Russia. Suddenly, it became clear to the young Russian Jewish men and women who were thinking of emigrating that the emerging Jewish community in Palestine was the most heterogeneous in the world: only one language united its varied groups – Hebrew.

The pogroms were the catalyst for an historic encounter between the Russian Jewish lower middle class and the Hebrew intelligentsia, leading to a phenomenal increase in Hebrew journalism and in Hebrew readers, which may have reached 100000 already in the 1880s (Miron 1987, p. 59ff.) For the first time, Hebrew writers could, in theory, make a living from their writings, and publishers could make substantial profits. In the short story *Bi-Yme ha-Ra'ash* (*Earthquake Days*, 1890), Mendele gives a brilliant satiric picture of the time: a bedraggled *melamed* attempting to escape the pogroms to Palestine via Odessa is converted literally overnight into a private tutor of modern Hebrew. The upsurge of interest in the study and creation of modern spoken Hebrew and journalism naturally increased the market for creative Hebrew. As a result, the artistic standard of this literature rose impressively after 1881. Hebrew readers of important writers such as Mendele, Bialik, Brenner, and Gnessin during this period rarely exceeded a few thousand, but this was far more than during the pre-1881 period. These readers constituted an elite, widely read and discerning, though mostly self-taught, and familiar with European and Russian literature. Hebrew literature, previously imitative, became competitive. It now aimed, largely successfully, to become an important part of European literature. The optimism and didacticism of Haskalah literature were turned round. Much post-1881 Hebrew literature is pessimistic and anxiety-ridden, foreshadowing the tone of post-First World War European literature. Yet, this literature also includes two outstanding humorists – Mendele and Sholom Aleichem (again, in Berkowitz's translation) – who convey a Yiddish comic sensibility which, in retrospect, appears to have been virtually a condition of survival in the Pale. As mentioned previously, Mendele's comic novella *The Travels of Benjamin the Third* was recast from a Yiddish original of

1878. However, it is highly significant in considering 1881 as a psychological divide in Jewish history and literature that whereas in the Yiddish draft of *The Travels* the quixotic Benjamin does not reach Palestine, in the Hebrew draft of 1896 he does. In the Hebrew version, Benjamin emerges in the end more as a courageous visionary than an unbalanced figure of fun.

Following the 1903 pogrom in Kishinev, Bialik developed a programme of *kinnus*, the "ingathering" of fragments of Jewish culture in an effort to give new force and direction to the growing Jewish national consciousness. *Kinnus* found practical expression in Bialik's work as a publisher and his co-editing of the legends and folklore of the Talmud and Midrash, as well as of the medieval Hebrew poetry of Solomon Ibn Gabirol and Moses Ibn Ezra. But his poems, particularly the prophetic "poems of wrath," are themselves a major contribution to *kinnus*, a harmonious amalgam of Hebrew strata parallel to Mendele's achievement in prose.

Maxim Gorky, who read the "poems of wrath" in Russian translation, called Bialik a modern Isaiah. Most of these poems were written during and in response to the pogroms of 1903–06. They express the outrage and impotence felt by the Russian Jews as well as the aggressiveness which led to increased militancy, especially among the young. It is estimated that by 1903 about half of those arrested for revolutionary activities in Russia were Jews. The official tendency to identify revolutionaries with "the Jews" – though the vast majority of Russian Jews were not – is exemplified in a letter of Tsar Nicholas II to his mother on 27 October 1905: "nine-tenths of the revolutionaries are Yids" (in Pipes 1990, p. 48). Bialik's "poems of wrath" are the outstanding literary expression of the growing radicalization of the post-1881 generation (Aberbach 1988). They mark a turning point in modern Jewish history, the beginning of a far-reaching change in Jewish consciousness and the emergence from powerlessness:

> As our voices entreating lift into the darkness –
> Whose ear will turn?
> As our raw blasphemy streams to heaven –
> Over whose crown will it trickle?
> Grinding tooth, knuckling ire-veined fists –
> On whose scalp will the fury drift?
> all will fall windily
> Down the throat of chaos;
> No comfort remains, no helping hand, no
>   way out –
> And heaven is dumb;

> Murdering us with dispassionate eyes,
> Bearing its blame in blood-torn silence.
>
> *Davar* (1904)

The art which Russian Jewish writers created from then until the revolution is built upon the conviction of holding the moral high ground. Their alienation from Russia, painful though it was, forced them to break from Russia and from the ideology of assimilation, to seek inner sources of strength and freedom. The following lines from Feierberg's novella *Le'an? (Whither?,* 1899), though put into the mouth of a madman, sums up the metamorphosis which turned many disillusioned young Russian Jews back to their semitic roots and to Palestine:

> The greatest enemy that Judaism has ever had has been ... the West, which is why I believe it to be unnatural that we Hebrews, we Easterners, should throw in our lot with the West as we set out for the East ... I believe that this great people, without whose books and spiritual genius the world could not possibly have achieved what it has, will again give a new civilization to the human race, but this civilization will be Eastern (1973, p. 214).

The collapse of rabbinic authority

Unlike the relatively emancipated and enlightened Jews in the cities of Western Europe, the East European Jews until the latter part of the nineteenth century accepted Jewish orthodoxy as an immutable fact of existence, knowing little else, and with deep distrust of secular education. A number of social forces caused the breakdown of rabbinic authority and of Jewish orthodoxy. This breakdown was so total that after the 1917 revolution most Russian Jews would for the most part willingly accept the atheist ideology of socialism.

The most radical force for change was the growing availability and attraction of secular education, inspired in the first place by the Haskalah ideology. The Russian Haskalah did not dismiss Jewish orthodoxy and rabbinic authority outright. Rather, it aimed to adapt Judaism to the modern world while preserving rather more than the Western European reform movement the traditional character of Judaism. There was no internal reform movement in the rabbinate in the Russian Pale of Settlement. The government under Alexander II set up rabbinical training schools designed to produce modern rabbis who would not be opposed to secular education. Whether for liberal or anti-Semitic motives, it aimed to weaken traditional rabbinic authority. The Haskalah was in a sense a willing instrument of government policy and inevitably conveyed a strong measure of Jewish self-hate.

This is the background to a unique phenomenon in the history of Hebrew literature: a literary movement opposed in many ways to Jewish orthodoxy but consisting of writers who, though heretics, themselves had much of the erudition, the devotion, the puritanism, the sense of spiritual calling associated – ideally – with the rabbinate. They bore something of the same tense relationship of tradition and modernity as writers such as Joyce, Yeats, and Eliot who, similarly, came from a theological environment and in an earlier age might have become clergymen. The Hebrew writers were steeped in Judaism and Jewish learning. They were the children of rabbis and scholars; they almost all had a classical Jewish education consisting of the *cheder* and the *bet midrash*; and they included some of the outstanding scholars in the *yeshivot* in Eastern Europe. Had they been born a generation or two earlier, most of them would almost certainly have become rabbis. Mendele and Sholom Aleichem were, in fact, trained as government rabbis. Mendele apparently failed his preaching examination and never practised, but Sholom Aleichem actually worked as a rabbi for several years. These writers in effect were the founding fathers of modern Hebrew (and Yiddish) literature. In their writings, they give not just a critique of Jewish life in Eastern Europe but also of Judaism. They provide a remarkable artistic picture of the problems, conflicts and revolutionary changes brought about by the violent clash between traditional, almost medieval Judaism and the modern world.

Hebrew literature of the Haskalah anticipates the anti-rabbinic thrust of post-1881 Hebrew literature. The importance of Haskalah literature is mostly historical rather than literary. It was created under the illusion that by gaining a secular education the East European Jews would, as it were, earn civil rights and emancipation. As we have seen, the Haskalah movement ended when this illusion was shattered in 1881. Nevertheless, this literature, led by writers such as Judah Leib Gordon (1830–92) and Abraham Mapu (1808–67), is the basis of modern Hebrew literature. Many of its elements, including the attacks on what its writers regarded as the unhealthy aspects of orthodoxy, look forward to the far greater literature of the post-pogrom years. The Haskalah writers invariably attack the rabbinate for being narrowminded and fanatical, stifling and imprisoning the people with halakhic rulings, and arresting their normal growth. The virulence of Haskalah attacks on rabbinic authority owes much to a suppressed resentment at the hundreds of anti-Semitic laws passed by the Russian government. The rabbis with their laws were a soft target, as were the Russian clergy in Russian literature who represented government authority: unlike the government itself, they could be attacked and their authority undermined. The greatest Hebrew poet of the Haskalah, Judah Leib Gordon, has a blistering attack on the emptiness and futility of rabbinic teaching in his poem *Bein shinei arayot* (*In the Lions' Jaws*, 1868): "They set up houses of study. What did they teach? To guard the wind, to plough the stone, to sieve water, to thresh chaff!"

In his novel *Religion and Life* (*Ha-Dat veha-Chayim*, 1876–77), Gordon's younger contemporary, the novelist Reuben Asher Braudes (1851–1902), attacks the demands of Judaism and of a normal life as being antithetical. He blames the rabbis for making Judaism unlivable:

> The Rabbis have so restricted every path of life, scarcely allowing the people to draw breath, that they have deadened their very spirit. And the people meekly bear the burden on their shoulders through blindness and fatigue, and have become a corpse among the living, without ever knowing that their Rabbis have overstepped the mark, broken the covenant of their *Torah*, and led them into the wilderness (Patterson 1964, p. 203).

Mendele, the outstanding Hebrew writer of the nineteenth century, bridges the Haskalah and the *dor ha-techiyah*, the post-1881 "generation of revival." In his writings, he subjects the rabbis to his unique brand of acerbic and often hilarious social satire. In the opening of *The Travels of Benjamin the Third*, the Hebrew version of which appeared in 1896, the rabbi as authority figure is an object of mockery as are those who naively believe in him:

> Once, on a boiling day in the month of Tammuz – I remember it as clearly as if it were today – our rabbi went for a dip in the lake outside town. I and two friends tracked after him, in awe of his presence, completely sure that nothing bad could happen, and with God's help we would come home safe and sound. No small matter, the protection of a rabbi, whose authority the whole world accepts, who can have no superior, whose honorary titles alone fill a whole page! The rabbi set a leisurely pace, some distance ahead of us: however, just as he reached the lake and began to undress, a peasant boy appeared and set his dog on him. The holy man was scared stiff.

He ran off – if you'll excuse my saying so – clutching his trousers in one hand and his round plush hat in the other. We boys were simply flabbergasted: if Leviathan himself was caught in the meshes, what were we minnows in the mud to do? (1947, p. 60).

Despite Mendele's affection and empathy toward Jews, such satire is evidence of severe disillusionment and a breakdown in rabbinic authority. The formative trauma in modern Jewish life and literature – the pogroms of 1881–82 and the May Laws of May 1882 in which the Jews were officially blamed for provoking the pogroms – in some ways confirmed and hastened this breakdown, but in other ways stimulated new pride in Jewish distinctiveness, expressed primarily, though not exclusively, in nationalism.

Among the effects of the pogroms and the May Laws was Jewish outrage at the injustice of these atrocities. The Jews were helpless victims. Consequently, they reacted against the Haskalah ideal of assimilation into the society that had victimized them. The May Laws increased the chronic pauperization of the Russian Jews. By the end of the century, it is estimated that as many as 40 percent of the Russian Jews were dependent partly or wholly on Jewish charity. The angry sense of injustice found an outlet in traditional Jewish life, with its alleged passivity and stagnancy. The rabbis could do little in the face of the massive crisis faced by the Russian Jews. They offered little in the way of practical leadership. At this time, Leon Pinsker wrote his treatise *Autoemancipation* (1882), coming to a conclusion shared by many Jews at the time: that the Jews could not appeal to universal justice but must take their fate into their own hands. Pinsker was one of the founders of *Hibbat Zion*, the organization based in Odessa responsible for the first *aliyah*, which brought about 25 000 Jews to Palestine by the end of the century.

Jewish heresy and the rejection of Russia

Modern Zionism was born out of the idea that the Jews had to master their own destiny and not depend on providence, but rather reject passive faith and rabbinic authority as potential dangers. Precisely at this point, Hebrew literature emerged as an important artistic expression of modern Jewish identity and aspirations. It was on one level a vote of no-confidence in Tsarist Russia. The pogroms of 1903–06 confirmed this movement toward internal and external Jewish independence: they, too, set off a wave of Jewish immigration to Palestine. At this time, in response to the pogrom in Kishinev, Bialik wrote his poem "On the Slaughter" (*Al ha-Shechitah*, 1903), in which, apparently for the first time in Hebrew poetry, the existence of God was questioned:

> Heaven! Beg mercy for me,
> If you have a God, and he can be found ...

Among the salient new elements in the Hebrew literature of this period is, in fact, the character of the heretic. This is hardly surprising as the majority of the Hebrew writers of the age – including Agnon and Greenberg, Galician Jews who later returned to a form of orthodoxy – were heretics in the sense that they broke away from orthodox Judaism: they were no longer part of a Jewish religious community, they ceased prayer and religious study, and they ceased general observance of the Sabbath, the festivals, and the dietary laws. In some cases, they had affairs with non-Jewish women. Shoffman and Tchernichovsky married outside the faith.

Micha Yosef Berdichevsky was the outstanding ideologue and one of the principal writers of this Hebrew literature of heresy. Berdichevsky had a decisive influence on the writers born around the 1881 watershed: Gnessin, Shoffman, and Brenner. After years of agonizing, he came to the conclusion that rabbinic Judaism was itself to blame for the exile and the diaspora of the Jews. The only way to overcome the psychological blows of exile was to deny Judaism and its values and return to a healthy pre-rabbinic, even pre-biblical identity. Berdichevsky was the son of a rabbi in the Ukraine and, like Bialik, spent time as a student in the distinguished Lithuanian yeshivah of Volozhin. As a teenager he was married off and, as was the custom, he lived with his in-laws. When his father-in-law discovered that he was reading Haskalah literature and having secret contact with *maskilim*, he forced Berdichevsky to divorce his wife. This is the background to the story "Across the River" (*Me-Ever la-Nahar*, 1899), whose chief symbol is a bridge crossing from the lower town, where the Jews live, to the upper town, home of the gentiles and the enlightened Jews. The young man in the story loves his wife and is fond of his father-in-law. But his questioning intellect does not allow him peace and draws him to secular study and to fraternity with a *maskil* across the river. The young man becomes a voice for the author's own questionings, in which the influence of Nietzsche is paramount: "Is there truly good and evil? Is there a God who watches over man and makes a covenant with man?" (1969, p. 13). On the night of Yom Kippur, his impatience and alienation from the community become almost unbearable:

> When two old men stood in front of the Ark holding *sifre Torah* and said *Kol Nidre*, permitting the congregation to pray with the

sinners, a strange lust burned in me to lift my *talit* above my head and cry out: "Wake up, my people!" (*ibid.*, p. 20).

Eventually his father-in-law discovers his heretical leanings. In a scene charged with conflict on the bridge, each renounces the other. The young man leaves his home and his wife forever.

The poet Saul Tchernichovsky was the type of new Jew that Berdichevsky admired: he seemed largely untouched by the neuroses of traditional Jewish life, by its backwardness, and poverty. He radiated energy, optimism, and health. Tchernichovsky was unusual among the Hebrew writers of the age in that he grew up in a largely non-Jewish rural part of southern Russia, and his family was well-integrated into their environment. By training a doctor, he was also a great linguist and, after Bialik, the most influential Hebrew poet of his generation. His poetry contains a radical protest against what were then seen as the life-denying qualities of Judaism. He was fascinated by paganism in a variety of cultures, but especially Canaanite, as a more authentic, freer and healthier way of life than monotheism which had in his view deadened the spirit of man. His ideal, not unlike Berdichevsky's, was a Nietzschean god of youth, power, and beauty. In the poem "Before the Statue of Apollo" (*Le-Nohakh Pesel Apollo*, 1898), the poet expresses anger at the Jews for having destroyed this god:

> I bow down to life, might and beauty.
> I bow to all beautiful things, robbed
> by rotten human carcasses,
> rebels against life, against *Tzuri Shaddai* –
> God of the gods of wondrous deserts,
> God of the gods of the conquerors of Canaan in storm –
> and tied him with *tefillin* straps ...

If Berdichevsky was the main ideologue of heresy and Tchernichovsky its main poet, Gnessin was the most dedicated and influential prose artist of this ideology. Gnessin describes in his fiction and was himself a type of uprooted Jewish intellectual of the turn of the century: alienated from tradition while being steeped in it; bound to the enlightened ideals of a universal Western culture but barred from entering this culture. This feeling of alienation, of not belonging, of marginality, is summed up in the titles of Gnessin's four most important prose works (which, incidentally, were inscribed on his tombstone): "Sideways" (*Hatzidah*), "Meanwhile" (*Bentayim*), "Beforehand" (*Be-Terem*), and "Next to" (*Etzel*).

These stories reflect alienation from Judaism. "Sideways," for example, tells of a young man named Hagzar who comes, as Gnessin did, from a distinguished rabbinical family – his father was a yeshivah head – but has abandoned the faith and lives a shiftless, bohemian, largely unsatisfied life in a small East European town. The elderly and sympathetic traditionalist Simcha Baer, father of one of Hagzar's girl friends, teases him with a jibe calculated to arouse guilt:

> ...enjoying his own joke, Simcha Baer inquired which synagogue Hagzar attended and had he said his evening prayers there – adding without waiting for an answer that it would have broken Rabbi Shmulka of Mogilev's heart to have lived to see his nephew's sinful ways" (Shaked and Lelchuk 1983, p. 24).

Gnessin's background was similar to that of Shoffman and Brenner – Brenner in fact once studied at the yeshivah run by Gnessin's father. Together these three writers created a new, highly experimental Hebrew style with an emphasis not upon communal values but upon the unique inner world of the individual. Their struggle for new forms and new subject matter was part of the struggle to reform Jewish tradition, using for its main weapons elements of the tradition itself. Invariably these writers were attracted to Zionism, and a number of them, notably Brenner and Agnon, lived in Palestine even prior to 1914, when the land was still a cultural backwater. The cultural nationalism promoted by Zionist ideology meant that Hebrew writers, even if they were not Zionists, found themselves with a growing market and an elite readership, unusually well-educated and discriminating.

The process by which Zionism came to replace Jewish orthodoxy among many young East European Jews at the turn of the century is depicted with great feeling in Feierberg's *Whither?* This was Feierberg's only major work before his death from tuberculosis at the age of 24 in 1899. In it a rabbi's son, Nachman, highly intelligent and sensitive, begins to question the relevance of rabbinic tradition. He rejects his family's ambition that he should himself become a rabbi. The climax of the story occurs during the service on Yom Kippur. Nachman suddenly declares his heresy in front of the congregation:

> ...it's all nonsense. What does the high priest mean to you? Why should you care about something that happened thousands of years ago?... And he picked up the candle that stood burning on the podium – and blew it out (1973, pp. 125–6).

Nachman the heretic, son of the rabbi, can remain within the community only if he is branded as a madman. Though tormented by guilt, Nachman is sure that he is right, that the Jews must have something more than a religious identity, for this is too narrow, at least in its present form:

> Why must he profane what is holy to so many people? – It's my curse, he thought, to belong to a nation that has nothing in this world but its religion. This leaves only two choices ... to attack the faith or defend it ... and yet all that I want for myself all is to be a free man. I can't spend my life being for or against religion ... there are other things for me to be and to do, for myself and among my people (*ibid.*, p. 127).

The writings of Feierberg and his contemporaries show in detail how for the first time in Jewish history the Jews in the late nineteenth and early twentieth centuries began to define themselves en masse in terms other than religion. The *yeshivot* themselves often served as clandestine halfway houses, where young men entered as strictly orthodox Jews and emerged with at least some secular education and, more importantly, with a conviction that they would not continue to live within the faith as their fathers did. Brenner's semi-biographical novel *Winter* (*Ba-Horef*, 1903–04) includes a classic account of this transition. The novel tells of Jeremiah, a highly sensitive and intelligent young man from a poor and troubled family who begins life at a yeshivah with an exalted sense of religious calling and an all-consuming thirst for learning – "life is nothing without God's Torah, for this is the foundation of the world" (1955, I 20). He discovers modern Hebrew literature which changes him slowly but inexorably. He develops critical distance toward Jewish observance, becomes a Zionist and secretly cultivates what he recognizes as a highly individual creative gift as a budding Hebrew writer. With a religious zeal and triumphalism bordering on illness – "like a priest worshipping his God" (*ibid.*, p. 22) – he writes imitations of the Hebrew poetry, parodies, feuilletons, and articles which he consumes indiscriminately and edits a collection of this work. Found out by the yeshivah head, he is disgraced and expelled. In a manner characteristic of his generation, he feels himself to be spiritually divorced from traditional Jewish life without yet having found a new life to fill the void.

Hebrew and Jewish continuity

Nevertheless, to say that Hebrew literature of 1881–1939 one-sidedly abandons the faith, and is itself a symptom of the decline of orthodoxy, is to miss its complexity. Virtually all the writers of this period, rebels though they were against tradition, were also dedicated to some form of continuity of the Jewish tradition, to a distinctive Jewish identity and culture. In some cases, they were quite clear about their identification with Jewish spiritual values, though often in a new, secular form, without what they felt to be the persecution of rabbinic authority in a sociopolitical environment already burdened with totalitarianism and anti-Semitism. They saw themselves rightly as a prophetic minority who might in the near future become the majority. At the same time that Gnessin and Brenner were depicting Jewish heretics, Peretz was writing stories in Hebrew as well as Yiddish in which the Hasidim are presented not satirically, as in the past, but with loving empathy. Berdichevsky and Bialik were mining the richness of the aggadic traditions.

The opening of Bialik's autobiography *Aftergrowth* (*Safiah*, 1903–23), published last, in 1923, reads almost like the testimony of a Jewish mystic. The poet recalls his childhood as a world of providence and faith and unceasing miracles. The origins of Judaism are in effect the origins of all religion, the mystery of creation, the soul of poetry:

> God in his mercy gathered me under the shadow of his wings… His hidden hand scattered miracles on every path, planting riddles wherever I looked. In every stone and twig a midrash of wonder, in every hole and ditch eternal mystery (Aberbach 2002, p. 63).

A large part of Bialik's enormous appeal as national poet was his capacity to translate the spiritual fervor of Judaism – and particularly Hasidism – into a secular Zionist form.

Many of Agnon's stories are, similarly, testimonies and contributions to the richness of Jewish tradition. While Agnon is often described as a secular artist, and in some ways a heretic, his art could hardly have been created if he did not have a very strong spiritual identification with Judaism. He is outstanding among Hebrew writers in emphasizing the creative, rather than the oppressive, side of the rabbinic tradition. (He once declared that if he had had a choice he would have lived in the eighteenth century, "when Torah ruled Israel.") The opening of the story "Agunot" (1908) from which Agnon took his pseudonym, is written in a style which seems to belong more properly to the midrash or kabbalah than to modernism but is, on close reading, a revolutionary synthesis of tradition and modernism:

> It is said: A thread of grace is spun and drawn out of the deeds of Israel, and the Holy One, blessed be He, Himself in His glory, sits and

weaves – strand on strand – a prayer shawl all grace and all mercy, for the Congregation of Israel to deck herself in. Radiant in the light of her beauty she glows, even in these, the lands of her exile, as she did in her youth in the Father's house, in the Temple of her Sovereign and the city of sovereignty, Jerusalem. And when He, of ineffable Name, sees her, that she has neither been sullied nor stained even here, in the realm of her oppressors, He – as it were – leans toward her and says, "Behold thou art fair, my beloved, behold thou art fair." And this is the secret of the power and the glory and the exaltation and the tenderness in love which fills the heart of every man in Israel. But there are times – alas! – when some hindrance creeps up, and snaps a thread in the loom. Then the prayer shawl is damaged: evil spirits hover about it, enter into it, and tear it to shreds. At once a sense of shame assails all Israel, and they know they are naked. Their days of rest are wrested from them, their feasts are fasts, their lot is dust instead of luster. At that hour the Congregation of Israel strays abroad in her anguish, crying, "Strike me, wound me, take away my veils from me!" Her beloved has slipped away, and she, seeking him, cries, "If ye find my beloved, what shall ye tell him? That I am afflicted with love" (Agnon 1970, pp. 30–1).

Agnon's generation felt strongly that the thread of tradition was broken, but also that they could continue this tradition through the fulfilment of Zionist ideals. To many of the *halutzim* (pioneers), the building of the land of Israel took the place of religious practice. Aharon David Gordon's ideology of the religion of labor is expressed memorably in the poetry of Shlonsky. Shlonsky, born into a Hasidic family, survived the Russian revolution and came to Palestine in the early 1920s. There, like many of the young Hebrew writers, he became a laborer. In his poem *Work* (*Amal*, 1927), the building of the roads is depicted in the imagery of prayer:

> My land is wrapped in light like a *talit*.
> Houses stand like *tefillin* boxes.
> Like *tefillin* straps the roads sweep down.
> This is how the lovely town
> says its morning prayers to its creator.

This is modernist poetry, influenced by the great revolution in European poetry in the early part of this century, and by Russian poets such as Mayakovsky, Esenin, and Blok. But it is also a distinctive Jewish modernism which attempts to preserve and create as well as deny and destroy. Destruction may bring about a spirit of creativity. The poet does not put on *tefillin*. But he puts *tefillin* on to the land of Israel. The writers of the period 1881–1939 were indeed heretics from the standpoint of the largely monolithic Judaism that existed up to that point in eastern Europe. In their writings, they described faithfully the defections from the faith as the Jews became increasingly aware of the world around them and critical of their own way of life. This self-criticism was to some extent at least a consequence of being a relatively small, powerless, impoverished and uneducated minority amid a hostile majority. But it also involved a natural process of adaptation to change which was general in Western society at the time.

Hebrew and Russian literature

While asserting Jewish continuity, nineteenth-century Hebrew literature was closely linked with contemporary Russian literature. In some respects, including its countercultural qualities, it might be regarded almost as a branch of Russian literature. The Russian and Hebrew writers came from radically different social and religious backgrounds. The first group was largely aristocratic and wealthy; the second, mostly from impoverished homes. Yet they lived in the same empire at the same time. They describe the same general world and confront similar problems. Repugnance at the poverty, backwardness and injustice of life in Tsarist Russia was common to Russian as to Hebrew and Yiddish literature. Each of these literatures explores social and psychological malaises which contributed to the break-up of the Tsarist empire. The humane depiction of the ordinary Jew in late nineteenth-century Hebrew fiction – a phenomenon which began before 1881, though initially without lasting artistry – was as revolutionary as that of the Russian peasants in Turgenev's *Notes of a Huntsman* (1852).

The quarter-century rule of Alexander II (1855–81) produced an unrivalled body of Russian prose fiction, including *Fathers and Sons* (1861), *Crime and Punishment* (1865–66), *War and Peace* (1865–68), *Anna Karenina* (1874–76), and *The Brothers Karamazov* (1880). The subtlety and depth of Russian literature, its moral power, the astonishing variety of its great characters, its heady blend of realism, idealism and universalism, its potential subversiveness – and its anti-Semitism – all left their mark on Hebrew literature. No Hebrew writer equalled the best of Tolstoy or Dostoyevsky. Chekhov, a major influence on Gnessin, Shoffman, and Brenner, is far and away their superior as an artist as they themselves would have admitted notwithstanding their crucial importance in the development of modern Hebrew fiction. For inasmuch as these writers set Russian literature as their chief model for the depiction of modern life, they inevitably came off second. Hebrew at the time was still too wooden and undeveloped. However, some Hebrew writers, notably Mendele and Bialik, adopted Western literary standards while creating a new style of Hebrew based on the full richness of the Hebrew literary tradition. (Often they did this after writing a first draft in Yiddish.) These writers had far greater artistic success. Mendele's dual achievement in Yiddish as well as Hebrew is comparable with that of Gogol or Turgenev, certainly of Saltykov-Shchedrin. Bialik's best poetry is not inferior to that of Lermontov or the young Pushkin. Characters such as Benjamin the Third or Tevye the Dairyman, both recast from Yiddish originals, are indigenous to Russia: though they are manifestly Jewish. Russia (or, to be more specific, the Ukraine) is their native soil. Also, as a charismatic literary figure in the Jewish national movement, Bialik had an influence on Russian Jewish society which was in some ways even greater than that of Tolstoy on Russian society (Aberbach 1996).

Perhaps at no other time was a secular literature valued so highly among its readers – to the point of acting as a compass of moral direction and social and political change – as in Russia in the second half of the nineteenth century. For the Russian-Jewish intelligentsia, this view of literature came easily, with the Bible and Talmud as its precedent. The Russian perception of literature as a means of changing society was largely adapted by Hebrew writers, though by the 1890s the "art for art's sake" movement affected both literatures.

The two often-overlapping streams of Hebrew literature, one drawing from native Jewish culture and the other from Western influences, are closely paralleled in the two main directions of Russian literature, the Slavophile and the Western. As in Russian literature, notably the fiction of Ivan Bunin, the village, or *shtetl*, became a stock setting of Hebrew literature, often treated with contempt, or in a sentimental or semi-satirical style. Gogol's description in *Dead Souls* (1842) of the "quixotic" element in the Russian character is duplicated among the Russian Jews: Mendele's *Travels of Benjamin the Third*, as indicated earlier, tells of a Jewish Quixote who sets off with his Sancho Panza for the Holy Land. Mendele's satiric juxtapositions of biblical and talmudic characters and allusions with contemporary realities bring to mind similarly absurd juxtapositions in Russian literature, for example, in Leskov's "Lady Macbeth of Mtsensk" or Turgenev's "A Hamlet of the Shchigry District."

The character of the "superfluous man" and the *talush* ("uprooted") is common to both literatures: the man with gifts which have no outlet, alienated and trapped in conditions over which he has little control. Russian and Jewish literatures of the late Tsarist period are united in their critical attitude to the role of education in a society in which the dominant problem was getting enough to eat from day to day (Aberbach 1993, pp. 80–2). The purpose of education, both secular and religious, is called into question. The most striking poetic expression in Hebrew of being at an educational crossroads is Bialik's *Lifne aron hasefarim* (*In Front of the Bookcase*, 1910). The poet stands in front of a bookcase whose sacred books no longer meet present day needs. This scene echoes Chekhov's *The Cherry Orchard* (1904), though without the comic irony, when Gayev addresses the family bookcase. Gayev and his family are about to lose their estate through bankruptcy. The bookcase is a symbol of loss, not only of the property but of noble ideals identical with those of the Haskalah:

> Dear bookcase! Most esteemed bookcase! I salute your existence, which for more than a hundred years now has been directed towards the shining ideals of goodness and truth. For a hundred years your unspoken summons to fruitful labour has never faltered, upholding [*in tears*] through all the generations of our family, wisdom and faith in a better future, and fostering within us ideals of goodness and of social consciousness (1978, p. 13).

The radical critique of orthodox religion is another feature which binds Russian and Hebrew literature in an age of imperial decline. This critique was especially vehement prior to 1881, when Haskalah ideology emerged in opposition to what was often seen as a stifling puritan tradition based on outmoded rabbinic authority. In some cases, as we have seen, the attacks on the rabbis may have been unnaturally severe because the Jewish clergy, in common with the Russian orthodox priests, represented the status quo and, therefore, became symbolic of oppressive authority. The rabbis, like some of the priests in Russian literature, were acceptable targets for social criticism and satire, unlike the totalitarian government which had subjected the Jews to hundreds of restrictive laws. The anti-clericalism of Hebrew literature remained after 1881 but in a toned-down fashion as the Jews were galvanized into unprecedented unity by Christian hatred.

Censorship deeply affected both Hebrew and Russian literature. It made open criticism of the government impossible and encouraged self-blame and self- hate. Jewish writers, intentionally or not, resorted to displacements or, following the lead of Saltykov-Shchedrin, used an "Aesopic" language of fables to hint at their intentions. In the greatest of these allegories, Mendele's *The Mare*, the battered mare is a symbol of the Jewish people whose miserable state is caused by prejudice and discrimination. However, when it came to the question of blame, the Jews are themselves held responsible for the mare's pathetic state. In much the same way, Gogol, in his tale of Captain Kopeikin in *Dead Souls*, was forced by the censors to alter his attacks on the uncaring Tsarist bureaucracy that denied a soldier mutilated in war a proper pension. Instead, he put the blame for Kopeikin's misfortune on Kopeikin, not on the authorities.

In Hebrew as in Russian literature both before and after 1881, censorship taxed the ingenuity of the writer, to convey a desired meaning subtly and allusively. In this way, Hebrew writers such as Bialik discovered that the resources of Jewish history and literature gave cover to thoughts and emotions which would otherwise have been banned. The poem quoted earlier beginning "Nothing but your fierce hounding" got past the censor as it was originally called "Bar-Kokhba," which set it safely in the second century CE.

Any challenge to authority was politically charged both in Hebrew and Russian literature. Under the Tsarist regime, literature became a vital outlet by which the depiction of individual consciousness was indirectly an act of rebellion against a social system in which there was scarcely room for individualism. The idea expressed by Ivan Karamazov in Dostoyevsky's *The Brothers Karamazov* that "If God is dead, all things are possible" is implicit in Hebrew literature. As we have seen, Bialik's poem *Al ha-Shehitah* (*On the Slaughter*), written after the Kishinev pogrom in 1903, questions the existence of God, apparently for the first time in Hebrew. In Feierberg's *Whither?*, the hero's break from the authority of family and religion, as well as his incipient Zionism, is signalled by the momentous act of blowing out a candle in synagogue on Yom Kippur. If such sacrilege is possible, then anything is possible – even the overthrow of the Tsar, the restoration of the Jews to their ancestral homeland, and the revival of Hebrew language and literature.

Hebrew literary stereotypes

Perhaps the most striking and important similarity in Hebrew and Russian literature is the low opinion – often coupled with great affection – the writers of each language appear to have of their own people (Aberbach 1993). This aspect of Russian literature may be taken to presage the need for revolution; in Hebrew literature it is part of Jewish self-criticism accompanying the national revival. Almost every Jewish literary stereotype crops up in Mendele's writings. Though vile and expressive at times of Jewish self-hate, these stereotypes are exploded through empathy and the passion for social change. They are seen as a symptom, not a cause, of poverty and backwardness whose elimination would allow a new type of Jew, free, strong and confident, to emerge. For this reason, though not a political Zionist, Mendele was adopted by the Zionist camp. His writings, with their ambivalence toward and satire of diaspora Jews, were interpreted as a justification of Zionism.[4]

Mendele's ambivalence toward his own people is often expressed in the pose of the impartial entomological observer. Like a natural scientist – in the 1860s and 1870s he had produced the first *Natural History* in Hebrew – the narrator of his stories constantly likens the Jews to ants or fleas. For example, in Mendele's fictional autobiography *Ba-Yammim ha-Hem* (*Of Bygone Days*, 1894, 1903–17), mostly recast from a Yiddish original of the same period, the narrator complains: "We are a congregation – no, a heap – of ants. In a book on natural history you find a chapter on ants, not on any one ant" (1947, p. 259). In *Ha-Nisrafim* (*The Fire Victims*, 1897), an indigent Jew complains to Mendele the Bookseller that the house of study where he slept has burned down in a fire which destroyed the whole town – this often happened in Russia – and Mendele cruelly remarks to himself: "Fleas if they could talk would argue so after losing their lodgings in houses and beds" (*ibid.*, p. 445). Blatant anti-Semitic stereotyping occurs frequently in Mendele's description of typical Jewish noses, the Jews' uncleanliness and unhygienic manners, their ridiculous appearance, and love of money.

Russian literature prior to the 1880s was full of similar anti-Semitic stereotyping, though without the empathy and reforming zeal which mark Mendele's fiction far more strongly than self-hate. Lermontov's play *The Spaniards*, Turgenev's story "The Jew," Gogol's novels *Taras Bulba* and *Dead Souls*, Dostoyevsky's fictional memoir *The House of the Dead* (1860), the satires of Saltykov-Shchedrin, Tolstoy's *Anna Karenina*, among others, betray shameful prejudice and hatred nourished by the Church and kept alive in the popular imagination. Whatever their personal views of the Jewish people, pre-1881 Russian writers fell short of their liberal, humanistic ideals when they wrote of Jews. The literary stereotype built largely on Church anti-Semitism poisoned the image of living Jews. In *The House of the Dead*, Dostoyevsky tells of the Jew whom he met while imprisoned in Siberia:

> He was the only Jew in our barrack, and even now I cannot recall him without laughing. Every time I looked at him I would think of the Jew Yankel in Gogol's *Taras Bulba* who, when he undressed in order to climb, together with his Jewess, into some sort of cupboard, looked uncommonly like a chicken (1965, p. 93).

In *Crime and Punishment* (1866) Dostoyevsky cannot resist describing the odious moneylender whom Raskolnikov murders as "rich as a Jew" (1975, p. 83); and in *The Brothers Karamazov* (1880), when the invalid girl, Lisa Khokhlakov, asks the saintly Alyosha, "is it true that at Easter the Jews steal a child and kill it?" Alyosha replies, "I don't know" (1976, p. 552). Even so, the anti-Semitism here as elsewhere in Dostoyevsky's major writings is muted in comparison with the virulent hatred spewed out in his publicistic works (Goldstein 1981).

Perhaps the most disturbing and dangerous side to this literary stereotype was the fact that while most Russian Jews lived in conditions of unspeakable poverty and degradation, Russian literature persisted in depicting "the Jew" as being wealthy and in the habit of using his wealth to oppress Russians. Russian writers prior to 1881 seen to have been largely unable to contemplate a Jew without medieval associations of moneylending, miserliness, trickery, and extortion. In *Dead Souls*, for example, Chichikov tries to persuade Nozdryov to sell his dead souls and Nozdryov, sensing a trick, keeps urging him to buy something of value: "what Jewish instincts you have," thinks Chichikov (p. 89). The Jewish revolutionary Liamshin in Dostoyevsky's *The Devils* (1871–72) is singled out as a traitor to Russia, a new Judas (Goldstein 1981), though Jewish involvement in the Russian revolutionary movement at that time was minimal. Even in *Anna Karenina* the only Jewish character is presented stereotypically. Prince Oblonsky covets a lucrative post on the railway board and is kept waiting to his annoyance by Bulgarinov, a Jew whose support he needs (1968, p. 775).

A measure of the extraordinarily poor image of the Jew in Russian society prior to 1881 (and, to a large extent, afterwards) is that although these Russian works are counted among the classics in world literature and are peopled with a wide range of characters, the negative image of the Jew is the only one which appears in them. There are no realistic or even sympathetic portraits to balance them, as, for example, Dickens' *Our Mutual Friend* is a corrective to *Oliver Twist*. Jewish nationalism and the accompanying creation of a vibrant Hebrew literature became a means of fighting this racist stereotype by means of more balanced self- portrayals.

Russian literary stereotypes

The distorted perception of the Jews is in most respects equalled by the generally low view of the Russian people in Russian literature. This sense of inferiority made the Russians especially vulnerable (as were the Germans in the 1920s and 1930s) to the projective identification of anti-Semitism. The self-hatred expressed by the characters in Russian literature (who in some cases are authorial mouthpieces) might be seen as foreshadowings of the collapse of the Romanov empire inasmuch as it implicitly calls for radical change. This self-image is reflected in Hebrew literature of 1881–1917. Bazarov puts it succinctly in Turgenev's *Fathers and Sons*: "The only good thing about a Russian is the poor opinion he has of himself" (1965, p. 116). Gogol's particular genius was to delineate with sharp, precise strokes of satire this allegedly inferior side of the Russian character.[5] It is uncanny how closely Mendele's satires against the Jews resemble the jibes at the Russians in Gogol's works, notably in *Dead Souls*: "no Russian likes to admit before others that he is to blame" (p. 99); "You know perfectly well what a Russian peasant is like: settle him on new land and set him to till it, with nothing prepared for him, neither cottage nor farmstead, and, well, he'll run away, as sure as twice two makes four" (p. 164); "In general, we somehow don't seem to be made for representative assemblies" (p. 208); "a Russian is wise after the event" (p. 215); "a Russian likes spicy words; he needs them as much as a glass of vodka for his digestion" (p. 307); "A Russian, to judge by myself, cannot carry on without a taskmaster: otherwise he will only drowse off and go to seed" (p. 339). The contempt which Jewish writers often felt for the Yiddish language had its parallel in the disdain which the Russian intelligentsia had for Russian. As the narrator puts it sarcastically in *Dead Souls*, "To ennoble the Russian tongue even more, almost half its words were banished from their conversation, and because of that they had very often to have recourse to French" (p. 169).

Russia's weaknesses were betrayed in her perception and treatment of the Jews and in the Jews' vulnerability. It is a lesson of history that a nation's Jewish policy is a gauge of its self-image. The psychologist Erik Erikson has described how individuals belonging to a hated minority might in any case come to hate their own people:

> The individual belonging to an oppressed and exploited minority
> which is aware of the dominant cultural ideals but prevented from
> emulating them, is apt to fuse the negative images held up to him by
> the dominant majority with the negative identity cultivated in his
> own group (1974, p. 303).

The "negative images" are likely to be all the more vicious if the
dominant majority has a strongly negative self-image. Indeed, it is striking how the main criticisms of Russia in Russian literature are echoed in
pre-1881 Hebrew literature: for example, in the charges of the lack of
dignity, parasitism, backwardness, and demonic corruption. Prior to
1881, the attacks on Jewish society in Hebrew (and Yiddish) literature
are mainly a clarion for social reform; after 1881, for national revival. In
his letter to Gogol of 1847, for example, Belinsky writes that what Russia
needs is "the reawakening in the people of a sense of their human dignity lost for so many centuries amid the dirt and refuse" (1981, p. 537).
A similar attitude prevailed among enlightened Jews toward the Jewish
masses in the Pale of Settlement. In *Dead Souls*, likewise, the charge of
parasitism is implicitly leveled by Gogol against the privileged classes,
the landowners and the bureaucracy who treat human beings like property. Identical charges against the Jewish upper class appear frequently
in nineteenth-century Yiddish and Hebrew literature (for example, in
Mendele's novel *Dos Kleyne Mentschele* [*The Parasite*, 1864–65]). The
critic Chernyshevsky's attack in the 1840s upon the total lack of originality in Russian intellectual life – "What have the Russians given to
learning? Alas, nothing. What has learning contributed to Russian life?
Again, nothing" (in Treadgold, 1973, I 181) – is echoed in the critique of
traditional Jewish life in Haskalah literature. Turgenev went so far in his
novel *Smoke* as to suggest that if Russia were destroyed it would be no
great loss to civilization.

The low national self-image in Russian literature, though not unmixed
with pride and empathy, came largely out of the awareness that most of
the empire's population was desperately poor and ignorant. The
disgust and condescension often felt by educated Russians toward the
peasants is well expressed in Dostoyevsky's *Crime and Punishment*, set
shortly after the liberation of the serfs in 1861. The examining
magistrate Porphiry jokes sardonically with Raskolnikov that no educated murderer would take refuge in the Russian countryside: "our modern educated Russian would sooner be in jail than live among such

foreigners as our peasants" (1975, p. 355). In *The House of the Dead*, Dostoyevsky expresses amazement at the number of literate prisoners among whom he was incarcerated for four years in Omsk, Siberia, in the early 1850s:

> In what other place where ordinary Russians are gathered together in large numbers would you be able to find a group of two hundred and fifty men, half of whom could read and write? (1985, p. 31).

Even the idea that the Jews are in some way possessed by the Devil, in Mendele's *The Mare* as in the traditional anti-Jewish stereotype, is echoed in Russian literature of the same period. At the end of Dostoyevsky's *The Devils*, the dying progressive scholar Stepan Verhovensky retells the New Testament story of the devils entering the swine as a parable of contemporary Russia:

> That's exactly like our Russia, those devils that come out of the sick man and enter into the swine. They are the sores, all the foul contagions, all the impurities, all the devils great and small that have multiplied in that great invalid, our beloved Russia, in the course of ages and ages (1952, II 288).

This roughly corresponded with Dostoyevsky's own view of Russia, the germ of his novel which, he wrote in a letter of 9/21 October 1870 to A.N. Maikov, "describes how the devils entered into the herd of swine" (1987, p. 343).

Not surprisingly, then, Russia's leading satirist of the late nineteenth century, Saltykov-Shchedrin, who influenced Mendele in his satiric portrayal of towns such as Glupsk and in beast fables such as *The Mare* – he used the battered mare as a symbol of the exploited Russian peasant – took a deeply negative view of Russian society and institutions, which he characterized as being ruled by "arbitrariness, hypocrisy, lying, rapacity, and vacuity" (1986, p. vii).

A further sign that Russian Jewish writers often took their cue from Russian writers may be seen in the fact that when Russian writers, in part because they were shocked by the pogroms of 1881–82, began to depict Jews favorably – for example, in works by Leskov, Chekhov, Korolenko, and Gorky – the image of the Jew in Mendele and other Jewish writers became markedly less satirical and more realistic and positive. The negative image in Hebrew literature, as in Russian, might represent on one level a breaking away from this image, a declaration of "not us," a function not unlike that of anti-Semitic literary stereotypes in Russian and other literatures. This splitting away from diaspora Jewry, which was perhaps inevitable in the creation of a new national identity, has resulted to this day in a deeply ambivalent Israeli view of the diaspora.

Conclusion

Hebrew literature of 1881–1917 in some ways marks a revolutionary point of departure from Jewish tradition and the predominantly sacred Hebrew literature of the past and also, in its assertion of Jewish distinctiveness, from Russian and European literature. At the same time, the social and political causes which forged Hebrew into an artistic instrument for Jewish cultural nationalism also gave Russian literature its revolutionary impetus. The extraordinary artistic quality of Hebrew literature of this period must be ascribed to the convergence of cultural influences in which each major stratum of Hebrew literature in the past and much of the most important nineteenth-century world literature played their part. Imitation came to serve the cause of Jewish national assertion. The growth of European nationalism and anti-Semitism in the latter part of the nineteenth century drove many of the Russian Jews to rediscover their religious–cultural roots while rejecting traditional clerical authority. In doing so, they redefined their national identity with new aggressive creativity, mainly through massive development of literary and spoken Hebrew. This revival of an ancient language has no parallel in cultural history. Following its meteoric ascent, in 1881–1917, Hebrew was exiled by the Soviet empire, driven back to its birthplace and only homeland. In the land of Israel, Hebrew has continued as a critical mouthpiece for Jewish national identity. It has grown with confidence and creative vigor lacking since the time of the Bible.

Notes

1 The Iron Age, Imperialism, and the Prophets

1. For a selection of some of the more important ancient near eastern documents, see Winton Thomas (1958) and Pritchard (1969).
2. "Amid the clamour of the multi-racial metropolis [Babylon in the sixth century BCE] the exiles must have watched the kings of many nations bring their tribute to Nebuchadrezzar and have envisaged the long-promised Day when the same would be done not for a man but for their God as King of Kings in his new city" (Wiseman 1985, p. 115).

2 Trauma and Abstract Monotheism: Jewish Exile and Recovery in the Sixth Century BCE

1. It is a commonplace among biblical scholars (e.g. Wellhausen 1885, Oesterley 1930, Pedersen 1940, Bright 1960, von Rad 1965, Aberbach 1993c) that the acceptance by the Jews of exclusive abstract monotheism in the sixth century was linked in some way to national loss of the kingdom of Judah and the Temple in Jerusalem and the exile to Babylonia. Although the degree to which exile marked a radical theological break with the past is debatable (cf. Albright 1957, pp. 250–1; and Hayes and Miller 1986, pp. 447–8), few dispute that the sixth century was a turning point. In Kaufmann's view, "With land, temple and king gone, only one contact with the holy was left: the divine word ... it was precisely in exile that the full stature of Israelite religion began to manifest itself" (pp. 447, 450–1). Cohn (1993) sums up: "The experience of the Babylonian exile ensured the final victory of 'Yahweh alone' " (p. 149).
2. Exile could be, and sometimes was seen – for example, by Judean exiles in Egypt (Jeremiah 44:18) – as an unanswerable argument against monotheism and in favor of polytheism: "there were Jews who regarded Josiah's reform not as a step that might have saved the nation, but as one that had contributed to its downfall" (Bright 1965, pp. 265–6).
3. There are vehement attacks on Jews who failed in other areas of observance of the Sabbath and festivals – and who intermarried (Ezra chs 9–10, Nehemiah ch. 13). The religious obligations undertaken by Jews newly returned to the Land of Israel do not include the rejection of idolatry (Nehemiah 10:28). This omission is all the more striking as the Jewish theology deriving from the exclusive acceptance of monotheism did not demand of non-Jews belief in the one and only God – only the turn away from idols as a false morality (Epstein 1959, pp. 143–4). It seems, therefore, that by the end of the sixth century, idolatry was no longer tolerated in mainstream Judaism.
4. See, for example, Langer (1951), Worringer (1951), Koestler (1964), Storr (1972), and Aberbach (1989, 1996). There is some critical recognition of the

importance of traumatic loss in the history of ideas, for example, Gedo (1978) on Nietzsche, Nelson (1981) on Pascal, Friedman (1981) on Buber, Atwood (1983) on Sartre, and Scharfstein (1980) on philosophers generally.

5. See Stern (1966) and Dyer (1986).
6. See Aberbach (1982, 1989, 1993, 1995, 1996).
7. See Stern (1966), Storr (1972), Dyer (1986), and Aberbach (1989).
8. See Lifton (1967), Bettelheim (1979), and Bowlby (1980).

3 The Roman–Jewish Wars and Hebrew Cultural Nationalism

1. On the spiritual Jerusalem in the Talmud, see, for example, *Kiddushin* 49b and *Ta'anit* 5a.
2. For general introductions to the talmudic period and its literature, see Stemberger (1996) and Steinsaltz (1976). The outstanding literary anthology of non-legal rabbinic texts (much of which dating, however, from the post-tannaitic period) is that of Bialik and Ravnitsky (1992). For a detailed analysis of effects of the Roman–Jewish wars on Hebrew creativity and Jewish identity, see Aberbach and Aberbach (2000).
3. On the view that nationalism is a modern phenomenon, see, for example, Kedourie (1960), Gellner (1964), Deutsch (1966), Anderson (1983), and Hobsbawm (1990); the opposing view, that nations do indeed have ancient "navels", is argued among others by Kohn (1946), Seton-Watson (1977), Armstrong (1982), and Hutchinson (1987), and Smith (1991).
4. On this paradox, see Aberbach (1966) and Feldman (1993).
5. Smallwood (1975) links the Roman annexation of Egypt as a province in 30 BCE with anti-Semitic eruptions in Alexandria soon after. These were the first pogroms in history: mob attacks on Jews and their property. They came at a time when Rome seemed to be favoring the Jews under Herod and in the diaspora. The Egyptian Jews had given the Roman invaders military help and were naturally hated by the Greeks. But on a deeper level, in Smallwood's view, Greek anti-Semitism might have been a displaced expression of humiliation over defeat and resentment at Roman domination: "[The Greeks] could make indirect attacks on Rome through her proteges the Jews, who were at hand and far more vulnerable, and whose ambitions were causing friction and tension" (p. 234).
6. On the attraction of Judaism in the Roman empire, see Millar (1986, pp. 160–1). Competitive incentives for Jewish mission might have derived from the fact that Greeks and Persians also required conversion for membership in the nation. When foreigners were initiated into the Eleusinian mysteries, they became Greek nationals. Those initiated into Mithraism became Persians. Cf. Baron (1952, I 181). The spread of Hellenism might itself have spurred imitative missionary forces in Judaism (Smith 1978). For texts which demonstrate or hint at Jewish religious expansion see Stern (1974).
7. According to Josephus, Titus gave a speech to the besieged Jews in Jerusalem in 70 CE in which he declared: "You have been in a state of revolt from the time Pompey's army crushed you" (BJ VI 6, 2 [329]). See pp. 48–9 below.

8. The high moral code of Judaism was not tied to messianic nationalism. Rabban Yochanan ben Zakkai, for example, was a model of this moral code while having reservations as to the value of messianism.

9. See Josephus, *Antiquities* XX 7, 1 (139–40); 7, 3 (145f.); also XVI 7, 6 (225); XVIII 5, 4 (133, 139, 140); XIX 9, 1 (355). No doubt partly because of the close affinity between the Judaean client kingdoms and Parthia, a congress of princes from these kingdoms held by Agrippa I at Tiberias (c. 42 CE) was dispersed by the Roman governor of Syria (*Antiquities* XIX 8, 1 [338–41]). Rome's distrust of any political or religious movement that might undermine the empire is apparent also in its suppression of various cults. See, for example, *Antiquities* XVIII 3, 4 (65–80); Tacitus, *Annals* II 85; Suetonius, *Tiberius* 36. Roman concern about the Parthian threat continued after 120 CE, when the post of legate of praetorian rank was upgraded to consular status and two permanent divisions were introduced: these were due, Goodman (1983) writes, "as much for possible Parthian campaigns as to prevent internal rebellion" (p. 135).

10. For a brief, comprehensive survey, with bibliography, of the history of anti-Semitism, showing its roots in the early imperial period, see Alexander (1992).

11. Tanna (Heb.) = teacher of the tannaitic (Mishnaic) age (first two centuries CE). According to Cohen (1992, p. 157), the Mishnah records dicta of 54 figures in the period between c. 80–135 CE (the Yavnean period); 29 figures in the generation after the Bar-Kokhba war (the Ushan period); and 16 contemporaries of Judah Hanasi. A few additional names appear in other tannaitic literature.

12. This state of *faute de mieux* had a precedent in the aftermath of the destruction of the First Commonwealth, the burning down of the Temple in Jerusalem in 586 BCE and the Judean exile to Babylonia: "With land, temple and king gone, only one contact with the holy was left: the divine word" (Kaufmann 1960, p. 447).

4 Entry to Powerlessness: The Tannaim, Marcus Aurelius, and the Politics of Stoicized Judaism

1. On Roman religion see Beard *et al.* 1998 and Rüpke 2001. On the ethical concerns of Stoicism, see Kidd (1978) and Inwood and Donini (1999).

2. For versions and interpretations of the Midrash on the escape of Rabban Yochanan ben Zakkai from Jerusalem, see Schalit (1975) and Schäfer (1979).

3. On Stoicism as a guide to the art of living, see Rist (1969), Rutherford (1989), and Hadot (1998).

4. Among biblical texts which teach the virtue of passive acceptance and faith, see Psalms 116:15, Lamentations 3:27, Proverbs 16:32, and Job 42:1–6.

5. Rabbinic texts which blame the Jews for their defeats include: *Gittin* 55b–56a, *Yoma* 9b, *Shabbat* 119b, and *Bava Metzia* 30b.

6. On textual parallels between Stoicism and Jewish literature, see Bacher (1903), Krauss (1910), Bergmann (1912), Kaminka (1926), Daube (1949), Baer (1955), Fischel (1973), Urbach (1975), Seltzer (1980), Wasserstein (1994), and Gruen (2002).

7. The first possible allusion to Marcus Aurelius' *Meditations* is by Themistius in 364 CE.

5 Secular Hebrew Poetry in Muslim Spain 1031–1140

1. Bilingual selections of medieval Hebrew poetry include Carmi (1981) and Scheindlin (1986, 1991). For a brief but comprehensive introduction to medieval Hebrew poetry by an important modern Hebrew poet, see Pagis (1971). Also, see Goldstein (1971) and Stillman (1979). Texts are taken mostly from Schirmann (1959). On the artistic problems of being a Hebrew poet in Muslim Spain, see Brann (1991).

2. From a sociological viewpoint, Spain was unique in a number of other ways: in having been a Roman province, then later an undifferentiated province of Western Christianity, and in having undergone Germanic conquest, with the result that "Even the Christians displayed a degree of assimilation that is scarcely paralleled in the east" (Crone and Cook 1977, p. 115).

3. "Abd ar-Rahman III's Umayyad predecessors repeatedly sought to exert Cordoba's centralizing authority over a territory and population torn by numerous tribal, ethnic, and social cleavages, socio-economic and religious struggles, and factional rivalries: Arabs battled with Berbers, Syrian Arabs quarreled with Yemenis, and Arab Muslims competed with native Iberian neo-Muslims and their descendants (Ar. *muwalladun*). The *saqaliaba* or 'Slavs', praetorian guards of diverse European origin, brought to Spain as slaves at a young age, were involved in revolts against Umayyad authority as well as Mozarabic Christians, not without considerable ambivalence, occasionally resisted the idea of living with an Islamic polity. Under such complex and unpredictably shifting political circumstances, it is easy to appreciate why the Jewish community, which had no stake in the various internecine disputes among Muslims and which could be neither accused of harbouring a subversive allegiance to any sovereign power nor suspected of entertaining an obligation to any anti-Umayyad cause, might have warranted the trust of the Umayyads" (Brann 1991, p. 4). The diversity in Muslim Spain was, at the same time, part of the wider unified Islamic empire: "It is precisely this pattern of regional disjunction within a broader context of fundamental social unity, as part of the universal society of Islam, which marks Iberian Islam from start to finish" (Wasserstein 1985, p. 294).

4. The translation of this and the other Arabic verse quoted next has been revised by David Aberbach.

5. For a more detailed and convincing argument that the most original Arabic poetry was written in its earliest phase, in the ninth to eleventh centuries, see Giffen (1971).

6. *Malkah resha'ah* (Evil queen, i.e. Christian Spain) is apparently a play on *malkhut resha'ah* (evil kingdom) which in the Talmud (e.g. *Berakhot* 61b) describes Rome. The collected poems of Hanagid are edited by Jarden (1966). For a bilingual edition of Gabirol's poetry by Hillel Halkin, see Gabirol (2000).

7. The imagery and language here owe much to the Book of Nahum. See p. 13 above.

8. Jarden (1975, p. 33). Schirmann (1959, I 231) has *lihyot* (to be) rather than *liḥyot* (to live).

9. Schirmann (1959, p. 202) dates this poem 1039–40.
10. Schirmann (*ibid.*, p. 243) notes the biblical references in this poem: Genesis 16:12; 21:17; Psalms 80:14 with its gloss in *Lev. Rab.* 13, "The pig is Edom" (i.e. Rome).
11. For a literary study of Ibn Ezra's poetry, see Pagis (1970).
12. See, for example, Schirmann (1959, pp. 386, 460), where Halevi describes Andalusia in biblical language reminiscent of his poems of Zion. Halevi's hope that messianic redemption from what he describes as arrogant and oppressive Muslim rule would occur in 1130 is expressed in the poem beginning *Namta ve-nirdamta* (*ibid.*, p. 480).

6 The Baal Shem Tov, Mystical Union, and Individualism

1. This work includes substantial bibliography on grief and on mysticism.
2. Also see the chapter on *devekut* in Scholem (1971), reprinted in Hundert (1991). For a disccussion, with illustrations, of *devekut* as practised by the Besht, see A. Rapoport-Albert, "God and the Zaddik," in Hundert (*ibid.*), pp. 299–329. A survey of the varieties of *devekut* in Jewish mysticism is given by Idel (1988). On the character of Hasidic prayer, see Jacobs (1972); and for a general introduction to Hasidic theology and sources pertaining to the Besht's life and work, see Dan (1983).
3. The entire text of the letter is reprinted in English translation by Jacobs (1977).
4. See Etkes (1988); and Rosman (1987), reprinted in English translation in Hundert, (1991, pp. 209–25). For a discussion, with bibliography, of the social and political forces underlying Hasidism, see the articles by Dubnow, Dinur and Ettinger in Hundert (ed.) *ibid.*, as well as Scholem (1971) and Weiss (1985).
5. The idea of charisma as a reflection of an intersection between external social and political reality and personal inner fantasy is developed by Aberbach (1993b, 1995).
6. Poe's *Eureka* reflects similar mystical tendencies. See pp. 26–7.
7. On grief and semi-mystical union in the writings of Donne, Wordsworth, Byron, Bialik, Masefield, Sartre, and others who experienced severe bereavement in childhood, see Aberbach (1989). For further illustrations in Bialik and Wordsworth, see Aberbach (1982).

7 Marx and Freud: Emancipation and the End of Rabbinic Dominance

1. See, for example, Aron (1956–57), Simon (1957), Grollman (1965), Berkower (1969), Lowenberg (1971), Gordis (1975), Vogel (1975), Gay (1987), who, however insightful, for the most part draw on the same limited sources. For further bibliography on Freud and Judaism, see Miller (1981).
2. On Freud and the crisis of Jewish adaptation to modern life, see, among others, Heer (1972), Cuddihy (1974), Gay (1987), and Blatt (1988).
3. For full-length interpretations of Judaism and its possible effects on psychoanalysis, see Robert (1976) and Klein (1985).

4. On the generation gap between Jewish fathers and their children as a factor in the development of psychoanalysis, see Robert (1976) and Aberbach (1980).
5. On Freud's Zionist sympathies, see Loewenberg (1970) and Falk (1978).
6. On Freud and Moses, see Bergman (1976), Handelman (1982), Rice (1990), and Yerushalmi (1991).

8 Conflicting Images of Hebrew in Western Civilization

1. On the transition from the Haskalah to Zionism as reflected in Hebrew literature, see Chapter 9.
2. The effects of the Roman–Jewish wars on Jewish identity are discussed in Chapter 3.
3. On the status of scholars in traditional Jewish society, see Zborowski and Herzog (1969). Also see pp. 58, 66, 121.
4. For a comprehensive dictionary of biblical motifs in English literature, see Jeffrey (1992); broad selections of English literature influenced by the Bible are given by Jasper and Prickett (1999) and Atwan and Wieder (2000).
5. On Marx's remarks on the influence of the prophets on the English Revolution in *The Eighteenth Brumaire of Louis Napoleon* (1852), see pp. 118–19 above.

9 The Renascence of Hebrew and Jewish Nationalism in the Tsarist Empire 1881–1917

1. Mostly because it asserted Jewish national distinctiveness, Hebrew was banned under Soviet rule; and it is highly significant that many leading Soviet dissidents in the 1970s and 1980s, such as Scharansky, were teachers and students of Hebrew.
2. On Mendele and his milieu, with literary and historical bibliography, see Aberbach (1993). The most comprehensive recent history of Hebrew literature of the period 1881–1917 is Shaked's (1977).
3. On Ahad Ha'am's rivalry with Herzl, see Zipperstein (1993).
4. Only one other major Hebrew writer – Agnon – followed Mendele in this ambivalent, satiric mode of depiction of European Jews, which became the essence of his style (Aberbach 1984). But in contrast with Mendele a generation earlier, Agnon was totally committed to Zionism, and he wrote most of his works in Jerusalem.
5. Gogol's claim to love Russia seems to have been true for the most part when he was out of the country (which he was while writing *Dead Souls*). When he lived in Russia, he appears to have despised it (Maguire 1994, pp. 176–7).

Bibliography

Aberbach, David (1980) "Freud's Jewish Problem." *Commentary* 69, 6: 35–9.

Aberbach, David (1982) "Loss and Separation in Bialik and Wordsworth." *Prooftexts* 2, 2: 197–208.

Aberbach, David (1983) "Screen Memories of Writers." *International Review of Psycho-Analysis* 10, 1: 47–62.

Aberbach, David (1984a) *At the Handles of the Lock: Themes in the Fiction of S.J. Agnon.* Oxford University Press: The Littman Library.

Aberbach, David (1984b) "Childlessness and the Waste land in Bialik and T.S. Eliot." *Hebrew Union College Annual* 55: 283–307.

Aberbach, David (1988) *Bialik.* London: Peter Halban; New York: Grove Press.

Aberbach, David (1989) *Surviving Trauma: Loss, Literature and Psychoanalysis.* New Haven and London: Yale University Press.

Aberbach, David (1993a) *Realism, Caricature and Bias: The Fiction of Mendele Mocher Sefarim.* Oxford: The Littman Library.

Aberbach, David (1993b) "Grief and Mystical Union: The Baal Shem Tov and Krishnamurti." *Harvard Theological Review* 86, 3: 309–21.

Aberbach, David (1993c) *Imperialism and Biblical Prophecy 75–500 BCE.* London: Routledge.

Aberbach, David (1993d) " 'Infidel Jew': Freud, Jewish Ritual and Psychoanalysis." In L. Spurling (ed.) *From the Words of my Mouth: Tradition in Psychotherapy.* London and New York: Tavistock/Routledge.

Aberbach, David (1995) "Charisma and Attachment Theory." *International Journal of Psycho-Analysis* 76, 4: 845–55.

Aberbach, David (1996) *Charisma in Politics, Religion and the Media: Private Trauma, Public Ideals.* London: Macmillan; New York: New York University Press.

Aberbach, David (1997) "Hebrew Literature and Jewish Nationalism in Tsarist Russia 1881–1917." *Nations and Nationalism* 3, 1: 25–44.

Aberbach, David (1998) *Revolutionary Hebrew, Empire and Crisis.* London: Macmillan; New York: New York University Press.

Aberbach, David (2001) "Mendele's 'Shelter from the Storm.' " *Jewish Quarterly* 48, 3 (183): 6–10.

Aberbach, David (2002) "The Village and I: Chapter 1 of Bialik's *Safiah.*" *Jewish Quarterly* 49, 3 (187): 61–6.

Aberbach, Moshe and Aberbach, David (2000) *The Roman–Jewish Wars and Hebrew Cultural Nationalism.* Basingstoke: Macmillan; New York: St. Martin's Press.

Aberbach, Moses (1966) *The Roman–Jewish War 66–70 CE.* London: R. Golub and The Jewish Quarterly.

Abraham, H.C. and Freud, E. (eds) (1965) *A Psychoanalytic Dialogue: The Letters of Sigmund Freud and Karl Abraham, 1907–1926.* London: Hogarth.

Abrams, M.H. (ed.) (1972) *Wordsworth: A Collection of Critical Essays.* Englewood Cliffs, NJ: Prentice Hall, Inc.

Agnon, S.Y. (1970) *Twenty-One Stories*. N. Glatzer (ed.). New York: Schocken Books.

Albright, W.F. (1957) *From the Stone Age to Christianity*. Baltimore: Johns Hopkins University Press.

Alexander, Philip S. (1992) "The Origins of Religious and Racial Anti-Semitism and the Jewish Response." In D. Englander (ed.) *The Jewish Enigma: An Enduring People*. Milton Keynes: The Open University; London: Peter Halban.

Allen, Woody (1990) *Three Films of Woody Allen*. London and Boston: Faber & Faber.

Alter, Robert (1988) *The Invention of Hebrew Prose: Modern Fiction and the Language of Realism*. Seattle: University of Washington Press.

Amichai, Yehuda (1975) *Akhshav ba-Ra'ash* [Poems in Hebrew]. Tel Aviv: Schocken.

Anderson, Benedict (1983) *Imagined Communities*, London: Verso.

Ansky, S. (1992) *The Dybbuk and Other Writings*. (ed.) D. Roskies. Tr. G. Werman *et al.* New York: Schocken Books.

Arberry, A.J. (1965) *Arabic Poetry: A Primer for Students*. Cambridge University Press.

Armstrong, John (1982) *Nations Before Nationalism*. Chapel Hill: University of North Carolina Press.

Aron, W. (1956–57) "Notes on Sigmund Freud's Ancestry and Jewish Contacts." *YIVO Annual of Jewish Social Science* 11: 286–95.

Ashtor, Eliyahu (1973, 1979, 1984) *The Jews of Moslem Spain*. 3 vols. Tr. from the Hebrew by A. Klein and J.M. Klein. Philadelphia: Jewish Publication Society.

Asmis, Elizabeth (1986) "The Stoicism of Marcus Aurelius." *ANRW* II 36, 3: 2228–52.

Atwan, Robert and Wieder, Laurance (eds) (2000) *Chapters into Verse: A Selection of Poetry in English Inspired by the Bible from Genesis through Revelation*. Oxford University Press.

Atwood, G. (1983) "The Pursuit of Being in the Life and Thought of Jean-Paul Sartre." *Psychoanalytic Review* 70, II: 143–62.

Aune, David C. (1994) "Mastery of the Passions: Philo, 4 Maccabees and Earliest Christianity." In Wendy C. Helleman (ed.) *Hellenization Revisited: Shaping a Christian Response within the Greco-Roman World*. Lanham MD, New York and London: University Press of America, pp. 125–58.

Aurelius, Marcus (1964) *Meditations*. Tr. M. Staniforth. Harmondsworth, Middlesex: Penguin Books.

Avi-Yonah, Michael (1976) *The Jews of Palestine: A Political History from the Bar-Kokhba War to the Arab Conquest*. Oxford: Basil Blackwell.

Bacher, Wilhelm (1903) *Die Agada der Tannaiten*. Strassburg: Trubner.

Baer, Yitzhak (1955) *Israel Among the Nations* (Hebrew), Jerusalem: Mossad Bialik.

Balbry, H.C. (1965) *The Unity of Mankind in Greek Thought*. Oxford University Press.

Baron, Salo (1952–) *A Social and Religious History of the Jews*. 18 vols. New York: Columbia University Press.

Baron, Salo (1971) "Population, Second Commonwealth." *Encyclopedia Judaica* 13: 870–2.

Barraclough, R. (1984) "Philo's Politics, Roman Rule and Hellenistic Judaism." *ANRW* II 21, W. Haase (ed.). Berlin and New York: Walter de Gruyter, pp. 417–553.

Beard, Mary, North, John, and Price, Simon (eds) (1998) *Religions of Rome. Vol. 1: A History.* Cambridge University Press.

Beckett, J.C. (1976) *The Anglo-Irish Tradition.* Dundonald, Belfast: Blackstaff.

Belinsky, Vissarion (1981) *Selected Philosophical Works.* Westport, Connecticut: Hyperion Press.

Bellow, Saul (1976; orig. 1964) *Herzog.* London: Penguin Books.

Ben-Amos, Dan, and Mintz, Jerome R., eds & trs (1970) *In Praise of the Baal Shem Tov: the Earliest Collection of Legends about the Founder of Hasidism* [*Shivhei ha-Besht*]. Bloomington, Indiana: Indiana University Press.

Ben Shalom, Israel (1993) *The School of Shammai and the Zealot Struggle against Rome* [Hebrew]. Jerusalem: Yad Itzhak Ben-Zui.

Berdichevsky, M.J. (1969) *Selected Stories* [Hebrew]. Tel Aviv: Dvir.

Bergman, M.S. (1976) "Moses and the Evolution of Freud's Jewish Identity." *The Israel Annals of Psychiatry and Related Disciplines* 14: 3–26.

Bergmann, Judah (1912) "Die stoische Philosophie und die judische Frommigkeit." In I. Elbogen *et al.* (eds) *Judaica (Festschrift Hermann Cohen).* Berlin: Cassire.

Berkower, L. (1969) "The Enduring Effect of the Jewish Tradition Upon Freud." *American Journal of Psychiatry* 125: 1067–73.

Berlin, Isaiah (1979) "Benjamin Disraeli, Karl Marx and the Search for Identity" (1970), in *Against the Current: Essays on the History of Ideas.* Oxford: Clarendon Press.

Bettelheim, Bruno (1979) *Surviving and Other Essays.* London: Thames & Hudson.

Bialik, C.N. (1965) *Selected Poems of Hayyim Nahman Bialik.* I. Efros (ed.). New York: Bloch.

Bialik, C.N. (1999; orig. 1903–23) *Random Harvest: The Novellas of Bialik.* Tr. D. Patterson and E. Spicehandler. Boulder, Colorado: Westview Press.

Bialik, C.N. and Ravnitsky, J.H. (eds) (1992; orig. 1908–11) *The Book of Legends.* Tr. W.G. Braude. New York: Schocken.

Blatt, D.S. (1988) "The Development of the Hero: Sigmund Freud and the Reformation of the Jewish Tradition." *Psychoanalysis and Contemporary Thought* 11: 639–703.

Boulton, W.F. (ed.) (1966) *The English Language: Essays by English and American Men of Letters 1490–1839.* Cambridge University Press.

Bowlby, John (1980) *Loss: Sadness and Depression.* Vol. 3 of *Attachment and Loss.* London: The Hogarth Press and The Institute of Psycho-Analysis.

Boyce, Mary (1984) "Persian Religion in the Achemid Age." In W.D. Davies and L. Finkelstein (eds) *The Cambridge History of Judaism*, vol. 1, *The Persian Period.* Cambridge: Cambridge University Press.

Brann, Ross (1991) *The Compunctious Poet: Cultural Ambiguity and Hebrew Poetry in Muslim Spain.* Baltimore and London: Johns Hopkins University Press.

Brenner, J.H. (1955, 1960, 1967) *Collected Works* [Hebrew]. 3 vols. Tel Aviv: Ha-Kibbutz Hame'uchad.

Bright, John (1960) *A History of Israel.* London: SCM Press.

Bright, John, (ed. & tr.) (1965) *Jeremiah*, The Anchor Bible, vol. 21. Garden City, New York: Doubleday & Co.

Brink, Andrew (1977) *Loss and Symbolic Repair: A Psychological Study of Some English Poets.* Hamilton, Ontario: The Cromlech Press.

Bronte, Emily (1989; orig. 1847) Wuthering Heights. New York/London: Norton.

Brown, Peter (1973) *The World of Late Antiquity*. New York: Harcourt Brace Jovanovich.

Brown, Terence (1981) *Ireland: A Social and Cultural History, 1922–79*. London: Fontana.

Brunt, P.A. (1977) "Josephus on Social Conflicts in Roman Judaea." *Klio*: 149–53.

Buber, Martin (1964; orig. 1913) *Daniel: Dialogues of Realization*. Tr. M. Friedman. New York: Holt, Rinehart & Winston.

Buber, Martin (1970; orig. 1923) *I and Thou*. Tr. W. Kaufmann. Edinburgh: T. & T. Clark.

Buber, Martin (1973) *Meetings*. (ed.) M. Friedman. La Salle, Illinois: Court.

Carlebach, Julius (1978) *Karl Marx and the Radical Critique of Judaism*. London: Routledge & Kegan Paul.

Carmi, T. (ed.) (1981) *The Penguin Book of Hebrew Verse*. New York: Viking; Harmondsworth, Middlesex: Penguin Books.

Chadwick, Henry (1999) "Philosophical Tradition and the Self." In G.W. Bowersock, Peter Brown, and Oleg Grabar (eds) *Late Antiquity: A Guide to the Postclassical World*. Cambridge, Massachusetts and London, England: The Belknap Press of Harvard University Press.

Chekhov, Anton (1978; orig. 1904) *The Cherry Orchard*. Tr. M. Frayn. London: Methuen.

Clare, John (1984) *John Clare*. In E. Robinson and D. Powell (eds) *The Oxford Authors*. Oxford University Press.

Cohen, Shaye J.D. (1992) "The Place of the Rabbi in Jewish Society of the Second Century." In L.I. Levine (ed.) *The Galilee in Late Antiquity*. New York and Jerusalem: Jewish Theological Seminary of America.

Cohn, Norman (1993) *Cosmos, Chaos and the World to Come: The Ancient Roots of Apocalyptic Faith*. New Haven and London: Yale University Press.

Coleridge, Samuel Taylor (1975; orig. 1817) *Biographia Literaria: or Biographical sketches of my Literary Life and Opinions*. (ed.) G. Watson. London: Dent; New York: E.P. Dutton.

Colish, Marcia L. (1985) *The Stoic Tradition from Antiquity to the Early Middle Ages*. London: E.J. Brill.

Crone, Patricia and Michael Cook (1977) *Hagarism: The Making of the Islamic World*. Cambridge University Press.

Cuddihy, J.M. (1974) *The Ordeal of Civility: Freud, Marx, Levi-Strauss, and the Jewish Struggle with Modernity*. New York: Basic Books.

Cullingford, Elisabeth (1981) *Yeats, Ireland and Fascism*. London: Macmillan.

Curtis, E.M. (1992) "Idols and Idolatry." In D.N. Freedman (ed.) *The Anchor Bible Dictionary*. New York: Doubleday, 3: 376–81.

Daiches, David (1997; orig. 1956) *Two Worlds: An Edinburgh Jewish Childhood*. Edinburgh: Canongate Books.

Dan, Joseph (ed.) (1983) *The Teachings of Hasidism*. New York: Behrman House.

Daube, David (1949) "Rabbinic Methods of Interpretation and Hellenistic Rhetoric." In C. Carmichael (ed.) *Collected Works of David Daube*, vol. 1 (1992): *Talmudic Law*. Berkeley: Robbins Collection Publication, University of California.

Davidson, Israel (1966; orig. 1907) *Parody in Jewish Literature*. New York: AMS Press.

De Quincey, Thomas (1966) *Confessions of an English Opium Eater and Other Writings*. New York: Signet.

Descartes, René (1970; orig. 1911) *The Philosophical Works of Descartes*. 2 vols. Tr. E.S. Haldane and G.R.T. Ross. Cambridge: Cambridge University Press.

Deutsch, Karl (1966) *Nationalism and Social Communication*. New York: MIT Press.

Diamond, John (2001) *Snake Oil and Other Preoccupations*. New York: Vintage.

Dickens, A.G. (1970; orig. 1964) *The English Reformation*. London: Collins, The Fontana Library.

Dostoyevsky, Fyodor (1952; orig. 1871–72) *The Possessed (The Devils)*. 2 vols. Tr. C. Garnett. London: Dent.

Dostoyevsky, Fyodor (1975; orig. 1865–66) *Crime and Punishment*. Tr. D. Magarshak. Harmondsworth, Middlesex: Penguin.

Dostoyevsky, Fyodor (1976; orig. 1880) *The Brothers Karamazov*. Tr. C. Garnett, rev. and edited by R.F. Matelow. New York: W.W. Norton & Co.

Dostoyevsky, Fyodor (1987) *Selected Letters*. (eds) J. Frank and D.I. Goldstein. Tr. A.R. MacAndrew. New Brunswick, NJ, and London: Routledge.

Dostoyevsky, Fyodor (1995; orig. 1860) *The House of the Dead*. Tr. D. McDuff. Harmondsworth, Middlesex: Penguin.

Duff, A.M. (1958) *Freedmen in the Early Roman Empire*. Cambridge: W. Heffer & Sons, Ltd.

Dyer, A.R. (1986) "Descartes: Notes on the Origins of Scientific Thinking." *The Annual of Psychoanalysis* 14: 163–76.

Edwards, Ruth Dudley (1977) *Patrick Pearse: The Triumph of Failure*. London: Gollancz.

Ellmann, Richard (1966) *James Joyce*. Oxford: Oxford University Press.

Ellmann, Richard (1969) *Yeats: The Man and the Masks*. London: Faber.

Elon, Amos (1975) *Herzl*. London: Weidenfeld & Nicolson.

Elton, G.R. (1971; orig. 1963) *Reformation Europe 1517–1559*. London and Glasgow: Collins.

The Epic of Gilgamesh (1960) Tr. N.K. Sanders. Harmondsworth: Penguin.

Epstein, Isidor (1959) *Judaism: A Historical Presentation*. Harmondsworth, Middlesex: Pelican.

Erikson, Erik (1963) *Childhood and Society*. New York: Norton.

Erikson, Erik (1974) *Identity: Youth and Crisis*. London: Faber.

Etkes, Emanuel (1988) "Hasidism as a Movement: The First Stage." In B. Safran (ed.) *Hasidism: Continuity or Innovation*? Cambridge, MA: Harvard University Press, 1–26.

Even-Shoshan, Avraham (1983) *Modern Hebrew Dictionary* [Hebrew] 3 vols. Jerusalem: Kiryath Sepher.

Ezra, Moses Ibn (1934, 1942, 1977) *Shire ha-Hol* (Secular Poems), vol. I, (ed.) H. Brody. Berlin and Jerusalem: Schocken; vol. II, (ed.) H. Brody, Jerusalem: Schocken; vol. III, (ed.) D. Pagis. Jerusalem: Schocken.

Falk, A. (1978) "Freud and Herzl." *Contemporary Psychoanalysis* 14: 357–87.

Feierberg, M.Z. (1973) *Whither? and Other Stories*. Tr. H. Halkin. Philadelphia: Jewish Publication Society of America.

Feldman, Louis H. (1993) *Jew and Gentile in the Ancient World: Attitudes and Interaction from Alexander to Justinian*. Princeton, New Jersey: Princeton University Press.

Feldman, Louis H. (1996) *Studies in Hellenistic Judaism*. Leiden: E.J. Brill.

Feuer, L. (1963) "The Dreams of Descartes." *American Imago* 20: 3–26.

Fisch, Harold (1964) *Jerusalem and Albion: The Hebraic Factor in Seventeenth-Century Literature*. New York: Schocken Books.

Fischel, Henry A. (1969) "Story and History: Observations on Greco-Roman Rhetoric and Pharasaism." In Denis Sinor (ed.) American Oriental Society, Middle West Branch, Semi-Centennial Volume. Bloomington and London: Indiana University Press: 59–88.

Fischel, Henry A. (1971) "Spiritual Resistance." *Encyclopedia Judaica* 8: 301–3, s.v. "Hellenism."

Fischel, Henry A. (1973) *Rabbinic Literature and Greco-Roman Philosophy.* Leiden: E.J. Brill.

Foster, R.B. (1997) *W. B. Yeats. A life: The Apprentice Mage 1865–1914.* Oxford: Oxford University Press.

Fox, Robin Lane (1986) *Pagans and Christians.* Harmondsworth, Middlesex: Penguin Books.

Frankel, Jonathan (1981) *Prophecy and Politics: Socialism, Nationalism, and the Jews, 1862–1917.* Cambridge: Cambridge University Press.

Freud, E.L. (ed.) (1960). *The Letters of Sigmund Freud.* Tr. T. and J. Stern. New York: Basic Books.

Freud, Martin (1957) *Glory Reflected.* London: Angus & Robertson.

Freud, Sigmund (1899)* *The Interpretation of Dreams.* SE IV, V.

Freud, Sigmund (1907) "Obsessive Acts and Religious Practises." SE IX 117–27.

Freud, Sigmund (1914) "The Moses of Michelangelo." SE XIII 211–36.

Freud, Sigmund (1921) "Group Psychology and the Analysis of the Ego." SE XVIII 67–143.

Freud, Sigmund (1926) "Address to the Society of B'nai Brith." SE XX 273–4.

Freud, Sigmund (1927) *The Future of an Illusion.* SE XXI 5–56.

Freud, Sigmund (1939) *Moses and Monotheism.* SE XXIII 7–137.

Frieden, Ken (1990) *Freud's Dream of Interpretation.* Albany: State University of New York Press.

Friedman, Maurice (1981) *Martin Buber's Life and Works.* 3 vols. New York: Dutton.

Fuller, William C. (1985) *Civil–Military Conflict in Imperial Russia 1881–1914.* Princeton, NJ: Princeton University Press.

Furman, Erna (1974) *A Child's Parent Dies: Studies in Childhood Bereavement.* New Haven and London: Yale University Press.

Gager, John G. (1983) *The Origins of Anti-Semitism: Attitudes toward Judaism in Pagan and Christian Antiquity.* New York and Oxford: Oxford University Press.

Garvin, Tom (1987) *Nationalist Revolutionaries in Ireland 1858–1928.* Oxford: Clarendon.

Gay, Peter (1987) *A Godless Jew: Freud, Theism and the Making of Psychoanalysis.* New Haven: Yale University Press.

Gay, Peter (1988) *Freud: A Life for Our Time.* New York: Norton.

Gedo, J.E. (1978) "Nietzsche and the Psychology of Genius." *American Imago* XXXV, 1–2: 77–91.

Gellner, Ernest (1964) *Nations and Nationalism.* Oxford: Blackwell.

Giffen, Lois Anita (1971) *Theory of Profane Love Among the Arabs: The Development of the Genre.* New York: New York University Press; London: London University Press.

* The abbreviation SE denotes *The Standard Edition of The Complete Works of Sigmund Freud,* translated by J. Strachey and published in 24 volumes by The Hogarth Press Ltd., London, and distributed in America by W.W. Norton, New York.

Glick, Thomas (1979) *Islamic and Christian Spain in the Early Middle Ages*. Princeton: Princeton University Press.

Gogol, Nikolai (1976; orig. 1842) *Dead Souls*. Tr. D. Magarshak. Harmondsworth, Middlesex: Penguin.

Goldmann, Lucien (1964; orig. 1956) *The Hidden God: A Study of Tragic Vision in the Pensees of Pascal and the Tragedies of Racine*. Tr. P. Thody. London: Routledge & Kegan Paul.

Goldstein, David (1971) *The Jewish Poets of Spain*. Harmondsworth, Middlesex: Penguin Classics.

Goldstein, David I. (1981; orig. 1976) *Dostoyevsky and the Jews*. Austin, Texas, and London: University of Texas Press.

Goodman, Martin (1983) *State and Society in Roman Galilee*, A.D. 132–212. Totowa, New Jersey: Rowman & Allanheld.

Goodman, Martin (1987) *The Ruling Class of Judaea: The Origins of the Jewish Revolt Against Rome* A.D. 66–70. Cambridge University Press.

Goodman, Martin (1996) "Judaea." In A.K. Bowman, E. Champlin, and A. Lintott (eds) *Cambridge Ancient History* vol. X, 2nd edn. *The Augustan Empire, 43 B.C.–A.D. 69*. Cambridge University Press.

Goodman, Martin (1997) *The Roman World 44 BC–AD 180*. London and New York: Routledge.

Gordis, Robert (1975). "The Two Faces of Freud." *Judaism* 24: 194–200.

Grant, Michael (1971) *Herod the Great*. New York: American Heritage Press.

Griffin, Miriam (2000) "Seneca and Pliny." In C. Rowe *et al.* (eds) *The Cambridge History of Greek and Roman Thought*. Cambridge University Press, pp. 532–58.

Grollman, E.A. (1965) *Judaism in Sigmund Freud's World*. New York: Appleton-Century.

Gross, John (2001) *A Double Thread: A Childhood in Mile End – and beyond*. London: Chatto & Windus.

Gruen, Erich S. (1998) *Heritage and Hellenism: The Reinvention of Jewish Tradition*. Hellenistic Culture and Society 30. Berkeley: University of California Press.

Gruen, Erich S. (2002) *Diaspora: Jews Amidst Greeks and Romans*. Cambridge, MA, and London: Harvard University Press.

Haberer, Erich E. (1995) *Jews and Revolution in Nineteenth-Century Russia*. Cambridge University Press.

Haddad, G. (1981) *L'enfant illegitime: Sources talmidiques de la psychoanalyse*. Paris: Hachette.

Hadot, Pierre (1998) *The Inner Citadel: The Meditations of Marcus Aurelius*. Cambridge, Massachusetts and London, England: Harvard University Press.

Halkin, Simon (1950) *Modern Hebrew Literature*. New York: Schocken Books.

Hall, John (1979) *The Sociology of Literature*. London and New York: Longman.

Hanagid, Shmuel (2000) *Grand Things to Write a Poem on: A Verse Autobiography of Shmuel Hanagid*. Ed. & tr. H. Halkin. Jerusalem and New York: Gefen Books.

Handelman, S.A. (1982) *The Slaying of Moses: The Emergence of Rabbinic Interpretation in Modern Literary Theory*. Albany: State University of New York.

Hastings, Adrian (1997) *The Construction of Nationhood: Ethnicity, Religion and Nationalism*. Cambridge University Press.

Hayes, J.H. and Miller, J.M. (1986) *A History of Ancient Israel and Judah*. London: SCM Press.

Heer, F. (1972). "Freud, the Viennese Jew." In J. Miller (ed.) *Freud: The Man, his World, his Influence*. London: Weidenfeld.

Heller, J.B. (1956) "Freud's Mother and Father." *Commentary* 21, 5: 418–21.

Hengel, Martin (1981; orig. 1973) *Judaism and Hellenism: Studies in their Encounter in Palestine During the Early Hellenistic Period*. 2 vols. Tr. J. Bowden. London: SCM Press.

Herr, Moshe David (1968) "The Meeting of Greece and Israel." In "Greek Language and Culture" (Hebrew), *Encyclopedia Hebraica* 19: 624–7.

Hertzberg, Arthur (1968; orig. 1959) *The French Enlightenment and the Jews*. New York: Columbia University Press.

Hobsbawm, Eric J. (1990) *Nations and Nationalism since 1780*. London: Clarendon.

Hobsbawm, Eric J. (1997; orig. 1975) *The Age of Capitalism 1848–1875*. London: Abacus.

Hourani, Albert (1991) *A History of the Arab Peoples*. London: Faber.

Hundert, Gershon D. (ed.) (1991) *Essential Papers on Hasidism: Origins to Present*. New York: New York University Press.

Hutchinson, John (1987) *The Dynamics of Cultural Nationalism*. London: Allen & Unwin.

Hutchinson, John (1994) *Modern Nationalism*. London: Fontana.

Idel, Moshe (1988) *Kabbalah: New Perspectives*. New Haven and London: Yale University Press.

Ignatieff, Michael (1998) *Isaiah Berlin: A Life*. London: Penguin Books.

Inwood, Brad, and Donini, Pierluigi (1999) "Stoic ethics." In K. Algra *et al.* (eds) *The Cambridge History of Hellenistic Philosophy*. Cambridge University Press: 675–738.

Jacobs, Louis (1972) *Hasidic Prayer*. London: Routledge & Kegan Paul.

Jacobs, Louis (1977) *Jewish Mystical Testimonies*. New York: Schocken Books.

Jacobs, Louis (1989) *Helping with Inquiries: An Autobiography*. London: Valentine, Mitchell.

Jacobson, Dan (1977) *Through the Wilderness: Selected Stories*. Harmondsworth, Middlesex: Penguin Books.

Jacobson, Dan (1985) *Time and Time Again*. London: Andre Deutsch.

Jarden, Dov (ed.) (1966) *Divan Shmuel Hanagid* (Hebrew). Jerusalem: Hebrew Union College Press.

Jarden, Dov (ed.) (1975) *The Secular Poetry of Rabbi Solomon Ibn Gabirol* (Hebrew). Jerusalem: Kiryat Noar.

Jasper, David, and Prickett, Stephen (eds) (1999) *The Bible and Literature: A Reader*. Oxford: Blackwell.

Jeffrey, David Lyle (1992) *A Dictionary of Biblical Tradition in English Literature*. Grand Rapids, Michigan: William Eerdmans Publishing Company.

Jenkyns, Richard (ed.) (1992) *The Legacy of Rome*. Oxford: Oxford University Press.

Johnson, Paul (1994; orig. 1987) *A History of the Jews*. London: Phoenix.

Jones, Arnold H.M. (1938) *The Herods of Judaea*. Oxford University Press.

Jones, Ernest (1953–57) *Sigmund Freud: Life and Work*. 3 vols. New York: Basic Books.

Joyce, James (1973; orig. 1922) *Ulysses*. Harmondsworth, Middlesex: Penguin Books.

Kafka, Franz (1978) *Wedding Preparations in the Country and Other Stories.* Tr. E. Kaiser, E. Wilkins, *et al.* Harmondsworth, Middlesex: Penguin Books.

Kaminka, Armand (ed. & tr.) (1923) *Marcus Aurelius' Meditations* (Hebrew). Warsaw: Stybel.

Kaminka, Armand (1926) "Les rapports entre le rabbinisme et la philosophie stoicienne." *Revue des Eudes Juives* 82: 233–52.

Katz, Jacob (1980) *From Prejudice to Destruction: Anti-Semitism 1700–1933.* Cambridge, MA: Harvard University Press.

Kaufmann, Yehezkel (1960). *The Religion of Israel.* Tr. & abridged by M. Greenberg. London: Allen & Unwin.

Kaufmann, Yehezkel (1970) *History of the Religion of Israel,* vol. IV, *The Babylonian Captivity and Deutero-Isaiah.* Tr. M. Greenberg. New York: Union of American Hebrew Congregations.

Kedourie, Elie (1960) *Nationalism.* London: Hutchinson.

Kermode, Frank (ed.) (1965) *Spenser.* Oxford University Press.

Kiberd, Declan (1995) *Inventing Ireland: The Literature of the Modern Nation.* London: Cape.

Kidd, I.G. (1978) "Moral Actions and Rules in Stoic Ethics." In J.M. Rist (ed.) *The Stoics.* Berkeley and Los Angeles: University of California Press.

Klein, D. (1985) *Jewish Origins of the Psychoanalytic Movement.* Chicago: The University of Chicago Press.

Klier, John (1995) *Imperial Russia's Jewish Question, 1855–1881.* Cambridge: Cambridge University Press.

Klier, John, and Lambroza, Shlomo (eds) (1992) *Pogroms: Anti-Jewish Violence in Modern Russian History.* Cambridge University Press.

Koestler, Arthur (1964) *The Act of Creation.* London: Hutchinson.

Kohn, Hans (1946) *The Idea of Nationalism.* New York: Macmillan.

Kraemer, David Charles (1995) *Responses to Suffering in Classical Rabbinic Literature.* New York: Oxford University Press.

Krauss, Samuel (1910) *Antoninus und Rabbi.* Frankfurt: Sanger & Friedberg.

Krupp, G.R. (1965) "Identification as a Defence against Anxiety in Coping with Loss." *International Journal of Psychoanalysis,* 46: 303–14.

Laing, R.D. (1969) *The Divided Self.* Harmondsworth, Middlesex: Pelican Books.

Lange, Nicholas de (1987) *Judaism.* Oxford University Press.

Lange, Nicholas de (1991) "The Origins of Anti-Semitism: Ancient Evidence and Modern Interpretation." In Sander L. Gilman and Steven T. Katz (eds) *Anti-Semitism in Times of Crisis.* New York and London: New York University Press: 21–37.

Langer, S. (1951) *Philosophy in a New Key.* Oxford University Press.

Lawrence, D.H. (1972) *The Complete Poems of D.H. Lawrence.* 2 vols (eds) V. de Sola Pinto and W. Roberts. London: Heinemann.

Lederhendler, Eli (1989) *The Road to Modern Jewish Politics: Political Tradition and Political Reconstruction in the Jewish Community of Tsarist Russia.* New York and Oxford: Oxford University Press.

Leoussi, Athena S. and Aberbach, David (2002) "Hellenism and Jewish Nationalism: Ambivalence and its Ancient Roots." *Ethnic and Racial Studies* 25, 5: 1–23.

Levin, Bernard (1983) *Enthusiasms: An Irresistible Celebration of the Joys of Life.* London: Jonathan Cape.

Levin, Gabriel (1992) "Yehuda Halevi and Moshe Ibn Ezra." *Ariel* 87: 35–6.

Levine, Lee I. (1998) *Judaism and Hellenism in Antiquity: Conflict or Confluence?* Seattle and London: University of Washington Press.

Lewis, Bernard (1984) *The Jews of Islam*. London: Routledge.

Lieberman, Saul (1950) *Hellenism in Jewish Palestine*. New York: Jewish Theological Seminary of America.

Lieberman, Saul (1963) "How Much Greek in Jewish Palestine?" In A. Altmann (ed.) *Studies and Texts*, vol. 1: *Biblical and Other Studies*. Cambridge, MA: Harvard University Press.

Lifton, R.J. (1967) *Death in Life: The Survivors of Hiroshima*. London: Weidenfeld & Nicolson.

Lindner, Amnon (1987) *The Jews in Roman Imperial Legislation*. Detroit, Michigan: Wayne State University Press.

Loewenberg, P. (1970) "A Hidden Zionist Theme in Freud's 'My Son, the Myops ... ' Dream." *Journal of the History of Ideas* 31: 129–32.

Loewenberg, P. (1971). " 'Sigmund Freud as a Jew': A Study in Ambivalence and Courage." *Journal of the History of the Behavioural Sciences* 7: 363–9.

Long, A.A. (1978) "Dialectic and the Stoic Sage." In J.M. Rist (ed.) *The Stoics*. Berkeley and Los Angeles: University of California Press.

Long, A.A. (1996) *Stoic Studies*. Cambridge University Press.

Löwe, Heinz-Dietrich (1993) *The Tsars and the Jews: Reform, Reaction and Anti-Semitism in Imperial Russia, 1772–1917*. Chur, Switzerland: Harwood Academic Publishers.

Lutyens, Mary (1975) *Krishnamurti: The Years of Awakening*. New York: Farrar, Straus, & Giroux.

Lutyens, Mary (1983) *Krishnamurti: The Years of Fulfilment*. London: Murray.

Lyons, F.S.L. (1979) *Culture and Anarchy in Ireland 1890–1939*. Oxford: Clarendon Press.

MacMullen, Ramsay (1988) *Corruption and the Decline of Rome*. New Haven and London: Yale University Press.

Maguire, Robert A. (1994) *Exploring Gogol*. Stanford, California: Stanford University Press.

Manning, C.E. (1986) "Stoicism and Slavery in the Roman Empire." *ANRW* II 36, 3, W. Haase (ed.) Berlin and New York: Walter de Gruyter: 1518–43.

Margalioth, Mordechai (ed.) (1976) *Encyclopedia of Talmudic and Geonic Literature* (Hebrew) 2 vols. Tel Aviv: Yavneh.

Marx, Karl (1969; orig. 1852) *The Eighteenth Brumaire of Louis Napoleon*. New York: International Publishers.

Marx, Karl (1934; orig. 1867) *Capital*. 2 vols, Everyman Edition, Tr. Eden and Cedar Paul. London: J.M. Dent; New York: E.P. Dutton.

Marx, Karl and Engels, Friedrich (1971; orig. 1848) *Manifesto of the Communist Party* Moscow: Progress Publishers.

Mendele Mocher Sefarim (1947) *Collected Works* [Hebrew]. 1 vol. Tel Aviv: Dvir.

Mendels, Doron (1992) *The Rise and Fall of Jewish Nationalism*. New York: Doubleday.

Mendes-Flohr, Paul and Reinharz, Judah (eds) (1980) *The Jew in the Modern World: A Documentary History*. New York and Oxford: Oxford University Press.

Meyers, Eric M. (1992) "Roman Sepphoris in Light of the Archaeological Evidence." In Lee I. Levine (ed.) *The Galilee in Late Antiquity*. New York and Jerusalem: The Jewish Theological Seminary of America.

Millar, Fergus (1986) "Gentiles and Judaism: God-Fearers and Proselytes." In Emil Schürer, *The History of the Jewish People in the Age of Jesus Christ*. Edinburgh: T. & T. Clark, vol IIIi, pt. 150–76.

Millar, Fergus (1993) *The Roman Near East 31 BC–AD 337*. Cambridge, MA: Harvard University Press.

Miller, Arthur (1987) *Timebends: A Life*. London: Methuen.

Miller, J. (1981) "Interpretations of Freud's Jewishness, 1924–1974." *Journal of the History of the Behavioural Sciences* 18: 357–74.

Mintz, Alan (1989) *Hurban: Responses to Catastrophe in Hebrew Literature*. New York: Columbia University Press.

Miron, Dan (1987) *When Loners Come Together: A Portrait of Hebrew Literature at the Turn of the Twentieth Century* (Hebrew). Tel Aviv: Am Oved.

Mommsen, Theodor (1996; orig. 1882–86) *A History of Rome Under the Emperors*. Tr. C. Krojzel (ed.) T. Weidemann. London: Routledge.

Monroe, James T. (ed.) (1974) *Hispano-Arabic Poetry: A Student Anthology*. Berkeley and Los Angeles: University of California Press.

Nelson, R.J. (1981) *Pascal: Adversary and Advocate*. Cambridge, MA, and London: Harvard University Press.

O'Brien, Conor Cruise (1988) *Passion and Cunning*. New York: Simon and Schuster.

O'Day, Alan (1977) *The English Face of Irish Nationalism*. Dublin: Gill and Macmillan.

Oesterley, W.O.E. (1930) *A History of Israel*. Oxford: Clarendon Press.

Orlinsky, H. (1977). "The Situational Ethics of Violence in the Biblical Period." In S.W. Baron and L. Goodman (eds) *Violence and Defense in the Jewish Experience*. Philadelphia: Jewish Publication Society.

Pagis, Dan (1970) *Secular Poetry and Poetic Theory: Moses Ibn Ezra and His Contemporaries* (Hebrew). Jerusalem: Mossad Bialik.

Pagis, Dan (1971) "Medieval Hebrew Secular Poetry." *Encyclopedia Judaica*, 13: 681–90, s.v. "Poetry."

Parkes, C.M. (1986) *Bereavement: Studies of Grief in Adult Life*. 2nd edn. London: Tavistock.

Patterson, David (1964) *The Hebrew Novel in Czarist Russia*. Edinburgh University Press.

Patterson, David (1985) "The Influence of Hebrew Literature on the Growth of Jewish Nationalism in the Nineteenth Century." In R. Sussex and J.C. Eade (eds) *Culture and Nationalism in Nineteenth-Century Eastern Europe*. Columbus, Ohio: Slavica Publishers.

Payne, Robert (1968) *Marx*. London: W.H. Allen.

Pedersen, J. (1940) *Israel: Its Life and Culture*. vols 3–4. Copenhagen: Dyva and Jeppeson.

Pipes, Richard (1990) *The Russian Revolution 1899–1919*. London: Collins Harvill.

Poe, Edgar Allan (1984). *Poetry and Tales*. (ed.) P.F. Quinn. New York: The Library of America.

Poliakov, Leon (1965–85) *The History of Anti-Semitism*. Tr. R. Howard *et al*. 4 vols. New York: Vanguard Press Inc.

Pritchard, James B. (1969) *Ancient Near Eastern Texts Relating to the Old Testament*. 3rd edn. Princeton: Princeton University Press.

Proust, Marcel (1981) *Remembrance of Things Past*. Tr. C.K. Scott Moncrieff *et al*. New York: Random House.

Rad G. von (1965) *Old Testament Theology*. 2 vols. Tr. D.M.G. Stalker. London: SCM Press.

Rajak, Tessa (1983) *Josephus: The Historian and his Society*. London: Duckworth.
Rapoport-Albert, Ada (1991) "God and the Zaddik." In G.D. Hundert (ed.) *Essential Papers on Hasidism: Origins to Present*. New York: New York University Press, pp. 299–329.
Rees, W.D. (1971) "The Hallucinations of Widowhood." *British Medical Journal* 4: 37–41.
Reid, Forrest (1925) *Apostate*. London: Faber.
Reif, Stefan (1993) *Judaism and Hebrew Prayer: New Perspectives on Jewish Liturgical History*. Cambridge University Press.
Reznikoff, Charles (1976) *Poems 1918–1936*. (ed.) S. Cooney. Santa Barbara: Black Sparrow Press.
Rice, E. (1990) *Freud and Moses: The Long Journey Home*. Albany, NY: State University of New York Press.
Richler, Mordecai (1985; orig. 1969) *The Street*. London: Penguin Books.
Rist, John M. (1969) *Stoic Philosophy*. Cambridge University Press.
Roazen, Paul (1975) *Freud and His Followers*. New York: Alfred A. Knopf.
Robert, Marthe (1976) *From Oedipus to Moses: Freud's Jewish Identity*. Tr. R. Manheim. Garden City, New York: Anchor Books.
Roberts, J.M. (1997) *The Penguin History of the World*. London and New York: Penguin Books.
Rogger, Hans (1986) *Jewish Politics and Right-Wing Politics in Imperial Russia*. London: Macmillan.
Rosman, M.J. (1987) "Miedzyboz and Rabbi Israel Baal Shem Tov" (Hebrew). *Zion* 52, 2: 177–89.
Rostovtzeff, Michael (1957) *The Social and Economic History of the Roman Empire*. 2 vols, 2nd edn. revised by P.M. Fraser. Oxford: Clarendon Press.
Roth, Henry (1960; orig. 1934) *Call It Sleep*. New York: Avon Books.
Roth, Philip (1989) *The Facts: A Novelist's Autobiography*. London: Jonathan Cape.
Roth, Philip (2001) *Shop Talk: A Writer and His Colleagues and their Work*. London: Jonathan Cape.
Rüpke, Jörg (2001) *Die Religion der Romer*. Munich: Verlag C.H. Beck.
Rushdie, Salman (1991) *Imaginary Homelands*. London: Granta.
Rutherford, R.B. (1989) *The Meditations of Marcus Aurelius: A Study*. Oxford: Clarendon Press.
Sachar, Howard M. (1981; orig. 1958) *The Course of Modern Jewish History*. New York: Dell.
Sachar, Howard M. (1993) *A History of the Jews in America*. New York: Vintage.
Saénz-Badillos, Angel (1993) *A History of the Hebrew Language*. Tr. J. Elwolde. Cambridge University Press.
Saggs, H.W. (1965) *Everyday Life in Babylonia and Assyria*. London: B.T. Batsford; New York: G.P. Putnam's Sons.
Saltykov-Shchedrin, Mikhail (1986; orig. 1875–80) *The Golovlets*. Tr. I.P. Foote. New York: Oxford University Press.
Schäfer, Peter (1979) "Die Flucht Johanan b. Zakkais aus Jerusalem und die Grundung des 'Lehrhauses' in Jabne." *ANRW* II 19, W. Haase (ed.) Berlin and New York: Walter de Gruyter, pp. 43–101.
Schäfer, Peter (1995; orig. 1983) *The History of the Jews in Antiquity*. Tr. D. Chowcat. Luxembourg: Harwood Academic Publishers.
Schalit, Abraham (1975) "Die Erhebung Vespasians nach Flavius Josephus, Talmud und Midrasch. Zur Geschichte einer messianischen Prophetie."

ANRW II 2, H. Temporini (ed.). Berlin and New York: Walter de Gruyter, pp. 208–327.

Scharfstein, Ben-Ami (1980) *The Philosophers: Their Lives and the Nature of their Thought*. Oxford: Basil Blackwell.

Schechter, Solomon (1975; orig. 1909) *Aspects of Rabbinic Theology*. New York: Schocken Books.

Scheindlin, Raymond P. (1986) *Wine, Women, and Death: Medieval Hebrew Poems on the Good Life*. Philadelphia: Jewish Publication Society.

Scheindlin, Raymond P. (1991) *The Gazelle: Medieval Hebrew Poems on Israel, and the Soul*. Philadelphia, New York: Jewish Publication Society.

Schirmann, Chaim (ed.) (1959) *Hebrew Poetry in Spain and Provence* (Hebrew), 2 books in 4 parts. Jerusalem: Mossad Bialik; Tel Aviv: Dvir.

Schofield, Malcolm (1999) *The Stoic Idea of the City*. Chicago and London: The University of Chicago Press.

Scholem, Gershom (1955) *Major Trends in Jewish Mysticism*. 3rd edn. London: Thames & Hudson.

Scholem, Gershom (1971) *The Messianic Idea in Judaism*. New York: Schocken Books.

Schumpeter, Joseph A. (1951) *Imperialism and Social Classes*. Tr. H. Norden (ed.) P.M. Sweezy. Oxford: Blackwell.

Schürer, Emil (1909) *The History of the Jewish People in the Age of Jesus Christ (175 B.C.–A.D. 135)*, vol. I (eds) G. Vermes, F. Millar, 1973; vol. II, (eds) G. Vermes, F. Millar, M. Black, 1979; vol. III, (eds) G. Vermes, F. Millar, M. Goodman, 1986, 1987; Edinburgh: T. & T. Clark. Translation and revision of *Geschichte des judischen Volkes im Zeitalter Jesu Christi*. 4th edn., vol. 3. Leipzig: Hinrichs.

Schwartz, Seth (2001) *Imperialism and Jewish Society, 200 B.C.E to 640 C.E.* Princeton and Oxford: Princeton University Press.

Seltzer, Robert (1980) *Jewish People, Jewish Thought: The Jewish Experience in History*. New York: Macmillan.

Seton-Watson, Hugh (1977) *Nations and States*. London: Methuen.

Shaked, Gershon (1977) *Hebrew Narrative 1880–1970* [Hebrew]. vol. 1. Tel Aviv: Hakibbutz Heme'uchad.

Shaked, Gershon and Lelchuk, Alan (1983) *Eight Great Hebrew Short Novels*. New York: New American Library.

Sheehy, Jeanne (1980) *The Rediscovery of Ireland's Celtic Past*. London: Thames and Hudson.

Shevchenko, Taras (1964) *Poetical Works*. Trs. C.H. Andrusyshen and W. Kirkconnell. Ukrainian Canadian Committee: University of Toronto Press.

Simon, Ernst (1957) "Sigmund Freud, the Jew." *Leo Baeck Institute Year Book* 2: 270–305.

Simon, Marcel (1996; orig. 1964) *Verus Israel: A Study of the Relations between Christians and Jews in the Roman Empire A.D. 135–425*. London: Littman Library.

Sinclair, Clive (1991) *For Good or Evil*. Harmondsworth, Middlesex: Penguin.

Smallwood, E. Mary (1976) *The Jews under Roman Rule: From Pompey to Diocletian*. E.J. Brill: Leiden.

Smith, Anthony D. (1981) "War and Ethnicity: The Role of Warfare in the Formation, Self-images and Cohesion of Ethnic Communities." *Ethnic and Racial Studies* 4, 4: 375–97.

Smith, Anthony D. (1991) *National Identity*. Harmondsworth: Penguin.

Smith, Anthony D. (1992) "Chosen Peoples: Why Ethnic Groups Survive." *Ethnic and Racial Studies* 15, 3: 436–56.

Smith, Anthony D. (1999) *Myths and Memories of the Nation*. Oxford University Press.

Smith, Morton (1978) "Rome and the Maccabean conversions – notes on I Macc. 8." In E. Bammel, C.K. Barrett, and W.D. Davies (eds) *Donum Gentilicum: New Testament Studies in Honour of David Daube*. Oxford: Clarendon Press.

Spicehandler, Ezra (1985) "Odessa as a Literary Center of Hebrew Literature." In G. Abramson and T. Parfitt (eds) *The Great Transition: The Recovery of Lost Centres of Modern Hebrew Literature*. Totowa, NJ: Rowman & Allanheld.

Stanislawski, Michael (1988) *'For whom Do I Toil? J.L. Gordon and the Crisis of Russian Jewry*. New York: Oxford University Press.

Steiner, George (1996) "A Preface to the Hebrew Bible." In *No Passion Spent: Essays 1978–1996*. London: Faber.

Steinsaltz, Adin (1976) *The Essential Talmud*. Tr. C. Galai. New York: Basic Books.

Stemberger, Günter (1996) *Introduction to the Talmud and Midrash*. 2nd edn., Tr. M. Brockmuehl. Edinburgh: T. & T. Clark. Revision of H.L. Strack, *Introduction to the Talmud* (1887).

Stern, Karl (1966). *The Flight from Woman*. London: Allen & Unwin.

Stern, Menahem (1974, 1980, 1984) *Greek and Latin Authors on Jews and Judaism*. 3 vols. Jerusalem: Israel Academy of Sciences and Humanities.

Stern, Menachem (1977) "Sicarii and Zealots." In M. Avi-Yonah and Z. Baras (eds) *Society and Religion in the Second Temple Period*, vol. 8 of *The World History of the Jewish People*. Jerusalem: Massada.

Stillman, Norman (1979) *The Jews of Arab Lands: A History and Source Book*. Philadelphia: Jewish Publication Society.

Storr, Anthony (1972). *The Dynamics of Creation*. London: Secker & Warburg.

Symons, Julian (1978). *The Tell-Tale Heart: The Life and Work of Edgar Allan Poe*. London: Faber.

Szakaly, F. (1990) "The Early Ottoman Period, Including Royal Hungary 1526–1606." In P.F. Sugar *et al.* (eds) *A History of Hungary*. London and New York: I.B. Tauris.

Talmon, Jacob (1967) *Romanticism and Revolt – Europe 1815–1848*. London: Thames & Hudson.

Tierney, Michael (1980) *Eoin MacNeill, Scholar, Man of Action*. Oxford: Clarendon Press.

Tolstoy, Leo (1968; orig. 1874–76) *Anna Karenina*. Tr. R. Edmonds. Harmondsworth, Middlesex: Penguin.

Treadgold, Donald W. (1973) *The West in Russia and China. vol. 1: Russia, 1472–1917*. Cambridge University Press.

Turgenev, Ivan (1965; orig. 1861) *Fathers and Sons*. Tr. R. Edmonds. Harmondsworth, Middlesex: Penguin.

Urbach, Ephraim E. (1975) *The Sages: Their Concepts and Beliefs*. Tr. I. Abrahams. Jerusalem: The Magnes Press.

Vermes, Geza (ed. & tr.) (1997) *The Complete Dead Sea Scrolls in English*. London and New York: Allen Lane, The Penguin Press.

Vital, David (1975) *The Origins of Zionism*. New York and Oxford: Oxford University Press.

Vital, David (1999) *A People Apart: The Jews of Europe 1789–1939*. Oxford University Press.

Vogel, L. (1975). "Freud and Judaism: An Analysis in the Light of His Correspondence." Tr. M. Sachs. *Judaism* 24: 181–93.

Wallach, Luitpold (1940–41) "The Colloquy of Marcus Aurelius with the Patriarch Judah I." *JQR* 31: 259–86.

Wasserstein, Abraham (1994) "Greek Language and Philosophy." In G. Abramson and T. Parfitt (eds) *Jewish Education and Learning (Festschrift* for David Patterson) Chur, Switzerland: Harwood Academic Publishers.

Wasserstein, David (1985) *The Rise and Fall of the Party-Kings: Politics and Society in Islamic Spain 1002–1086.* Princeton: Princeton University Press.

Watt, Montgomery W. (1984; orig. 1974) *The Majesty that Was Islam.* London: Sidgwick & Jackson.

Weber, Max (1952; orig. 1917–19) *Ancient Judaism.* Tr. H.H. Gerth and D. Martingale. New York: Free Press.

Weber, Max (1961; orig. 1923) *General Economic History.* Tr. F.H. Knight. New York: Collier Books.

Weiss, Joseph (1985) *Studies in Eastern European Jewish Mysticism.* (ed.) D. Goldstein. Oxford: Oxford University Press.

Wellhausen, Julius (1885) *Prolegomena to the History of Israel.* Tr. J.S. Black and A. Menzies. Edinburgh: Adam and Charles Black.

Wheen, Francis (2000) *Karl Marx: A Life.* New York: W.W. Norton.

Whittaker, Molly (1984) *Jews and Christians: Graeco-Roman Views.* Cambridge University Press.

Winston, David (1984) "Philo's Ethical Theory." *ANRW* II 21, 1, W. Haase (ed.) Berlin and New York: Walter de Gruyter: 372–416.

Winton, Thomas D. (1958) *Documents from Old Testament Times.* London: Thomas Nelson & Sons.

Wiseman, D.J. (1985) *Nebuchadrezzar and Babylon.* Oxford: Oxford University Press.

Worringer, W.R. (1953; orig. 1908) *Abstraction and Empathy.* Tr. M. Bullock. London: Routledge & Kegan Paul.

Wouk, Herman (1992; orig. 1959) *This Is My God.* London: Souvenir Press.

Yadin, Yigael (1963) *The Art of Warfare in Biblical Lands in the Light of Archaeological Study.* 2 vols. New York: McGraw-Hill.

Yerushalmi, Y.H. (1991) *Freud's Moses: Judaism Terminable and Interminable.* New Haven and London: Yale University Press.

Zborowski, Mark and Herzog, Elizabeth (1969; orig. 1952) *Life Is with People: the Culture of the Shtetl.* New York: Schocken Books.

Zipperstein, Steven J. (1985) *The Jews of Odessa: A Cultural History, 1794–1881.* Stanford, California: Stanford University Press.

Zipperstein, Steven J. (1993) *Elusive Prophet: Ahad Ha'am and the Origins of Zionism.* London: Peter Halban.

Index